20/9/1997

To Carolyn,

With best wishes

Yih yi-Fu To

賀 遠 飛

Other books by Eileen Yin-Fei Lo

The Dim Sum Book: Classic Recipes from the Chinese Teahouse

The Chinese Banquet Cookbook: Authentic Feasts from China's Regions

China's Food (co-author)

Eileen Yin-Fei Lo's New Cantonese Cooking

From the Earth: Chinese Vegetarian Cooking

The Dim Sum Dumpling Book

The Chinese Way

Healthy Low-Fat Cooking from China's Regions

中國地區性
健康低脂食饍

Eileen Yin-Fei Lo

Calligraphy by San Yan Wong

Macmillan • USA

MACMILLAN
A Simon & Schuster Macmillan Company
1633 Broadway
New York, NY 10019-6785

Library of Congress Cataloging-in-Publication Data

Lo, Eileen Yin-Fei.
   The Chinese way : healthy low-fat cooking from China's regions /
Eileen Yin-Fei Lo ; calligraphy by San Yan Wong.
     p.   cm.
   Includes index.
   ISBN 0-02-860381-8 (alk. paper)
   1. Cookery, Chinese. 2. Low-fat diet—Recipes. I. Title.
TX724.5.C6L59443   1997
641.5′638—dc20   96-43587
                                            CIP

Book Design: Heather Kern

Manufactured in the United States of America

10 9 8 7 6 5 4 3 2 1

Dedication and Acknowledgments

This book is dedicated, as always, to Stephen, Elena, and Christopher, and to my husband, Fred, for their encouragement and their tastings. Very special thanks are due to my indefatigable agent, Carla Glasser, upon whose shoulder I have often leaned, and to Justin Schwartz, my editor and sympathetic friend. I often call this book Fred's diet book and he knows what that means.

Contents

Introduction

The Chinese Way

This book is about flavor, what the Chinese call *mei doh,* or good taste. If a dish is pleasing and balanced it is said to have *mei doh,* and if it is exceptional, we say it has *ho mei doh,* or the finest of taste. No characteristic of food is more important to the Chinese than taste, and balance, which of course is the way one food, one ingredient, will complement another. To be sure, this book is about cooking with less fat than is customary in the Chinese kitchen, already a cuisine that is inherently low in fat, but more importantly, it is about flavor.

All of us have been subjected in recent times to low-fat recipe books that mask blandness with presentation, and substitute parades of spices for true and natural flavors. Many of them have been unsatisfactory because textures, tastes, and balance have been deemed to be unimportant, as long as recipes can be labeled as being low in fat. This is not the case with this book, which harkens to Chinese tradition for its cooking practices, and reaches back into moderately recent Chinese history for its inspiration.

Let me make the point first that Chinese low-fat cooking is virtually redundant; proper Chinese cooking, that is. In those corner neighborhood Chinese restaurants with which most Westerners have grown up, there has always been an extensive use of fats and heavy oils. This is not proper Chinese cooking. For subtlety and *ho mei doh,* the fine Chinese kitchen has always relied upon small amounts of oil, just enough to stir-fry vegetables, meats, and seafood to proper doneness. It has always relied heavily upon steaming to preserve the inherent nature and taste of whichever food is being steamed. That is the Chinese way.

Steaming food gives life. There is simply no better way, for example, to prepare fish than to steam it—not covering it with a *beurre blanc* or other sauce, not dredging it in flour or bread crumbs and allowing it to swim in hot fat. The emphasis on the use of animal fats in Chinese culinary traditions has changed greatly in the last few decades. Now the medium of choice is peanut oil, not beef suet, in which many of the West's fast foods are fried, and not vegetable oils that harden within the body. Peanut oil is delicious, fragrant, complementary, and flattering to foods.

For inspiration I have reached back to my childhood, an unpleasant time of need when some foods were scarce, as were the ingredients with which to prepare them. As a very small child I lived in Sun Tak, a suburb of Canton. In my father's house and that of my grandmother, my Ah Paw, we had never wanted for anything. Then the great war came to China and we found that money was not the wonderful thing it had always been. Inflation was rampant, and the money that our family had in the morning was of little value in the afternoon; it had been replaced with newly printed paper money.

In those days peanut and other vegetable oils were scarce, and of necessity were sold by the tael, about 1.3 ounces, rather than the 16-tael catty (units of weight and value). A family with a pig was said to be rich, because it had the pig's meat to eat and preserve, and its fat to render. Pigs were scarce in those war days—slaughtered for a community and their meat apportioned out on the basis of the number of males in a family. Woe if the male in your family was away in the military, and was considered missing, perhaps dead. There was no pork for that family. I recall vividly the parades of Buddhist nuns, mendicants, who would come to our courtyard to comfort us. They would not beg, but we and others would share with them our cooking oil. They did not eat pork or any other meat, so animal fat was of no use to them. And while they had an abundance of vegetables and fruits, they had to rely upon our donations for their cooking oil. We and other families would give them our scarce oil by the tael.

During this time our family cooks became experts in the art of water-blanching, a simple process that preserved flavors. When a piece of meat is dropped into boiling water, then quickly removed, it becomes sealed, and may be cooked with lesser amounts of oil. When vegetables are plunged into boiling water for blanching, their water content is removed, and they too can be cooked with less oil. Fish were always steamed, and seafood was steamed rather than fried. Hardship is the way we thought of it, but inherently natural and healthful was what it was. It was our time of *ho siu yau*, or very little oil, and it became our cooking technique. *Siu siu*, my Ah Paw would say, "use less," and she was generous with her praise for our cooks, whom she said were blessed with the skill of *ho sau sai*, their great skill in making scarcity seem like abundance.

We steamed, we "baked" foods in covered woks atop ovens, and we grilled foods over wood fires. We began to emphasize vegetables and seafood, natural and unadorned. Oil was expensive and often unobtainable. Water was free and plentiful; soups were made by boiling leftovers.

How have I brought this experience to this book? I embrace the concept of steaming, as you will see from the many steamed dishes to be found here. I have also taken the concept of blanching to another tasteful level. Traditionally we never blanched foods in stocks. Stocks were to be used as bases for soups or sauces, but I have created stocks in which I blanch meats, poultry, fish, seafood, and vegetables; using stocks the way others use water for blanching and poaching. When you blanch meat in stock, you not only seal it, but you add a dimension of flavor that is enhanced a second time when the meat is stir-fried. Not only does this prepare these foods for the next step in cooking, but they acquire a complexity and richness of flavor. For example, if a head of broccoli is blanched, it holds less water, its fiber has been softened ever so slightly, and it will accept the use of a mere touch of oil in a stir-fry. And the amount of oil in the stir-fry itself will be reduced by as much as 75 percent. For still more flavor, I have created a menu of scented and infused oils that confer flavor without excess.

I must say that in those early days we were never conscious of the fact that we were eating "low-fat" food. No, indeed, what we were doing was inventing and improvising. With great skill, the aim of our cooks was to provide flavor, foods that we could eat *sik dak fook*, with complete enjoyment, foods that would ensure our health in a generally unhappy time.

So often today when we eat low-fat foods we feel deprived. This should not at all be the case. If what we eat tastes good; if it provides nourishment; if it is balanced; if it ultimately satisfies, it is not "low-fat cooking," it is rather "cooking that is low in fat." And there is a difference.

In this book I am bringing balance and flavor to foods so that you who follow the recipes, cook the foods, and eat them will be happy and satisfied. I know that this has been the case with my family, particularly my husband who, largely by eating the foods in this book, lost more than fifty pounds in less than a year, without feeling deprived.

You will find the recipes in this book very low in their use of fat. In no recipe is animal fat used, except of course for the fat that is part of the meat's structure. This is not a low-salt book, but there is minimal use, with most of the sodium coming from the condiments used—soy sauces, oyster sauce, hoisin, bean sauces, and prepared stocks. As you seek out the nutritional breakdown of the recipes, and you find high percentages of calories from fat in individual servings, you will note how low the overall caloric content is.

Seasoning is the most important aspect of the recipes in this book. Although seasoning is important at any time, it is more so in a low-fat context because so much of the taste of food is traditionally derived from fat. The challenge thus is not to remove fat and replace it with something else, but to cook with care—to blend, complement, balance. I cannot use those words enough. Yet I have incorporated the principles of the Chinese way of eating into these recipes, and I urge you to consider them. If you eat a large meal of many courses—and that can happen with a collection of foods low in fat just as easily as it can with a fat-rich binge—then do not eat a rich dessert. Do as the Chinese do: Eat fresh fruit, cold fruit, perhaps fruit soups such as those in this book. If you eat heavily, counterbalance your excess with some herbal tea.

The modern Chinese way relies not on processed foods and oils, but on the naturalness of things. It has expanded beyond its birthplace, Hong Kong, to become fresher, lighter, more adventurous. We cook more with fruits than ever before. We cook with tea. We cook with an eye to balance and health.

An herbalist will listen to a cough, and if he considers it tight will suggest that at your next meal you should consume less ginger and more winter melon. If your cough is loose, he will tell you to increase your ginger intake and to have chicken. Soups made with tomatoes and soybean sprouts will lower your temperature in summer, as will watercress and lettuce. A hot and sour soup will, on the other hand, raise your interior temperature, as will most meats. Dates are said to keep one's lungs clear, and boxthorn seeds in soups are fine for one's eyes. As a child, my cousin could not eat a raw orange or chew on a piece of sugarcane. The orange had to be cooked, the sugarcane boiled. This is the sort of thing that is considered more and more in the Chinese way, food said to engender *ghin hong*, or "good health." I have put some of these considerations in my recipes, and noted them.

The point should be made as well that most Chinese cooking is by its nature low in fat. It relies heavily on many vegetables, eaten naturally, not preserved. Rice is plentiful and is the bed upon which most meals rest. I cannot recall knowing anyone in China who suggested he or she might have to go on, or considered going on, a diet to lose weight. Snacks are not processed sweets, but rather nuts, watermelon and pumpkin seeds, candied lotus seeds, and pickled fruits. When I was a child there was virtually no ice cream, for the simple reason that there was no milk. I first encountered ice cream when I was taken with my cousins to the city of Canton, where I also found sweet pies and Western pastries.

Yet, in many places where Chinese culture, and the Chinese kitchen, has been subjected to Western influences—in Hong Kong, Shanghai, Taipei, Singapore, for example—we find these days movements against fat in diets quite like such movements in the West. Menus are constructed with inserts emphasizing the low-fat concept. There is some evidence, as there is with most international food trends, that this small preoccupation could be a fad, an adaptation of what is perceived as going on elsewhere, something worth aping. Nevertheless it exists, and chefs are cooking with less fat and with better oils, often with more concern for healthful eating. A small note: *Lop cheung*, the classic Chinese pork and pork liver sausage, now has less fat and salt than before.

No one should be, as my Ah Paw would say with some scold in her voice, a *ho sai sik*, or "very small eater." Not at all. It is expected that you eat well, and that you be satisfied with what you eat, that its tastes bring a smile to your face. That is what she wished. That is what I wish for you.

Cooking in the Chinese Manner

The basic Chinese kitchen is simple, unencumbered by batteries of pots and pans and racks filled with knives. There is the wok, perhaps the finest all-purpose cooking pot ever devised, unchanged for more than a thousand years. And there is the cleaver, to cut, slice, chop, dice, mince, and mash.

Initially, because the wok and the cleaver are different from Western cooking tools, many people tend to think that cooking the Chinese way is difficult, arcane, impossible to master. This is nonsense. It is simply a matter of familiarity that comes with proper usage. I have taught hundreds of people to cook everything from perfectly boiled rice to stir-fried meats and fish to vegetable preparations of many steps and many ingredients. While it is true that representations of the foods of all of the regions of China can be eaten in restaurants these days, that ought not to be an excuse for not learning how to prepare what I and others consider the most creative and varied cuisine in the world. *Not* to learn is to deprive yourself of the satisfaction that comes with accomplishment.

Chinese cooking, perhaps more than any other, is a living, changing cuisine. Learning the techniques of Chinese cooking is anything but tedious—it is a delight. Nor should you be put off by the idea of preparing a meal of many courses. Many dishes can be prepared ahead, or those that require less preparation can be paired with those needing more. The fun is in the challenge. The reward is in the tasting. The need is patience.

The key to the enjoyment of Chinese cookery is to do things correctly and with economy. Ingredients and utensils should be prepared and at hand before your heat is turned on. Any cookery can be daunting and frustrating if you are ill prepared, and Chinese cuisine, with its disciplines, is no different. You will be free of most concerns if you attend to basics. This means not only familiarizing yourself with different meats, fish, shellfish, and vegetables, but with sauces, oils, and spices. It means learning their properties and the techniques that enhance them. It also means learning the capacities of the tools necessary to work with these foods.

Here are the basic tools of the Chinese kitchen:

Wok

The range of woks these days is extensive, and unfortunately, most of those available are the products of trendy designers and are inadequate. The best to use is one made of carbon steel, with a diameter of about 14 inches. It is the all-purpose Chinese cooking utensil, used for stir-frying, steaming, dry-roasting, and sauce-making. Historically, it was first made of iron, later of carbon steel, still later of stainless steel and aluminum. Shaped like an over-sized soup plate, its concave shape places its belly right into the flame or heat source of a stove and makes it the ideal cooker.

Though it is not a pot or a pan by Western cooking standards, it functions as both. Its shape permits food to be stir-fried, tossed quickly through tiny amounts of oil so that the food cooks yet does not retain the oil. This is especially advantageous in low-fat cooking. The shape of the wok permits one to make it a steamer simply by placing bamboo steamers in its well.

If you buy only one wok it should be of carbon steel. It conducts heat almost instantly. Available in Chinese or Asian markets, it will cost only $7 or $8 and will be perfect when properly seasoned. I do not recommend for general use the many other kinds of woks made of stainless steel, aluminum, and various thicknesses of iron, particularly for stir-frying, although the stainless steel and aluminum wok is fine for steaming. In most cases these woks are more expensive than the best of the carbon steel. Nor do I favor any of the coated woks. Chinese stir-frying requires intense, direct heat, and such heat can damage, or loosen, this coating. Avoid plug-in electric woks because you cannot control their heat as precisely as you must. Nothing is as versatile as the carbon steel wok.

If the wok is to be used several times in the course of a single cooking session, it should be wiped with a towel, over heat, before each use. The wok is best used with a wok ring that steadies it over the flame.

A wok of carbon steel must be properly cleansed when it is new, because of its coating of sticky oil. Once cleaned and seasoned, however, it is ideal and will last for years. A new wok should be immersed in extremely hot water with a little liquid detergent. The interior should be cleaned with a sponge, the outside with steel wool and cleanser; then the wok should be rinsed and, while wet, placed over a flame and dried with a paper towel to prevent instant rust. Discard the paper towel, and with the wok still over a burner, add one teaspoon of cooking oil and rub it around with another paper towel. This oiling procedure should be repeated until the paper towel is free of any traces of black residue. The wok is then ready for use. A new wok literally "drinks" oil until it is properly seasoned. Once this is accomplished very little oil is necessary to cook.

With a new wok I usually make a batch of french fried potatoes. I find the process a perfect way to season the wok. I pour in four cups of oil, heat the wok until I see a wisp of white smoke rising, then put in the potatoes. Since this is a low-fat cookbook, do not eat these french fried potatoes. Have a small feast for your, or a neighbor's, children.

鑊蓋 Wok Cover

Usually of aluminum, although lately there are covers of stainless steel. They are about 12 to 13 inches in diameter with a top handle. They sit firmly in the wok enabling it to be used for stews, steaming, and boiling. Years ago in China, the cover was made of wood.

鑊刷 Wok Brush

A slightly oversized, oar-shaped wooden scrub brush with long, very stiff bristles. It is used, with exceedingly hot water, to clean cooking residues from the wok, without any detergents.

鑊座 Wok Ring

A hollow steel base that nestles over a single stove burner. The round base of the wok settles into it firmly, thus ensuring that the wok will be steady on the stove and that the flames from the burner will surround it evenly.

蒸籠 Bamboo Steamers

Circular frames of bamboo with woven bamboo mesh bases and covers, these come in various sizes, but those 12 inches in diameter are preferred because they sit quite nicely in the wok. Foods rest on the woven bamboo, and steam passes up through the spaces. The steamers can be stacked two or three high so that different foods can be steamed simultaneously. Steamers are also made of aluminum and of wood with bamboo mesh bases. There are also small steamers, usually of bamboo and stainless steel, that are often used for individual servings. For the recipes in this book, two bamboo steamers and one cover should be sufficient.

As I explain later in detail, also useful for steaming are the steel insets that fit into pots, usually used for such items as asparagus, corn, or pasta. There are also pots with steaming insets, usually of steel, as well as those insets in which clams are steamed.

鑊 Chinese Spatula

鏟

A shovel-shaped tool available in carbon steel or stainless steel, and in different sizes. The carbon steel spatula has become rare in recent years. For the recipes in this book, a stainless steel spatula is recommended. If a carbon steel spatula is to be used several times in the course of a single cooking session, then it should be wiped with a towel, over heat, before each use.

菜 Chinese Cleaver

刀

This is the other all-purpose tool of the Chinese kitchen. It cuts and dices. It minces, and its flat blade and its handle can mash. Usually of carbon steel with a wood handle, it is also available in stainless steel, either with a wood handle or with blade and handle of one continuous piece of steel. There are different sizes and weights, from 3/4 pound to 2 pounds. I prefer, for the recipes in this book, a stainless steel cleaver with a wood handle, the blade of which is 8 inches long and 3 1/2 inches wide. Try to find a professional cleaver made by Dexter in the United States.

Most kitchens these days are equipped with electric food processors and mixers. Slicing and chopping can be done with a food processor, if you wish, but I prefer the control I can exert with my hand on a cleaver. It is the traditional way, the way of the finest Chinese chefs, and I recommend it. Once you become adept with the cleaver, I think you will prefer it as well.

Rather formidable looking, the cleaver occasionally causes trepidation; some people think that the first time they use it they will slice off one or more of their fingers. The cleaver, when held correctly so that its weight and balance are properly used, can do virtually anything a handful of lesser knives can. It slices, shreds, dices, and hacks, all with great ease. It scoops, and can also function as a dough scraper.

There is really no single correct way to hold a cleaver, except that it should be held comfortably and in such a way as to make the weight of the cleaver do the work, firmly and efficiently. There are two grips that will be helpful.

First, for chopping and mincing, I grip the handle in a fistlike grasp and swing it straight down. The strokes are long and forceful, as if I am cutting something quite thick. If I am mincing, the strokes are short, rapid and controlled. The wrist dictates the force.

Second, for slicing, shredding and dicing, I grip the handle as before but permit the index finger to stretch out along the side of the flat blade to give it guidance. The wrist, which barely moves with this grip, is virtually rigid and becomes almost an extension of the cleaver, as the blade is drawn across the food being cut. When you use this grip, your other hand becomes a guide. Your fingertips should anchor the food to be cut, and your knuckles should guide the cleaver blade, which will brush them ever so slightly as it moves across the food.

The handle of the cleaver is perfect for mashing. Hold the handle firmly, with the index finger and thumb at the base of the blade where it meets the handle. The other fingers are clenched. The blade faces outward. The handle thus becomes a hammer that can be used to make a paste, such as that of fermented black beans and garlic.

铣 Chinese Strainer

A circular steel-mesh strainer attached to a long split-bamboo handle. Strainers come in many sizes, from as small as a person's palm to as large as 14 inches in diameter. For all-purpose use, I prefer one 10 inches in diameter. As an option, there are rather large all stainless steel strainers fashioned by piercing holes in a circle of steel. They may either have wood handles or be of one piece of steel, their handles hollow steel tubes. Both of these come in 10-inch diameter sizes as well.

Chopsticks, Bamboo

In addition to being Chinese eating utensils, these are marvelous cooking tools. They make fine stirrers, mixers, and serving pieces and are available usually in packages of ten. Avoid plastic chopsticks. They cannot be used for cooking and are more difficult to manipulate than those of bamboo.

The following will complete your Chinese low-fat kitchen:

Round cake pan
Selection of steam-proof dishes
Strainer, fine all-purpose
Large ladle
Small hand grater
Garlic press
Kitchen shears

Techniques

Stir-Frying

This is surely the most well known of all Chinese cooking techniques. It is fascinating to watch finely sliced and chopped foods being whisked through a bit of oil and tossed with a spatula. The hands and arms move as the wok is often tipped back and forth. Stir-frying is all movement and rhythm. What leads to it is organized preparation.

The object of stir-frying is to cook foods precisely to the point at which they retain their flavor, color, texture, and nutritive value. All foods, evenly cut, must be next to the wok, ready to be put into the heated oil. This is simply organization, so that as you cook you will have everything within reach, and the rhythm of stir-frying will not be interrupted. The best stir-fried foods are those that retain their natural characteristics while absorbing and retaining the heat from the wok.

When I stir-fry I heat the wok for a specific time, usually from 30 seconds to 1 minute. I pour oil into the wok and coat its sides by spreading it with a spatula. I drop some minced or sliced ginger into the oil; when it becomes light brown, the oil is ready. I usually add a bit of salt to the oil, place the food in the wok and begin tossing it through the oil—I to 2 minutes for soft vegetables such as bok choy and scallions, about a minute longer for firmer vegetables such as cabbage, carrots, and broccoli. I usually poach meats and seafood in stock before stir-frying them later. This is particularly advantageous in low-fat cooking because poaching in stock imparts flavor and allows one to stir-fry with far less oil.

If vegetables are too wet they will not stir-fry well, so they should be patted dry with paper towels. If they are too dry, however, you may have to add a bit of stock, perhaps I to 2 tablespoons, to the wok while cooking. When stock is added in this manner, steam is created, which aids the cooking process.

Stir-frying may initially appear as a rather frenzied activity, but it is not. The more you do it, the more you will realize that it is simply establishing a cooking rhythm.

出 水 Water Blanching

Water blanching removes water from vegetables. Pour 3 to 4 cups of water into a wok, add 1/4 teaspoon of baking soda, and bring to a boil. The baking soda is optional; it ensures bright color for the vegetables. When their color becomes bright (green vegetables, for example, will become a color that I like to say is like imperial jade), remove them. This process usually takes no more than 30 seconds. Place the vegetables in the water and immerse them. Immediately drain them in a strainer, place them in a bowl, and run cold water over them to halt the cooking process. Drain well and set aside.

蒸 Steaming

Chinese-style steaming is at the heart of low-fat cooking. It is truly a life-giving process. Natural tastes are preserved when food is steamed. Dry food becomes moist when subjected to steam's wet and penetrating heat. That which is shrunken expands. Steaming bestows a glistening coat of moisture on foods.

It is artful as well, because foods can be arranged in attractive ways within bamboo steamers, and once cooked, they can be served without being transferred to other dishes. Steaming requires virtually no oil at all, except that which is used to brush the bamboo reeds at the bottom of the steamer to prevent sticking. Use stainless steel steamers exactly as you would bamboo.

To steam, pour 4 to 5 cups of water into a wok and bring it to a boil. Place the steamers in the wok so that they sit evenly above, but not touching, the water. You will be able to stack two steamers or more, should you wish. Cover the top one and the contents of all will cook beautifully. Boiling water should be on hand at all times during the steaming process, to replenish any water that evaporates from the wok. Steaming times vary with the foods being prepared. These times are specified in the recipes.

You may also steam in a wok without bamboo steamers. Use a large cake rack. Place it in the wok, over the boiling water. Place the food to be steamed in a steam-proof porcelain or glass dish on the rack. Cover the wok and steam. You may also steam in a metal dish, cake pan, or pie plate. If steaming in a metal dish the steaming time, in general, will be half that of porcelain or glass.

You may also use steamers of stainless steel or aluminum. There are Chinese steamers, self-contained, of holed inserts that nestle into pots. These are available in aluminum, with punched holes, or in steel, with woven steel strips. Using these, the process is again the same, with times indicated in the recipes. With these, most foods must be in steam-proof dishes. Some vegetables, however, may be steamed directly within the inserts.

You may also use asparagus, clam, or pasta steamers to steam foods. With these, food should be placed in the steam-proof dishes before cooking. The exceptions are some vegetables that can be steamed directly in the holed inserts.

Tempering Dishes for Steaming. If you do not have steam-proof dishes, or prefer not to use metal for steaming, here is the way to temper porcelain or Pyrex dishes for use in steaming: Fill a wok with 5 to 6 cups of cold water. Place a cake rack in the wok and stack the dishes to be tempered on the rack, making certain they are completely covered by the cold water. Cover with a wok cover and bring the water to a boil. Let the water boil for 10 minutes, turn off the heat, and allow the wok to cool to room temperature. The dishes are then seasoned and can be placed in steamers without fear that they will crack. Foods are placed in the seasoned, tempered dishes, which are in turn placed on cake racks within the wok. Cover and steam as described in the steaming section. Once tempered, the dishes will remain so for their lifetime. They need not be tempered again.

It has been suggested that it is unnecessary to temper Pyrex because it is already tempered glass. However this only applies if Pyrex is used in the oven. It has been my experience, and that of my students, that Pyrex will indeed crack occasionally during steaming. So it is best to temper Pyrex dishes along with porcelain. The process is simple and quick and provides a good measure of safety.

干 Dry-Roasting

炒

The advantage of dry-roasting is that there is no need for oil, salt, or anything else in the wok except the food to be roasted.

To dry-roast nuts, heat the wok over high heat for 30 to 45 seconds. Add the nuts and lower the heat to very low. Spread the nuts in a single layer and use a spatula to move them about and turn them over to avoid burning on one side. This process takes about 12 to 15 minutes, or until the nuts turn brown. Turn off the heat, remove the nuts from the wok, and allow them to cool. Nuts can be dry-roasted two to three days in advance of their use. After they cool, place them in a sealed jar.

Use the same process to dry-roast sesame seeds, except reduce the roasting time to only 2 to 3 minutes.

A Final Note

A gas range is best for cooking Chinese food, particularly those stir-fries that require high, direct heat. There is a technique to obtain high heat as well as necessary variance on an electric range—a method I have devised and taught with success.

I use two electric burners side by side. Turn one burner to the highest setting and allow it to heat for 10 minutes. After 5 minutes, turn the adjoining burner to medium. Place your wok on the highest heat and allow to heat up for 45 seconds to 1 minute, until the wok is very hot.

Begin your cooking process. Place the food in the wok. If it begins to cook too quickly or looks as if it might begin to burn, switch the wok to the burner with medium heat. Go back and forth between the burners as necessary. Once you have become accustomed to this method you will cook Chinese food perfectly, without a gas range, and with ease.

Once the use of these few tools and cooking techniques has been mastered, much of the mystery attached to Chinese cooking will have been removed. Familiarity breeds success.

The Foods of the Chinese Kitchen

The proper ingredients are essential to the authentic Chinese kitchen. Spices, flavorings, soys, flours, and noodles that are Chinese in origin, or which the Chinese have absorbed from other cultures, are what makes this cuisine, in all of its regional varieties, distinctive. Happily, more of these Chinese foodstuffs are becoming more widely available.

With this wider acceptance has come more extensive use, and these days more and more people, including chefs, shop in Chinese and other Asian groceries with confidence. Only a very few of the special foods and ingredients in this book are not available everywhere. The rest you will find in your local market or in Chinese and other Asian markets. Most of the spices, oils, and condiments, as well as the bottled, jarred, and canned foods and the soys, are of Chinese origin and are imported from the People's Republic of China, Hong Kong, Singapore, and Taiwan. Of late they have been joined by imports from Southeast Asia, the Philippines, Indonesia, Malaysia, Korea, and Japan.

Most are available by mail order as well, particularly those ingredients that are prepared, preserved, or dried, and advertisements for them can be found in the better cooking magazines. Brands have also proliferated. Except in particular instances where I consider a product to be far superior to its counterparts and in my opinion essential to a recipe, I have refrained from recommending brands.

Bamboo Shoots

These are the pale yellow spear-shaped young beginnings of bamboo trees. Rarely are fresh bamboo shoots available, and the few that reach other markets are often discolored or dried out. Use those that have been cooked and canned in water. Winter bamboo shoots are considered to be more desirable because they are more tender, less fibrous, and of better quality. Cans will read "winter bamboo shoots" or "bamboo shoots, tips." The latter are as good as those labeled "winter" and are less expensive. I prefer those that come in larger chunks, so they can be cut to specifications. Once the can is open, shoots must be moved to another container. Occasionally, shoots will be removed from cans, refrigerated and sold loose, by weight. They will keep for two to three weeks in water, in a closed container, if the water is changed daily.

Bean Curd, Fresh

Called *daufu* by the Chinese, tofu by the Japanese, fresh bean curd comes in square cakes, 2 1/2 to 3 inches on a side. Made from soybean liquid, called milk, the cakes are custardlike. Individual cakes are preferred rather than those that come several to a package or in large blocks. Bean curd has little taste of its own; its versatility lies in its ability to absorb the tastes of the foods with which it is combined. It may be kept refrigerated in a container of water, tightly closed, with the water changed daily. So treated, it will keep two to three weeks.

Bean Curd, Dried

When bean curd is being prepared, a film forms on top of the liquid, or milk. This is dried and cut into rectangular pieces about 1 1/2 by 5 inches and about 1/8 inch thick. Ideally it is sun-dried, but more commonly the drying is done in factories under heat. It is then packaged in paper wrap labeled "dried bean curd, slice type." It is brittle and should be handled carefully. Kept in a closed container in a cool, dry place, dried bean curd will keep for at least a year.

# Bean Curd Cakes

These begin as fresh bean curd formed into smaller cakes. They are pressed to remove almost all moisture, then cooked in water flavored with a five-spice seasoning and soy sauce. They are dried and packaged, six to an eight-ounce pack. They are brown in color and are usually labeled "soybean cake." They also come loosely bundled in a smaller size, about two dozen to the pack, and in larger bags of ten ounces to one pound. The larger cakes tend to be white inside and have a milder taste. The smaller ones are spicier, with an added taste of chili. I recommend those that come six to a package, with the faint taste of anise imparted by the five-spice seasoning.

Bean Cake, Preserved

Cubes of bean curd that have been preserved in salt and water. Their label will read "preserved bean curd," on jars that come from China, Hong Kong, or Taiwan. Once opened they must be refrigerated. They will keep at least six months.

Bean Sauce

This sauce is of whole soy beans, which remain after soy sauce is made, and thus are fermented. They are mixed with wheat flour, sugar, and salt. The jars are usually labeled "bean sauce." Once labels were "brown bean sauce," or "yellow bean sauce," and you may still see jars so labeled. There is also "ground bean sauce," which simply means the beans have been ground into a mash. I do not prefer these as they tend to be quite salty.

Bean Sprouts

There are two varieties. The first, mung bean sprouts, are white and plump, with a decided crunch, and are grown from mung beans. They are sold by weight not only in Chinese groceries but in packages in supermarkets. They can be stored in plastic bags in which holes have been punched, in the refrigerator, and will keep no more than four days, after which they become softened and colorless.

The second variety, soybean sprouts, are also white, but longer than mung bean sprouts, with a yellow soybean at the tip. Storage is exactly the same as for mung bean sprouts. These are not as widely available as mung bean sprouts and are to be found mostly in Chinese groceries.

Bean Thread Noodles

These are often called just bean threads, or vermicelli bean threads, or cellophane noodles. They are made when mung beans are moistened, mashed, strained, and formed into very thin, white noodles. They come in half-pound packages divided into eight two-ounce bundles. Avoid other large packs of irregularly shaped sheets and long, thick rough sticks, both of which are labeled "dried bean thread" and are sandy brown in color. They are made with soybeans and should not be confused with bean thread noodles. (Note: These latter are not used in this book. I mention them in order to avoid any confusion.)

Black Beans, Fermented

These fragrant beans are preserved in salt. They come either in plastic-wrapped packs or in cans. I prefer the packages, lightly flavored with ginger and orange peel. Before the beans are used, the salt must be rinsed off. They will keep for as long as a year, without refrigeration, as long as they are kept in a tightly sealed container.

白菜 **Bok Choy**

This white-stalked green-leafed vegetable, known to the Chinese as the "white vegetable," is quite versatile because of its crispness and sweetness. It is sold by weight. It is often referred to as Chinese cabbage, but that is an error because it bears no resemblance to cabbage. It will keep for about a week in the vegetable drawer of a refrigerator, but it tends to lose its sweetness quickly, so I recommend using it when fresh.

上海白菜 **Bok Choy, Shanghai**

Smaller than the usual bok choy, it is bulb-shaped at bottom and its stalks come together at the top, rather than flowering. The stalks are pale green and the leaves darker green. If you ask for Shanghai bok choy, you may be looked at strangely. In that case, simply ask for *tong choi*.

 **Chilis, Thai**

Small, thin chilis, colored red to green, about 1 1/2 inches long. These are quite hot and impart a heat that tends to linger in the mouth, yet they are, I believe, pleasant. They are the chilis I favor for the recipes in this book. I also find them dependable in terms of the numbers used to obtain desired hotness. They will keep refrigerated for about four weeks in an open container, lightly covered with plastic wrap. Do not seal the container because the chilis will deteriorate. They may be used dry as well, but their heat will be less intense.

韭菜 **Chives, Chinese**

These are also known as garlic chives. They are more pungent than the Western chive and are wider and flatter, though of the same deep green color. Yellow chives are the same vegetable, but they are deprived of sun and thus take on a lighter color. They are more delicate than green chives and milder, with more of the taste of onion than of garlic. If you can't find Chinese chives, you may use Western chives, but the taste of the recipe will be different.

Choi Sum

This is a green, leafy vegetable with thin, tender stalks. It is all green, from its large outside leaves to the smaller inside leaves to the light green stalks, which are crisp and sweet. *Choi sum*, like other leafy vegetables, tends to lose its sweetness and so should be eaten as quickly as possible. It is available usually in Chinese or Asian groceries.

Cloud Ears

Also called tree ears. They are fungi that when dried look a bit like round chips, either brown or brown-black. When they are soaked in water they soften and resemble flower petals. They may be kept indefinitely in a closed jar in a cool, dry place.

Coriander, Fresh

Also called cilantro and Chinese parsley. This is similar in appearance to parsley. It has a strong aroma and imparts a distinctive taste when used as a flavoring agent or a garnish. Often it is suggested that Italian parsley be used as a substitute. I do not agree with that. Their aromas are entirely different. There is no substitute for coriander. It should be used fresh so that its bouquet will be appreciated, but it may be kept refrigerated for a week to ten days.

Curry Powder

A blend of spices, such as turmeric, cumin, fennel, and coriander seeds, plus others. There are many brands of curry powder on the market. I prefer the stronger, more pungent brands from India, in particular the Madras brand.

Eight-Star Anise, or Star Anise

A tiny eight-pointed hard star, this spice has a flavor more pronounced than that of anise seed. It should be kept in a tightly sealed jar in a cool place. It will keep for a year, though it may gradually lose its fragrance.

Eggplant, Chinese

This bright purple eggplant is shaped somewhat like a cucumber, and is about the same size. Its taste is like that of the usual eggplant, but its skin is quite tender and need not be removed before cooking.

Five-Spice Seasoning

This is often used to flavor foods like soybean cakes and barbecued pork. The five spices can be of any combination from the following: star anise, fennel seeds, cinnamon, cloves, gingerroot, licorice, nutmeg, and Sichuan peppercorns. Different makers prefer different mixtures, though anise and cinnamon predominate. You may devise your own five-spice seasoning by asking for a ready-mixed packet at a Chinese herbal shop. The herbalist will be happy to oblige. Often the spices are ground into a powder that is quite pungent and used only sparingly in dishes that demand strong flavors.

 Ginger

Also known as gingerroot. When selecting gingerroots look for those with smooth outer skins, because ginger begins to wrinkle and roughen with age. It flavors well, and the Chinese believe that it greatly reduces stomach acidity. It is used sparingly and should be sliced, and often peeled, before use. Its strength is often dictated by its preparation. In this book I use ginger sliced, peeled and unpeeled, smashed lightly, julienned, minced, and shredded. When placed in a heavy brown paper bag and refrigerated, it will keep for four to five weeks. I do not recommend trying to preserve it in wine, or freezing it, because it loses strength. Nor do I recommend ground ginger or bottled ginger juice as substitutes, because in the Chinese kitchen

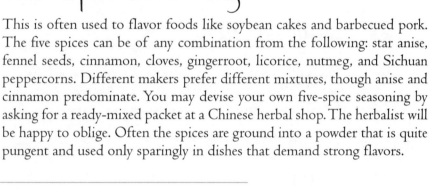

there is no substitute for fresh ginger. There is also young ginger, which is very smooth, slightly pink in color, and without the tough skin of older ginger. It is quite crisp. It is often called spring ginger, but that is a misnomer; it grows not in the spring, but twice each year—late in the summer and in January and February. Occasionally there is even a third crop. I use this young ginger to make my own Ginger Pickle. Pickled ginger is also available in jars and is a passable substitute.

Ginger Juice

Although this is available in small bottles, you can make a better quality juice yourself simply by grating fresh gingerroot into a bowl, then pressing it through a garlic press. Do not store it; make as needed.

Glutinous Rice

This is often called sweet rice and is shorter grained than other rice. When cooked, it becomes somewhat sticky. Its kernels stick together in a mass instead of separating the way long-grain rice does.

Ham

See Smithfield Ham (page 30).

Hoisin Sauce

A thick chocolate-brown sauce made from soybeans, garlic, sugar, and chilis. Some brands add a little vinegar to the mix; others thicken the sauce with flour. Often it is mistakenly called plum sauce, which it decidedly is not. Hoisin comes in large cans or jars, as well as in bottles. If purchased in a can, it should be transferred to jars and refrigerated. It will keep for many months.

Horse Beans, Preserved with Chili

The horse bean is the lima bean or fava bean. To make this sauce, the beans are cooked, mashed, and mixed with ground chilis. It is a very spicy sauce and adds good heat to many dishes. It comes in jars that, once opened, must be refrigerated. It will keep for months. This ingredient can be difficult to find. Hot pepper sauce could be substituted, but the taste of the recipe will not be the same.

Hot Pepper Oil

There are many brands of hot oil on market shelves. Often however, they are based on inferior oils. It is preferable that you make your own with peanut oil. It is not difficult. Also you will have as a by-product hot pepper flakes at the bottom of your oil, a bonus with many uses.

Ketchup

Ketchup from China comes in bottles, like its Western counterpart. The best brand is *Koon Yick Wan Kee*, manufactured in Hong Kong, and is made from tomatoes, vinegar, and spices. The difference between it and Western ketchup, with which we are familiar, is its use. In China, ketchup is used more as a food-coloring agent than as a flavoring. The Chinese version is difficult to obtain, however, so the use of Western ketchup will suffice.

Lotus Seeds

Lotus seeds are the olive-shaped seeds from the lotus pod. Most people are familiar with these as the cooked, mashed filling in Chinese sweets. They are regarded as a delicacy and are priced accordingly by weight. They may be kept for as long as a month at room temperature in a tightly sealed jar. I do not recommend keeping them that long, however, for their flavor weakens and their texture toughens with time.

Mushrooms, Chinese Black

These dried mushrooms come in boxes or cellophane packs. They are black, dark gray, or speckled in color, and their caps range in size from about that of a nickel to three inches in diameter. Those in boxes are the choicest, both in size and color, and are more expensive. Chinese black mushrooms must always be soaked in hot water for at least half an hour before use, their stems removed and discarded, and they should be thoroughly cleaned on the underside of the cap and squeezed dry. In their dried form they will keep indefinitely in a tightly closed container. If you live in an especially damp or humid climate they should be stored in the freezer.

Mushrooms, Straw

Small mushrooms with elongated domelike caps. They are common in southern China and highly prized. It is a mark of respect to serve these mushrooms to a guest. Occasionally to be found fresh, they are most often canned.

Mustard, Hot

This is made by mixing equal amounts of mustard powder and cold tap water. There are many hot mustards on the market, but I prefer the English-made Colman's Mustard, Double Superfine Compound. It must be dried mustard powder, not the Colman's prepared mustard that comes in jars. For normal use, combine 2 to 3 teaspoons of mustard with a similar amount of water.

Mustard Greens (Sour Mustard Pickle)

This leafy, cabbagelike vegetable is called *kai choi,* or "leaf-mustard cabbage." Its taste is strong and it is used fresh in soups or stir-fried with meats, but it is more commonly used in its preserved forms. Water-blanched and cured with salt and vinegar, it is used in stir-fries and soups. It comes loose, sold by weight, or in cans labeled "sour mustard pickle" or "sour mustard greens" or "mustard greens." If you buy the greens loose, place them in a tightly closed plastic container and refrigerate them. They will keep for three months. Once cans are opened, greens should be stored in the same manner and will have the same storage life.

Mustard Pickle

See Sichuan Mustard Pickle (page 29).

Mustard, Preserved

See Preserved Mustard (page 26).

Noodles

There are many variations on the noodle in China. There are wheat flour noodles, fresh and dried, of various widths, made from flour sometimes mixed with eggs, often just of flour and water. There are rice noodles, also fresh and dried, of various widths. Very fine rice noodles are often called rice sticks. And there are mung bean noodles, in addition to the bean threads listed earlier. These are usually shaped like linguine and need only be soaked in hot water before use.

For the noodle dishes in this book, most types of noodles will be quite suitable. (Even fine vermicelli or cappellini pastas, fresh or dried, will substitute quite well.) I have given my preferences with the individual recipes.

Oils

Peanut oil is the preferred oil of the Chinese kitchen, not only for its healthful attributes, but for the fine, nutty flavor it imparts. I have used peanut oil, and sesame oil, to create a series of flavored, spiced infused oils, to prepare various recipes in this book.

Oyster Sauce

A thick sauce, the base of which is ground dried oysters. It is a highly prized seasoning in China, not only for its distinctive taste, but for its richness of color. It is highly regarded by Buddhists, because the oyster is an allowed food in their vegetarian diet. Once opened, a bottle of oyster sauce should be refrigerated and it will keep indefinitely. Unrefrigerated, it will also keep for a good period of time if used often and quickly, but I prefer to refrigerate it.

Preserved Mustard

The Chinese call this *mui choi*. They are preserved mustard plants that have been cooked, then preserved in salt and sugar, then dried. Brown in color when dried and put into plastic bags, they are soft and pliable, with a texture quite like that of prunes. They are used in steaming as well as for stir-fried dishes, in braising, even in soups. They should be stored in a sealed jar at room temperature, and will keep at least six months.

Red Beans

These small, deep-red beans are used generally in sweets, although occasionally they are combined with other foods in casseroles. The beans are sold in plastic sacks by weight and will keep indefinitely. Red beans are most often used in their paste form, made by mashing cooked beans and sweetening them with sugar. Red bean paste comes in cans and is used as a filling in pastries and sweet desserts. Once a can is opened, the bean paste must be kept refrigerated in a closed container. It will keep from four to six weeks.

 ## Rice

The universal staple of the Chinese kitchen. It exists in many forms and can be prepared in many ways. A section of this book is devoted to rice and its preparations. At the beginning of that section there is my method for cooking perfect, foolproof rice.

 ## Rock Sugar or Rock Candy

This is a compound of white sugar, raw brown sugar, and honey. It comes in one-pound sacks and looks like a collection of small, amber rocks.

 ## Sah Gut

Commonly known in the West as jícama, this bulbous root is sweet and crisp, with a sand-colored exterior and white interior. It can be eaten raw or cooked. In Mexico and the Southwest it is known as jícama, reflecting its origin. Jícama has been widely adopted and cultivated in Asia. A fine use for it is as a substitute for water chestnuts when the fresh variety of these small sweet vegetables are unavailable. Stored in a brown paper bag and refrigerated, jícama will keep three to four days.

Sesame Oil

This is an aromatic oil with a defined nutlike smell. I prefer it as an additive or as a dressing. It tends to burn quickly when used to cook and when this occurs there is no benefit of its fine aroma, little of its distinctive taste. It is made from sesame seeds. Adding a bit of this oil to an already prepared dish imparts fine flavor, particularly in the case of some soups. It is thick and brown in versions from China and Japan, thinner and lighter from the Middle East. I recommend the former. Stored in a tightly closed bottle at room temperature, it will keep at least four months.

Sesame Seeds, Black and White

Black seeds, either roasted or not, are customarily used as a decoration or as an ingredient in the preparation of sweet fillings. Roasted white seeds are generally used in dumpling fillings, or as garnishes, and occasionally in the making of sweets as well.

Sesame Seed Paste

Also called tahini, this is a paste made by mixing ground white sesame seeds with soybean oil. It comes in jars. It is smooth, with the consistency of peanut butter. Its sesame taste is quite pronounced. After opening, the jar should be refrigerated. It will keep for six months.

Shao-Hsing Wine

This is a sherry-like wine made and bottled in China and Taiwan. There are several grades. I use not only the basic wine, but also the best refined grade of Shao-Hsing, which is labeled *Hua Tiao Chiew.* You may simply ask for "*far jiu*," which is a generic term, like "burgundy." Take care not to buy something called "Shao-Hsing Wine for Cooking," for it is of inferior taste. I use Shao-Hsing widely in this book, as you will see, for it adds a great deal to individual dishes. A dry sherry is an acceptable substitute.

蝦米 Shrimp, Dried

These are precooked, shelled, and dried shrimp, which come usually in packages of one-half and one pound, in various sizes. To be used they should be soaked, as instructed.

四川榨菜 Sichuan Mustard Pickle

Also called mustard pickle, it is made from Chinese radishes cooked with chili powder and salt. It can be added to soups and stir-fried with vegetables. It is never used fresh, only in its preserved form. It can be bought loose, by weight, but more often can be found in cans labeled "Sichuan Preserved Vegetables" or "Sichuan Mustard Pickle." As you can see, the labeling is not always precise, so be careful when you shop so that you obtain the correct vegetable. Sichuan Mustard Pickle should not be confused with "Sour Mustard Pickle" (see page 30).

花
椒

Sichuan Peppercorns

Quite different from the usual peppercorn, this is reddish in color and not
solid, but open. In Canton it is called "flower peppercorn" because of its
shape. It is not hot or peppery, but rather mild. Store these peppercorns
in a tightly capped jar as you would ordinary peppercorns. Several recipes
call for ground Sichuan peppercorns. These cannot be bought; you must
grind them yourself. To do so, use a mortar and pestle, or smash with the
broad side of a cleaver blade, then strain through a sieve. Store in a tightly
closed jar. Once ground, Sichuan peppercorns can be used as a base for an
infused oil.

維
苔
火
腿

Smithfield Ham

Cloth-wrapped hams cured in Virginia are used to replace the traditional
salted Yunnan ham of the Chinese kitchen. I use them often. It is not necessary to buy an entire ham. Slices of up to one pound are available in
butchers' shops. To prepare for use, soak in water for four hours to remove
salt, then place in a steam-proof dish, add 1/3 cup of brown sugar, and
steam for two hours. The ham is then ready for use and approximates quite
well the ham of Yunnan. After preparing the ham it may be kept refrigerated in a closed container. It will keep at least a month, or it may be frozen
for six months.

Sour Mustard Pickle

See Mustard Greens (page 25).

菜

Soy Sauce

This comes in light and dark varieties. The light soys are usually taken from the tops of the batches being prepared, the darker soys from the bottom. Both are made from soybeans, flour, salt, and water. The best are fermented in the sun. There are many brands from many countries, but I believe the very best quality soy sauce is a Hong Kong brand called *"Yeut Heung Yuen."* The light soy from this manufacturer is labeled "pure soybean sauce"; the dark soy (it is often called "double dark") is marked "C soy sauce." Dark soys are best for imparting a rich color to a dish; light soys are used for their somewhat sweeter taste. There is even a soy sauce flavored with mushrooms, and it is so labeled.

The Chinese believe soys give body and richness to cooking. I often combine the various soys for different tastes and colorings, as you will see. Some soys come in cans, though most are bottled. If in a can, transfer to a bottle. Soy can be kept indefinitely in a tightly capped bottle at room temperature. In this book "soy sauce" refers to light soy. All others are specifically indicated.

 ## Sugarcane Sugar

Made from sugarcane, it comes in caramel-colored blocks, either plastic wrapped, or loose in crocks. It is usually bought by weight in Asian markets.

 ## Tangerine Peel, Dried

The dried, wrinkled, brown skin of the tangerine is sold in packages and can be stored indefinitely. The darker the dried skins, the older they are; the older the better. The oldest are also the most expensive.

菱 粉 Tapioca Starch

Also called tapioca flour, this is made from the starch of the cassava root. Much of it comes packaged from Thailand. It is used as a basic ingredient in dumpling doughs, as a thickener for sauces, or as a coating. Store as you would any flour.

芋 頭 Taro Root

The starchy root of the taro plant is called *poi* in Hawaii and is somewhat like a potato, but more fibrous and tinged throughout its interior with fine purple threads. It must be eaten cooked, usually steamed or boiled. When the taro root steams, it emits a pleasant chestnut-like aroma. After cooking it can be mashed.

天津白菜 Tianjin Bok Choy

Often called Tianjin or Tientsin cabbage, or celery cabbage, or Napa cabbage, it comes in two varieties: a long-stalked type and a rounder one. In either of its shapes it is a sweet, crisp vegetable. It may be kept refrigerated in a plastic bag for about a week, but like bok choy, it tends to lose it sweetness, so I suggest using it early, if not immediately.

金針菜 Tiger Lily Buds

Elongated, reddish brown lily buds that have been dried are also known to the Chinese as "golden needles." The best are those that have a softness to them. If dry and brittle they are usually old. Sold in packages they will keep at least six months in a tightly covered jar stored in a cool place.

 Tree Ears

See Cloud Ears (page 20).

 Turnips, Chinese

These large, white vegetables are eight inches long, often longer, and two to three inches across at their thickest point. They have a fine crispness and can be nearly as hot as radishes. They will keep for a week in a refrigerator vegetable drawer, but are best used promptly.

 Vinegar, Chinkiang

This very strong, aromatic red vinegar made from rice is widely used in the kitchens of the Chiu Chau and Hakka people of southern China. It has a distinctive taste. Red wine vinegar may be used in it place, but it is not a true substitute.

  Water Chestnuts

These are not actually nuts. Rather they are bulbs, deep purplish brown in color, that grow in muddy water. To peel fresh water chestnuts is time consuming, but most rewarding once done. The meat of the water chestnut is white and sweet, juicy and crisp, and delicious even raw. Canned water chestnuts are a barely adequate, though serviceable substitute. As a matter of fact, if you cannot find fresh water chestnuts I would prefer that you use fresh jícama instead of canned water chestnuts. Quite versatile, they can be used in stir-fries or in soups. They are even ground into a flour that is used to make pastries. They should be eaten fresh for greatest enjoyment. As they age they become less firm, more starchy, less sweet. If you keep their skins on, with the mud remnants, and refrigerate them in brown paper bags, they will keep four to five weeks.

Winter Melon

This big melon looks like a watermelon and grows to the same oblong-round shape. Its skin is dark green and occasionally mottled, while the interior is white with a very pale green tinge and white seeds. The winter melon has no taste of its own, but has the characteristic of absorbing the flavors of whatever it is cooked with. When it is cooked, usually in soup, or steamed, the melon becomes translucent. Often the whole melon is used as a tureen, with other ingredients and stock steamed in it after it has been seeded and hollowed out. Winter melon should be used immediately, for it tends to dry quickly, particularly when pieces are cut from a larger melon. It is usually sold by weight, and by the piece. There is no reason to buy an entire melon unless you wish to try your hand at vegetable carving.

Won Ton Wrappers

Also known as won ton skins, occasionally spelled as "won tun," these thin wrappers are made of flour, eggs, water, and baking soda. They come in packages of one pound—about seventy-five to a hundred wrappers in a package—and can be found in the refrigerated sections of markets. They are also made without eggs, if you desire.

*C*hapter 1

My *S*pecial Preparations

In the introduction I discussed tools and ingredients used in the Chinese kitchen. There are, however, other ingredients that I have developed over my years of cooking and teaching that I believe enhance Chinese cooking that I wish to share with you.

*S*tocks

The basis for the best of Chinese cooking, particularly when cooking foods low in fat is a consideration, are stocks. You will note that in this book virtually every recipe uses one of these stocks as a base, as an ingredient for soups, for poaching, as a component of a sauce, and in marinades. They are essential, for the first step in cooking well is to have a fine base, which is what these stocks provide. They are simply made and you will enjoy the richness and tastes they provide.

齋上湯 Vegetable Stock

4 quarts cold water

I pound carrots, peeled and cut into thirds

2 pounds onions, quartered

2 bunches scallions, trimmed and cut into thirds

1/2 pound fresh mushrooms, cut into thirds

8 stalks celery, halved

1/4 pound fresh coriander (cilantro), cut into thirds (I cup)

1/4 cup Chinese preserved dates, soaked in hot water
    30 minutes and washed (or 4 preserved figs)

2 tablespoons boxthorn seeds, soaked in hot water
    30 minutes and washed (or 4 pitted sweet dates)

I teaspoon white peppercorns

3 ounces fresh ginger, lightly smashed

1/2 cup Fried Scallions (page 39)

Salt to taste

Yield:
3 to 31/2
quarts

I. In a large pot bring water to a boil. Add all ingredients to the boiling water, reduce heat, and simmer at a slow boil in a partially covered pot for 5 hours.

2. When the stock is cooked, remove from the heat and strain the liquid. Discard the solids. Store stock in a plastic container until needed. The stock will keep, refrigerated, for 4 to 5 days, or it can be frozen for up to 6 months.

Nutrition per serving (per tablespoon): 2.2 Calories; less than Ig Fat; Ig Carbohydrates; 0 Cholesterol; 26mg Sodium.

杞

子

Note: Preserved dates come in 1-pound plastic packages labeled either "red dates" or "dates" and can be found in Chinese and Asian markets. After opening the package, the dates should be placed in a glass jar, covered, and stored in a cool place. They will keep for 6 months. Boxthorn seeds, so labeled, come in 1/2-pound to 1-pound packages. Store likewise.

鶏 Chicken Stock
上
湯

2 whole chickens (8 pounds), fat removed, washed, also wash
  giblets. Cut each chicken into 4 pieces.

10 cups water

41/2 quarts cold water

1/4 pound fresh ginger, cut into thirds, lightly smashed

6 whole garlic cloves, peeled

1 bunch scallions, trimmed, washed, cut into thirds

4 medium onions, quartered

1/4 pound coriander, cut into thirds (1 cup)

1/2 cup Fried Scallions (page 39)

1/2 teaspoon white peppercorns

Salt to taste

Yield:
3 quarts

1. In a large stockpot bring 10 cups of water to a boil. Add chicken
   and giblets, allow to boil for 1 minute. This will bring blood and
   meat juices to the top. Turn off heat. Pour off water, run cold
   water into pot to rinse chicken. Drain.

2. Place chicken and giblets back into pot. Add 41/2 quarts cold water
   and all remaining ingredients. Cover pot and bring to a boil over
   high heat. Lower heat to simmer, leave a small opening at the cover
   and simmer for 4 hours.

3. Turn off heat. Allow to cool for 10 to 15 minutes. Strain and pour
   into containers. The stock will keep refrigerated for 4 to 5 days. It
   may be frozen. It will keep up to 6 months.

Nutrition per serving (per tablespoon): 1.5 Calories; less than
1g Fat; 0 Carbohydrates; 0 Cholesterol; 26mg Sodium.

*Note: You may eat the chicken used to make this stock if you wish. It will, unfor-
tunately, be quite bland, for all of its flavor will have gone into the stock.*

海鮮上湯 # Seafood Stock

8 pounds fish heads and bones, washed in cold running water

4 quarts cold water

2 pounds medium onions, quartered

6 stalks celery, cut into thirds

2 bunches scallions, trimmed and cut into thirds

1/4 pound ginger, lightly smashed

6 whole garlic cloves, peeled

1 teaspoon white peppercorns

1/4 cup Crisp Garlic (page 39)

1/4 pound fresh coriander (cilantro), cut into thirds

Salt to taste

Yield:
3 quarts

1. Place all ingredients in a large stockpot, cover and bring to a boil over high heat. Lower heat to simmer; leave a small opening at the lid and simmer for 3 hours.

2. Turn off heat. Allow to cool 10 to 15 minutes. Strain. Pour into containers. The stock will keep, refrigerated, for 3 to 4 days. Frozen, it will keep up to 6 months.

Nutrition per serving (per tablespoon): 1.1 Calories; 0.1g Fat; 0.1 Carbohydrates; 0 Cholesterol; 11mg Sodium.

調味油 # Infused Oils

I have developed these infused oils over time, as ingredients to add flavor—often unexpected—and thus interest to many recipes. With low-fat cooking they become increasingly important because, in conjunction with my stocks, they provide aroma, fragrance, and taste with minimal amounts of oil. There are, in addition, by-products of the infusion process that you will enjoy and use in these recipes as well. For nutritional purposes each of these oils contains, per teaspoon, 40 calories, 4.5 grams of fat, and no carbohydrates, cholesterol, or sodium.

葱 Scallion Oil

油

Scallion oil is used widely in this book, as you will see. The fried scallions that remain after the oil has been made are perfect ingredients for stocks, or even as additions to stir-fried dishes.

1 cup peanut oil

5 scallions, cut into 2-inch sections, white portions smashed

Yield:
3/4 cup

Heat wok over medium heat. Add peanut oil, then scallions. When the scallions turn deep brown, the oil is done. With a strainer remove the scallions. Strain the oil through a fine strainer into a bowl and allow to cool to room temperature. Pour oil into a glass jar, seal and store in a cool place until needed. Do not refrigerate.

蒜 Garlic Oil

油

The crisp garlic that results from this infusion is used in my seafood stock, in soups, and in other recipes in this book. My husband thinks it makes a great snack food.

3/4 cup of garlic (2 bulbs) peeled, thinly sliced

3/4 cup peanut oil

Yield:
2/3 cup

Heat wok over high heat for 30 seconds. Add peanut oil and garlic. Stir to separate. Cook for 3 minutes. Lower heat to low and cook for 8 minutes more or until garlic turns light brown. Turn off heat. Strain oil into a bowl and allow to cool to room temperature. Pour into a glass jar and seal. This will keep for 1 month at room temperature, or 6 months refrigerated.

Shallot Oil

The crisp shallots left over from this infusion may be drained on a paper towel, then stored in a closed container for further use, for one month at room temperature, or two months refrigerated. They are used in various recipes in this book.

I pound shallots, peeled thinly sliced (2 cups)
I cup peanut oil

Yield:
About
3/4 cup

Heat wok over high heat for 40 seconds. Add the peanut oil and shallots. Stir and cook for 5 minutes. Lower heat to medium, stir shallots frequently to ensure they cook evenly. Cook for 10 more minutes or until shallots turn golden brown. Turn off heat. Strain oil and allow to cool. Pour into a glass jar and seal. It will keep at room temperature for 1 month, or refrigerated for 6 months.

Onion Oil

The browned onions remaining from this infusion will be used in recipes throughout this book. They may be kept, in a closed container at room temperature for one month, or refrigerated for two months.

I pound onions, sliced very thinly (4 cups)
I 1/2 cups peanut oil

Yield:
About I 1/4
cups

1. Heat wok over high heat for 30 seconds. Add peanut oil and onions. Stir, making sure the onions are coated with the oil. Cook for 7 minutes, stirring and turning often to prevent burning and to ensure the onions brown evenly.

2. Lower heat to medium and cook for 15 minutes more, or until onions turn light brown. Turn off heat, strain oil. Use a ladle or a large spoon to press onions as they strain. Allow to cool. Place onion oil in a glass jar and seal. This will keep 1 month at room temperature, 6 months refrigerated.

芫茜油 Coriander Oil

This oil resembles the green of an extra-virgin olive oil after the infusion, but there the resemblance ends, since the green comes from the fresh coriander, also known as cilantro. The coriander leaves and stems that remain may be added to your next vegetable stock.

I cup fresh coriander (cilantro) stems and leaves (I large bunch of coriander should provide the correct amount of stems and leaves); stems cut into 2-inch pieces.

I 1/4 cups peanut oil

Yield:
About I cup

1. The coriander should be perfectly dry. Heat a wok over high heat for 40 seconds. Add peanut oil, stir briefly, and add coriander stems. Stir and bring the oil to a boil for about 4 minutes. Add the coriander leaves and stir, making certain they are coated. Cook until the coriander become dull in color, then brown.

2. Turn off heat, strain, and allow to cool. Pour into a jar and store in a cool place. It will keep, closed, for 6 to 8 weeks.

白椒油 White Peppercorn Oil

White pepper is a universal spice of choice throughout China, much preferred to black pepper. I use white pepper in most of my recipes for its flavor and fragrance. This infused oil reflects perfectly the essence of white pepper, its taste and its subtle aroma.

I tablespoon white peppercorns, crushed

1/4 cup peanut oil

Yield:
Under 1/4 cup

Place oil and peppercorns in a wok over medium heat. Bring to a boil. Reduce heat to low and cook for 2 minutes. Turn off heat. Allow to cool. Do not strain. Pour the oil and the peppercorns into a glass jar, close.

Because of its delicate nature this infused oil will not keep as long as others, so I make only a small amount at a time. I also retain the peppercorns in the oil to maintain its taste. This oil will keep, at optimum strength, no more than 2 months, refrigerated.

花椒油 Sichuan Peppercorn Oil

After making this infused oil, strain, but retain the Sichuan peppercorns for they make fine additions to stocks. They will keep indefinitely, in a closed container, refrigerated.

2 tablespoons Sichuan peppercorns
I cup peanut oil

Yield:
Under I cup

Heat a wok over high heat for 30 seconds. Add the Sichuan peppercorns to the dry wok and stir. Lower the heat to low. Stir for 1 1/2 minutes, or until the peppercorns release their fragrance. Add the peanut oil, raise heat to medium, and allow to come to a boil. Lower the heat and cook for 4 to 5 minutes, or until the peppercorns turn black. Turn off heat, strain the oil, and allow to cool. The oil will keep, in a covered jar, in a cool place, for I to 2 months.

辣油 Hot Pepper Oil

The hot pepper flakes that remain after this infusion should be kept with the oil. They will rest at the bottom of the storage jar and will be used in various recipes in this book.

1/2 cup hot red pepper flakes
1/3 cup sesame oil
1/2 cup peanut oil

Yield:
1 1/3 cups

Place all the ingredients in a large jar and mix well. Close the jar tightly and place in a cool, dry place for 2 weeks. The oil will then be ready for use. The longer it is stored, the more potent it becomes. Because the heat of hot pepper flakes varies, the oil may be ready for use in I week instead of 2. Taste it.

Alternately: Place the hot pepper flakes in a mixing bowl. Bring the peanut and sesame oils to a boil and pour over the flakes. (I caution you not to have your face over the bowl, for the fumes may cause discomfort and coughing.) After the oil cools, it is ready for use. Store as above.

Minced Garlic

Minced garlic is available in jars. Often it is mixed with oil or with vinegar. Neither of these are, in my opinion, sufficiently potent for the recipes in this book. It is best to make your own minced garlic. The process is simple.

In general a recipe in this book will call for 1 to 2 teaspoons of minced garlic. Occasionally whole cloves will be called for. Usually 3 medium cloves will yield sufficient minced garlic for one recipe. Any that is left over may be kept, covered and refrigerated, for up to 4 days for later use. When selecting garlic, I prefer to buy loose bulbs rather than those in packs. A good bulb will be quite hard and will have weight to it. If light, the garlic is older, dryer and has been on the shelf for awhile.

To make, separate the bulb into cloves. Smash the clove with the flat side of a cleaver blade. This permits easy removal of the skin. Discard the skins and mince finely until you have a 1/8-inch dice. Do not mince it any finer than this.

Ginger Juice

Ginger juice should be made for immediate use as well.

Peel a piece of fresh gingerroot, 11/2 inches long and 11/2 inches thick. Grate it into a pulp with a small hand grater. Press the pulp into the well of a garlic press and squeeze into a small bowl. This should yield about 11/2 teaspoons. Occasionally ginger will be dry and will yield less juice. Simply use a larger piece, if that is the case.

My Rice Wine Vinaigrette

I devised this dressing for salads in this book. It contains rice wine vinegar and Chinese rice wine in a pleasant, sweet and tart mix. It complements the salads it is used with quite well.

2 1/2 tablespoons soy sauce

I tablespoon rice wine vinegar

I tablespoon Shao-Hsing wine or sherry

2 1/2 teaspoons sugar

1/4 teaspoon salt

I 1/2 teaspoons minced ginger

I 1/2 teaspoons minced garlic

1/2 cup Chicken Stock (page 37)

Yield:
3/4 cup

Combine all ingredients, stirring to dissolve and blend well. This may be made in advance and kept, covered and refrigerated, for 2 to 3 days. I prefer it not be kept longer for its strength will fade.

For nutritional purposes, I tablespoon of this vinaigrette contains 70 calories, 8 grams of fat, no cholesterol, and only traces of carbohydrates and sodium.

Pickles

Pickling, to preserve or to change and enhance flavors, has been an integral part of the Chinese kitchen for centuries. Recipes for pickling vegetables and fruits have come from great-grandmother, to grandmother, to mother, and in my case, to me. Most Chinese pickling is simple, classic preparations that are traditional. In this book I use several of these in various recipes for their taste as well as for their crisp texture.

I constantly experiment with pickles to see how they will keep. I have made and used them at three-month intervals. However I have set some aside, refrigerated, and I can say that they will keep, with no loss of strength, nor any loss in texture, for a year. In fact the tastes seem to intensify with time. Because these are ingredients in recipes, the nutritional informational of these pickles is incorporated within the recipes, in which they are used.

和
味
子
薑

Ginger Pickle

Pickled ginger or, as I call it, Ginger Pickle, is not only a Chinese classic, but is versatile as well. It can be eaten as a first course, or as a snack; it is an ingredient in much of my cooking, and I also use it as a garnish. Only fresh, young ginger should be used to make these pickles. I have discussed this ginger in my listing of the foods of the Chinese kitchen.

Young ginger can be recognized by its creamy, white interior, the pinkish cast to its thin skin, and the green shoots that protrude from the root. Pickled ginger is also available, jarred, in markets, but I prefer the taste of that I make myself. You will too.

4 cups cold water

1/2 **teaspoon baking soda**

3/4 **pound fresh young ginger, washed thoroughly, any bark discarded, but pink skin left on, cut into** 1/8**-inch slices with shoots retained**

MARINADE

3/4 **teaspoon salt**

1/3 **cup white vinegar**

1/2 **cup sugar**

Yield:
About 11/4
to 11/2 cups

1. In a large pot bring water and baking soda to a boil. Add ginger and boil for 30 seconds. Remove from heat. Add cold water to reduce the temperature. Drain. Add cold water again and drain. Repeat a third time and allow ginger to sit in cold water for 10 minutes. Drain well and place ginger in a bowl.

2. Combine marinade ingredients and add to the ginger. Mix well, cover, and refrigerate for at least 24 hours before serving. Serve cold.

和味桃 Pickled Peaches

I use these pickles alone or with other pickles, in salads, in stir-fries, and in steaming. They are an ideal addition to any meal, at any level. These pickled peaches have a pleasing sweet and sour taste. If you prefer them sweeter, increase the amount of sugar to taste. But this must be done at preparation time. Sugar cannot be added after the peaches have been pickled, for it will not penetrate the fruit.

> **2 pounds fresh peaches, very hard, but with color indicating that they are ripening (about 8 peaches)**
>
> **2 cups white vinegar**
>
> **3 3/4 cups cold water**
>
> **2/3 cup sugar**
>
> **2 1/4 teaspoons salt**

Yield:
1 peach,
julienned,
about 1 cup

1. Wash peaches well, dry thoroughly. Do not slice or peel them. In an oversized glass jar place the vinegar, water, sugar, and salt. Mix well with a wooden spoon until sugar and salt are completely dissolved.

2. Add peaches and stir them in well. Cover the jar tightly. A jar with a screw top is preferred. Refrigerate for 3 days, untouched, before serving.

和味梨 Pickled Pears

For these pickles I recommend the Bosc pear, for it is closest to the hard, crisp pear in China referred to as sah leh, or "sand pear," which is almost round, and quite hard.

> **2 pounds pears, very hard, barely ripe (5 or 6 pears)**
>
> **1 1/3 cups white vinegar**
>
> **1 1/3 cups cold water**
>
> **1/2 cup sugar**
>
> **2 teaspoons salt**

Yield:
1 pear,
julienned,
about 1 to
1 1/4 cups

Peel, wash, and dry pears. In an oversized glass jar place the vinegar, water, sugar, and salt. Mix with a wooden spoon to dissolve the sugar and salt. Place the pears into the jar, mix thoroughly, and close the jar. A screw top jar is preferred. Otherwise place a sheet of plastic wrap over the top before putting the lid on. Allow to remain in the refrigerator for at least 3 days, untouched, to ensure the pears absorb the pickling. Serve cold.

和味木瓜 Green Papaya Pickle

Green papaya pickles are quite popular in the Philippines. This is my version of that pickle, which I find marvelous as a first course to pique the appetite, as a garnish, or combined with other foods as you will see in this book. A most versatile fruit, green papaya is simply an unripe papaya, quite hard and white inside.

4 1/2 cups cup cold water

1/2 teaspoon baking soda (optional)

1/2 cup sugar

I medium green, unripe papaya (I pound), peeled, seeded, quartered, then cut into 1/4-inch-thick slices

1/2 cup white vinegar

1/2 cup sugar

I teaspoon salt

Yield:
About 1 1/4
to 1 1/2 cups

1. In a pot bring water and baking soda to a boil over high heat. Add sliced papaya, stir, and cook for 45 seconds. Turn off heat. Run cold water into pot, drain. Repeat twice more. Drain thoroughly.

2. Combine vinegar, 1/2 cup of cold water, sugar, and salt in a jar and stir with a wooden spoon until the sugar and salt are dissolved. Add the blanched papaya, making certain it is covered with the liquid. Cover the jar, screw top preferred, and refrigerate until used. It will take about 3 days for the pickling to affect the papaya. It is best served cold.

I have taken you through a series of basics, the foods of the Chinese kitchen and those other preparations of my own that I believe are necessary to cook authentically in the Chinese manner. Finally, and this will serve as an introduction to the first selection of recipes in this book, there is what is perhaps the most necessary preparation of all: perfectly cooked rice. Virtually every steamed dish, every stir-fry in this book and beyond, benefits from being accompanied by perfectly cooked rice. It also is the basis upon which other recipes are built.

白 Basic Cooked Rice

Bak Fon

 The Chinese call cooked rice bak fon, or "white rice," for it is the whiteness of cooked rice that is prized. In parts of China brown rice is eaten, to be sure, but not nearly as often, or widely as traditional white rice. Here is a foolproof method of cooking it.

> 1 1/2 **cups of rice**
> 1 1/2 **cups cold water**

Yield:
4 cups

1. Place the rice in a pot with some cold water and wash it three times. As you wash it, rub it between your hands. Drain well after washing. Then add the 1 1/2 cups of cold water and allow the rice to sit for 2 hours before cooking. A good ratio of rice to water is 1 cup of rice to 1 cup, minus 1 tablespoon, of water (so-called "old rice," which has been lying about in sacks for extended periods of time, will absorb more water and will cook easier.)

2. Begin cooking, uncovered, over high heat and bring the water to a boil. Stir the rice with chopsticks and cook for about 4 minutes, or until the water evaporates. Even after the water is gone the rice kernels will be quite hard. Cover the pot and cook over low heat for about 8 minutes more, stirring from time to time.

3. After turning off the heat, loosen the rice with chopsticks. This will help retain fluffiness. Cover the pot tightly until ready to serve. Just before serving, stir rice with chopsticks once again. Well-cooked rice will have absorbed the water but will not be lumpy, nor will the kernels stick together. They will be firm, fluffy and separate.

In this book the usual serving, per person, of cooked rice as an accompaniment to stir-fried or steamed dishes, is 1/2 cup. Each of these servings contains 112 calories, 2 grams of fat, 16 percent of calories from fat, 25 grams of carbohydrates, and no cholesterol or sodium.

Chapter 2

Rice And Noodles

In China rice is customarily eaten at all three daily meals. In the morning rice is eaten generally as a basic breakfast porridge, or *congee*, made from a mixture of white long-grained rice and shorter-grain glutinous rice. At the afternoon and evening meals it is the core around which meals are built. A Chinese person will say *sik fon*, or "eat rice," when referring to a meal.

Typically an afternoon or evening meal will be cooked rice, accompanied by prepared meats, fish, seafood, and vegetables. A lunch will be referred to as *n'fon*, or "afternoon rice," dinner or supper as *mon fon*, or "evening rice." The emphasis is always on rice. When eating Chinese food in the West, the focus is on the cooked preparations, with rice as the accompaniment. Indeed, among the Chinese, a mark of wealth is to have a meal of many cooked courses, with but a small amount of rice. This shows one's neighbors, or guests, that the hosts wish their guests to satisfy themselves with the various foods served and not to fill themselves with rice.

In addition to rice being the most important of China's food staples, it possesses symbolism to the Chinese. A person who has possessions and is able to care for his family is said to have a "rice bowl that is full." Someone who has fallen upon leaner times is said to possess a "broken rice bowl."

The rice most favored in China is white, and when cooked, its grains should be fluffy and separate. This is achieved with long-grain or extra-long-grain rice. In Chinese and Asian markets there is a distinction between these, but in Western food markets no such distinction is made. The basic long-grain kernel is generally about four times as long as it is wide; extra-long-grain a bit longer and thinner. When cooked properly, the kernels are separate, fluffy, and have a pleasant bite. An especially fragrant version of extra-long-grain rice is that from Thailand. It has a most pleasing aroma of jasmine when cooking and tastes faintly of that flower. I recommend it.

Short-grain rice kernels are round, plump, and short. They become soft when cooked, and stick together in clumps. I favor short-grain rice as a component in congees where I mix it with glutinous rice, for a smooth mouth-filling feel. Glutinous rice, often called "sticky rice" or "sweet rice," is short-grained and when cooked becomes a mass of kernels that adhere.

Rice is not as common in the north of China where there is a bread and noodle culture as is wheat. This is not to say, however, that noodles are not highly regarded in other parts of China. Indeed, noodles are universal, whether of wheat or rice flour, and are regarded as symbolic, because of their length, of longevity and happy old age. Noodles are always served on birthdays and at the lunar New Year, on which everybody's birthday is celebrated.

Noodles in China are fresh or dried, made with eggs or without. There are even noodles fashioned from the processed starch of mung beans, known as bean thread noodles. Soft, fresh noodles are found in the refrigerated compartments of markets and are best used fresh, though they may be refrigerated for two to three days. Frozen they will keep from four to six weeks. One of these soft noodles is the supple skin used to make won ton. Dried noodles come packaged in as many sizes and thicknesses as one finds with pastas. Indeed for many recipes, including those in this book, the substitution of Italian pastas is not only possible, but pleasing.

Fried Rice with Asparagus and Capers

Heung Mai Lo Sun Chau Fan

This is one of my adaptations of the classic version of fried rice, what the Chinese call chau fon. *No longer is this the case. These days fried rice can be what you wish, a fresh dish with different tastes.*

SAUCE

> 2 tablespoons oyster sauce
>
> 2 tablespoons Chicken Stock (page 37)
>
> 1 1/2 teaspoons soy sauce
>
> 2 teaspoons white wine
>
> 1 teaspoon sugar
>
> 1/2 teaspoon sesame oil
>
> Pinch of white pepper

To continue the dish

1 recipe Basic Cooked Rice (page 48)

3 large eggs, beaten

4 teaspoons Scallion Oil (page 39)

To complete the dish

1 1/2 teaspoons minced ginger

12 medium asparagus stalks, hard ends removed, cut across into 1/4-inch slices (1 3/4 cups)

1/4 cup capers

5 to 6 fresh water chestnuts, peeled, cut into 1/4-inch dice (2/3 cup)

2 tablespoons Chicken Stock (page 37)

3 scallions, finely sliced (3/4 cup)

3 tablespoons minced fresh coriander (cilantro)

Yield:
6 servings

1. Combine sauce ingredients and reserve. Prepare Basic Cooked Rice. Allow to cool to room temperature. Scramble eggs with 2 teaspoons Scallion Oil over medium heat until cooked; cut up coarsely and reserve.

2. Heat wok over high heat for 30 seconds. Add remaining Scallion Oil, coat wok with spatula. When a wisp of smoke appears, add ginger, stir for 30 seconds until its fragrance is released. Add asparagus and capers, stir and cook for 1 minute. Add water chestnuts, stir, then add chicken stock and cook for 2 minutes. Add rice, mix thoroughly, making certain the rice is coated and very hot. Add egg pieces and combine. Stir reserved sauce and drizzle into rice. Mix well. Cook for 2 more minutes. Add scallions, and coriander, and mix well. Turn off heat, transfer to a heated serving dish and serve.

Nutrition per serving: 254 Calories; 11.2g Fat; 4% calories from fat; 40g Carbohydrates; 106mg Cholesterol; 347mg Sodium.

Shallot Fried Rice with Coriander

Chung Tau Yeun Sai Chau Fon

Herewith another variation on the theme. In this the flavors of barbecued pork and shrimp complement the rice. Using more traditional ingredients, this dish demonstrates the adaptability of rice.

1 recipe Basic Cooked Rice (page 48)

SAUCE

2 tablespoons oyster sauce

11/2 teaspoons soy sauce

2 teaspoons Shao-Hsing wine or sherry

1/2 teaspoon sugar

Pinch white pepper

3 tablespoons Chicken Stock (page 37)

TO COMPLETE THE DISH

21/2 teaspoons Shallot Oil (page 40)

11/2 teaspoons minced ginger

2 ounces Barbecued Pork (page 236) sliced into 1/2-inch pieces (1/2 cup)

1/4 pound medium shrimp, shelled, deveined, halved lengthwise, then each length cut into 4 pieces

1/2 teaspoon salt

2 large eggs, beaten with a pinch of white pepper

3 tablespoons Crisp Shallots (page 40)

1/4 cup minced fresh coriander (cilantro)

Yield:
6 servings

1. Prepare Basic Cooked Rice recipe. Allow to cool to room temperature, reserve. Combine sauce ingredients and reserve.

2. Heat wok over high heat for 30 seconds. Add I teaspoon Shallot Oil and coat wok with spatula. When a wisp of white smoke appears, add the minced ginger and stir briefly. Add the barbecued pork, mix, and cook for I minute. Add the shrimp, mix, and cook for I1/2 minutes more or until shrimp turn pink. Turn off heat, remove pork and shrimp mixture and reserve.

3. Turn heat back to high. Add remaining Shallot Oil and salt and coat wok with spatula. When a wisp of white smoke appears, add the cooked rice, stir and mix well. Lower heat to medium and continue to turn rice for 2 minutes. Turn heat back to high. Make a well in the center, add the beaten egg, cover, and stir and cook for 2 minutes more. Add the pork and shrimp mixture and mix well. Again make a well in the center, pour in sauce, and mix thoroughly making certain the rice is well coated. Add the Crisp Shallots and coriander and stir to mix. Turn off heat, transfer to a heated dish and serve.

    Nutrition per serving: 248 Calories; 11.6g Fat; 7% calories from fat; 36.2g Carbohydrates; 102mg Cholesterol; 369mg Sodium.

Shrimp Fried Rice with Sun-Dried Tomatoes

Tai Gawn Keh Har Chau Fon

Here is a meatless version of chau fon, *with the color of the sun-dried tomatoes fooling the eye into thinking it might be barbecued pork. The tongue will tell you differently. The variations of fried rice are limitless. I have even made it with dried, salted fish, for example. I encourage you to try your own combinations.*

1 Basic Cooked Rice recipe (page 48)

3 large eggs, beaten with a pinch of white pepper and salt

1 tablespoon plus 1 teaspoon peanut oil

SAUCE

1 1/2 teaspoons oyster sauce

1 tablespoon Chicken Stock (page 37)

2 teaspoons soy sauce

1 teaspoon white wine

3/4 teaspoon sugar

Pinch white pepper

1/2 teaspoon sesame oil

TO COMPLETE THE DISH

1 1/2 teaspoons minced ginger

2 cups broccoli stems, peeled, cut into 1/4-inch dice

1/4 pound medium shrimp, shelled, deveined, and cut into 1/2-inch pieces

1/4 cup sun-dried tomatoes, washed in warm water, cut into 1/2 × 1/4-inch pieces

1/2 cup scallions, finely sliced

3 tablespoons minced fresh coriander (cilantro)

Yield:
6 servings

1. Prepare Basic Rice recipe. Allow to cool to room temperature. Scramble eggs in I teaspoon of peanut oil over medium heat until cooked; then cut into small pieces and reserve. Combine sauce ingredients and reserve.

2. Heat wok over high heat for 30 seconds. Add I tablespoon peanut oil and coat wok with spatula. When a wisp of white smoke appears, add ginger, stir briefly. Add broccoli stems, stir and cook for 20 seconds. Add shrimp, stir and cook for 30 seconds. Add the cooked rice and mix well, turning, for 5 minutes until the rice mixture is very hot.

3. Stir the sauce, pour over rice, and mix thoroughly. Add eggs and stir. Add sun-dried tomatoes and mix to combine thoroughly. Add the scallions and coriander and mix well. Turn off heat, transfer to a heated dish, and serve.

Nutrition per serving: 251 Calories; 10g Fat; 6% calories from fat; 41g Carbohydrates; 128mg Cholesterol; 330mg Sodium.

粥 Congee

Congee is what it is known as to the West. The Chinese call it *jook,* a quick little word that translates as "soft rice." Jook is an infant cereal, a nourishing preparation for the aged, and adored by all ages in between. In this day of lighter meals, congees are becoming the meals of choice for many young Chinese professionals in places such as Hong Kong and Taiwan.

The origin of congee is mythological. Once, it is said, there was a rich but miserly man who, faced with the need to produce sufficient rice to feed ten guests, kept urging his cook to add spoonfuls of water to the rice pot to stretch it. What resulted was a rice porridge rather than cooked rice. Today's congees are quite a bit more sophisticated than that and definitely not for penny-pinchers.

Congee is the thickened rice soup on which Chinese babies have been raised for centuries. Often it is one of the preparations for wedding banquets or sixtieth-birthday celebrations. The variations, of this happy mixture of short-grain and glutinous rices, are infinite. It is for vegetarians, for meat eaters, and for fish lovers. Once regarded as a poor man's meal, it has become, as you will see, a thick soup of much elegance.

白 **Basic Congee**

Jook

粥
1/2 cup short-grain rice
1/4 cup glutinous rice
4 cups cold water
4 cups Chicken Stock (page 37)

Yield:
6 servings

1. Place both kinds of rice in a 4-quart pot. Wash the rice 3 times in cold water. Drain.

2. Return the washed rice to the pot, then add the water and chicken stock and bring to a boil over high heat. Cover the pot, leaving the lid partially open. Reduce the heat to medium-low and cook for 1 hour, stirring occasionally to prevent the rice from sticking to the bottom of the pot. Cook until the rice thickens to the desired consistency of porridge. Remove to a heated tureen and serve.

Nutrition per serving: 44.6 Calories; 2g Fat; 4% calories from fat; 6.3g Carbohydrates; 0mg Cholesterol; 423mg Sodium.

鶏 Chicken Congee

Gai Jook

粥 1 recipe Basic Congee (page 59)
1/2 pound lean chicken cutlet, thinly sliced into 2-inch-long pieces

MARINADE

2 teaspoons soy sauce

2 teaspoons Shao-Hsing wine or sherry

2 teaspoons cornstarch

1 1/2 teaspoons sugar

1/4 teaspoon salt

2 tablespoons finely shredded ginger

1 tablespoon Scallion Oil (page 39)

Pinch white pepper

TO COMPLETE THE DISH

3 tablespoons scallion greens, finely sliced

Yield:
6 servings

1. While you prepare Basic Congee, marinate the chicken in the combined marinade ingredients for 10 minutes.

2. Bring congee to a boil and add chicken and marinade. Stir until well mixed. Allow the congee to return to a boil. Lower heat and simmer for 2 minutes, or until chicken is cooked. Stir to avoid sticking. Turn off heat, transfer to a heated tureen, sprinkle scallions on top of congee and serve.

Nutrition per serving: 91.5 Calories; 4g Fat; 4% calories from fat; 10g Carbohydrates; 0mg Cholesterol; 320mg Sodium.

魚、Fish Congee

Yueh Jook

粥

I recipe Basic Congee (page 59)

3/4 pound fillet of carp, cut into slices 2 × 1/8 inch
(any firm, thick fish such as halibut may be used if
desired)

MARINADE

I teaspoon white vinegar

2 teaspoons Shao-Hsing wine or sherry

2 teaspoons soy sauce

I tablespoon White Peppercorn Oil (page 41)

1/2 teaspoon salt

3 tablespoons ginger, finely shredded

Pinch of white pepper

TO COMPLETE THE DISH

2 scallions, greens finely sliced

I tablespoon chopped fresh coriander (cilantro)

Yield:
6 servings

1. While preparing basic congee, marinate the fish in the combined
   marinade ingredients briefly, no more than 5 minutes.

2. Bring congee to a boil, stirring so it does not stick. Add fish slices
   and marinade. Stir to mix well. Return congee to a boil. Stir in
   scallions and coriander. Turn off heat, transfer to a heated tureen,
   and serve.

   Nutrition per serving: 99 Calories; 2.3g Fat; 2% calories from fat;
   8.2g Carbohydrates; 0mg Cholesterol; 720mg Sodium.

Tianjin Bok Choy Congee

Tianjin Bok Choy Jook

天津白菜粥

1 Basic Congee recipe (page 59)

1 pound Tianjin bok choy

1 slice fresh ginger, 1 inch thick, lightly smashed

3/4 teaspoon salt

2 teaspoons soy sauce

Pinch white pepper

1 tablespoon Scallion Oil (page 39)

Yield:
6 servings

1. Prepare the basic congee. As congee cooks prepare the Tianjin bok choy. Remove the individual stalks, wash and drain. Cut each stalk in half lengthwise, and these halves into 1/2-inch pieces on the diagonal. Cut leaves into 1/2-inch slices. Reserve.

2. When congee is cooked, add ginger, salt, and bok choy stalks and stir to mix well. Return the congee to a boil, lower heat, and simmer 5 to 7 minutes or until stalks are tender. As the congee simmers, stir frequently to avoid sticking. Bring back to a boil, add leaves, soy sauce, and white pepper. Cook for 2 minutes, stirring, until leaves soften. Add scallion oil, stir in. Turn off heat, transfer to a heated tureen, and serve.

Nutrition per serving: 80.3 Calories; 4g Fat; 0.4% calories from fat; 8.5g Carbohydrates; 0mg Cholesterol; 704mg Sodium.

Chiu Chow Congee

Chiu Chow Jook

To purists, this would not be recognized as a traditional congee. To the Chiu Chow people of southern China, however, it most assuredly is. The seafood-loving Chiu Chow often eat this congee instead of plain cooked rice; they claim it is far smoother, easier to digest, and serves to enhance the appetite. For this congee I strongly recommend fresh oysters. My choice would be those tiny Olympias from Washington, or their Kumamoto siblings. However, any fresh oyster will do.

2 cups Chicken Stock (page 37)

1 cup cold water

2 tablespoons shredded ginger

Pinch of white pepper

1 1/2 cups of cooked rice (see note)

1 1/2 dozen small oysters, whole, or 1/4 cup large oysters chopped

2 tablespoons minced fresh coriander (cilantro)

**Yield:
4 servings**

Place chicken stock, water, ginger, and white pepper in a pot. Cover and bring to a boil over high heat. Add the cooked rice, stir to mix. Bring back to a boil, add the oysters. Immediately turn off heat. Stir to mix. Transfer to a heated tureen, garnish with minced coriander, and serve.

Nutrition per serving: 44 Calories; 1.4g Fat; 3% calories from fat; 7g Carbohydrates; 5mg Cholesterol; 221mg Sodium.

Note: For this recipe use the rice of the Basic Cooked Rice recipe (page 48), either freshly made, or leftover.

Noodles with Black Bean Shrimp

See Jup Har Mien

6 cups cold water

1/2 pound thin egg noodles (or vermicelli)

1/3 cup cold water

I slice ginger, 1/2 inch thick, lightly smashed

1/2 pound large shrimp (16) shelled, deveined and washed

SAUCE

I tablespoon oyster sauce

I teaspoon soy sauce

I teaspoon white vinegar

I 1/2 teaspoons Shao-Hsing wine or sherry

1/2 teaspoon sugar

I tablespoon cornstarch

Pinch of white pepper

1/3 cup Chicken Stock (page 37)

TO COMPLETE THE DISH

I 1/2 teaspoons peanut oil

I teaspoon minced garlic

I tablespoon fermented black beans, washed twice, soaked for 10 minutes and drained

1/2 small red bell pepper, julienned (1/3 cup)

2 scallions, ends discarded, cut into I 1/2-inch sections, white portions quartered

2 teaspoons Shao-Hsing wine or sherry

Yield:
4 servings

1. In a large pot place 6 cups water, cover and bring to a boil over high heat. Add noodles, stirring and loosening with chopsticks. Cook for 1 minute or until *al dente.* Turn off heat. Run cold water into pot. Drain. Repeat again. Transfer to a serving platter. Reserve.

2. Heat wok over high heat, add 1/3 cup cold water and ginger and bring to a boil over high heat. Add shrimp, stir and cook for 1 minute or until shrimp begin to curl and turn pink. Turn off heat. Reserve shrimp. Reserve liquid.

3. Combine sauce ingredients and set aside.

4. Heat wok over high heat for 30 seconds. Add peanut oil and coat wok. When a wisp of white smoke appears, add minced garlic, stir briefly, and add black beans. Stir and cook for 30 seconds, add peppers and scallions, stir and cook for 45 seconds. Add the wine and mix well. Add reserved shrimp liquid and mix well. When the mixture boils, add reserved shrimp and stir and cook for 1 minute. Stir sauce, pour into mixture, and mix thoroughly. Cook for 1 minute or until sauce darkens and bubbles. Turn off heat, spoon mixture over the noodles, and serve.

    Nutrition per serving: 305 Calories; 5g Fat; 13% calories from fat; 45g Carbohydrates; 65mg Cholesterol; 449mg Sodium.

玉
花
蝦
麵

Noodles with Shrimp and Broccoli

Yuk Far Har Mien

The "jade flower" of the Chinese kitchen, broccoli enhances this dish of taste and other colors, including pink shrimp and red tomatoes, all atop the bed of noodles.

12 cups cold water

I slice ginger, 1/2 inch thick, lightly smashed

1/4 teaspoon baking soda (optional)

2 small heads broccoli, florets separated and cut into
    3/4-inch pieces (3/4 pound), (reserve stems for other use)

6 ounces medium shrimp (15), shelled, deveined, washed,
    cut into 1/2-inch pieces

1/2 pound Chinese egg noodles (or vermicelli)

SAUCE

I 1/2 tablespoons oyster sauce

I 1/2 teaspoons soy sauce

1/2 teaspoon sugar

I teaspoon Shao-Hsing wine or sherry

Pinch white pepper

I tablespoon cornstarch

3/4 cup Chicken Stock (page 37)

TO COMPLETE THE DISH

2 teaspoons Garlic Oil (page 39)

I small onion, cut into 1/4-inch dice

I 1/2 teaspoons minced garlic

10 sun-dried tomatoes (2 ounces), soaked briefly in warm
    water until soft and cut into 1/2-inch pieces

I 1/2 tablespoons Shao-Hsing wine

2 tablespoons Chicken Stock (page 37)

Yield:
6 servings

1. In a large pot bring 6 cups water, ginger, and baking soda to a boil over high heat. Immerse broccoli florets and blanch for 5 seconds. Turn off heat, run cold water in pot, drain. Remove florets and reserve.

2. Place other 6 cups of water into pot. Bring to a boil over high heat. Add noodles, stir and loosen, bring back to a boil and cook for 1 minute or until *al dente.* Turn off heat, run cold water into pot, drain. Remove noodles and reserve on a heated platter.

3. Combine sauce ingredients and reserve.

4. Heat wok over high heat for 30 seconds. Add 1 teaspoon of Garlic Oil, coat wok with spatula. When a wisp of white smoke appears, add onion, cook for 2 minutes until softened. Turn off heat, remove from wok, reserve.

5. Heat wok over high heat for 15 seconds, add remaining Garlic Oil, coat wok. Add garlic and stir briefly. Add shrimp and stir well. Add sun-dried tomatoes, stir. Add reserved broccoli and mix. Add wine, stir and mix well. Add reserved onions and mix. Add chicken stock and mix well. Make a well in the center of the mixture, stir sauce, pour in. Stir-fry for 1 1/2 minutes until sauce thickens and begins to bubble. Turn off heat, pour over noodles and serve.

Nutrition per serving: 215 Calories; 4.2g Fat; 17% calories from fat; 34g Carbohydrates; 43mg Cholesterol; 312mg Sodium.

冬
菇
瓣
麵

Mushroom Noodles

Dong Gu Ban Mien

This dish, with the fragrant, pungent mushrooms and chives offset by the cooked noodles, is a perfect example of a balanced dish. Classically, this is made with scallops. I prefer it as I have adapted it.

8 cups cold water

3/4 pound Chinese egg noodles (or vermicelli)

SAUCE

1 1/2 tablespoons oyster sauce

1 1/2 teaspoons soy sauce

2 teaspoons Shao-Hsing wine or sherry

1 teaspoon sugar

Pinch white pepper

1/2 cup Vegetable Stock (page 36)

TO COMPLETE THE DISH

1 1/2 teaspoons Garlic Oil (page 39)

1 tablespoon shredded ginger

1/4 pound Chinese chives, cut into 1-inch sections

6 medium Steamed Black Mushrooms (page 206) julienned (1/3 cup)

Yield:
6 servings

1. In a large pot bring water to a boil over high heat. Add noodles, stir to separate. Allow to return to a boil. Turn off heat, run cold water into pot, drain. Repeat. Reserve.

2. Combine sauce ingredients and set aside.

3. Heat wok over high heat for 30 seconds. Add Garlic Oil and coat wok. When a wisp of white smoke appears, add ginger, stir and cook for 20 seconds. Add chives, stir and mix, cook for 30 seconds. Add

mushrooms, stir and cook for 30 seconds more. Stir sauce, pour into wok, and mix well. Allow the sauce to come to a boil. Add noodles, stir and mix thoroughly. When the noodles absorb the liquid, turn off heat. Transfer to a heated platter and serve.

Nutrition per serving: 244 Calories; 4g Fat; 14% calories from fat; 44g Carbohydrates; 65mg Cholesterol; 294mg Sodium.

Cool Sesame Noodles

Ji Mah Mien

This dish is widely eaten in both Hunan and Sichuan. Contrary to what many people might think, there is peanut butter in China. It is called "peanut sauce" and is readily available.

8 cups cold water

1/2 pound Chinese egg noodles (slightly thicker than vermicelli)

1 teaspoon sesame oil

SAUCE

1 teaspoon sesame seed paste (tahini)

1 1/2 tablespoons peanut butter

2 teaspoons white vinegar

1 tablespoon mushroom soy sauce

1 1/4 teaspoons Hot Pepper Flakes (page 42)

2 teaspoons sugar

1/4 cup Chicken Stock (page 37)

Pinch of white pepper

2 tablespoons finely sliced scallion greens

2 sprigs fresh coriander (cilantro), broken into pieces

Yield:
4 servings

1. In a pot bring water to a boil over high heat. Add noodles, stirring to loosen. Cook for 1 1/2 minutes, until *al dente*. Run cold water into pot and drain noodles. Repeat. Drain thoroughly.

2. Place drained noodles in a mixing bowl, and toss with sesame oil. Refrigerate uncovered for 1 hour. Meanwhile combine the sauce ingredients.

3. When noodles are cool, toss with the sauce, place in a platter, garnish with coriander sprigs, and serve.

    Nutrition per serving: 131 Calories; 2.5g Fat; 14% calories from fat; 29g Carbohydrates; 0mg Cholesterol; 291mg Sodium.

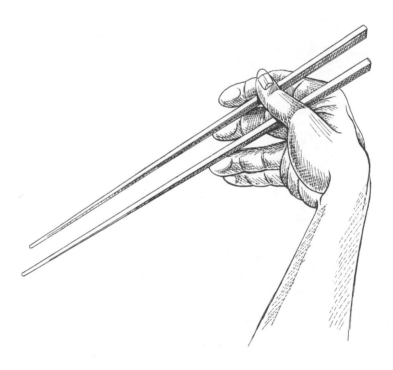

Tainan Noodles

Toi Lam Mien

In Tainan, in the southern part of Taiwan, there is a tiny noodle shop, Du Shao Yueh, in which this spicy soup originated. The shop is still there, and it still turns out pots and pots of these marvelous noodles. At the shop, this dish is not regarded as a soup, but as noodles in a broth. Traditionally it is made with pork and chicken broths, noodles, deep-fried pork, and pork meatballs. I have simplified it and lightened it considerably, with no loss of flavor. If you can't find horse beans with chili, you can substitute hot pepper sauce, but the flavor will not be the same.

1/4 pound lean ground pork

MARINADE

1 1/2 teaspoons mushroom soy sauce

1 1/2 teaspoons oyster sauce

2 Thai chilies, minced

1 teaspoon Shao-Hsing wine or sherry

1/2 teaspoon sesame oil

1/2 teaspoon sugar

TO COMPLETE THE DISH

4 cups plus 2 tablespoons Chicken Stock (page 37)

1 1/2 tablespoons horse beans with chili

1 teaspoon sesame oil

1 large piece of ginger, 2 inches long, smashed

1/4 teaspoon white pepper

2 teaspoons Shao-Hsing wine or sherry

1 tablespoon soy sauce

6 cups cold water

1/2 pound thin Chinese egg noodles (or spaghetti #10)

1/4 pound Chinese chives, cut into 1-inch pieces

Yield:
6 servings

1. Place ground pork in combined marinade ingredients. Mix well and allow to stand for 15 minutes.

2. Heat wok over high heat. Add 2 tablespoons chicken stock and bring to a boil. Add pork and marinade. Stir to loosen pork. Cook for 10 minutes, or until all liquid is absorbed and the meat is dry and crumbly. You must continue to stir so that the meat does not burn. Turn off heat, remove pork and reserve.

3. Pour the 4 cups of chicken stock into the wok, add horse beans, sesame oil, ginger, white pepper, wine, and soy sauce. Cover wok and bring mixture to a boil. Lower heat to simmer (this is to collect and blend the residue remaining in the wok after the pork has been cooked). Simmer for 4 minutes, raise heat back to high, and allow to come back to a boil.

4. As the broth simmers, prepare the noodles. Boil the 6 cups of cold water. Add noodles and boil for 1 minute or until they are *al dente*. Turn off heat, run cold water into pot. Drain. Repeat again, drain thoroughly. Remove noodles and divide into 6 soup bowls.

5. Add the chives to the boiling broth, stir in briefly until they become bright green. Turn off heat. Sprinkle the reserved pork over the noodles, and ladle the broth with chives over them. Serve immediately.

Nutrition per serving: 316 Calories; 5.1g Fat; 26% calories from fat; 36g Carbohydrates; 37mg Cholesterol; 971mg Sodium.

Shanghai Spiced Noodles

Seung Hoi Ja Jeung Mien

This noodle dish is a Shanghai specialty, where touches of heat and sweetness characterize the regional cooking. It was so popular that immigrants from Shanghai brought it to Hong Kong with them, and now it is popular there as well.

1/4 pound fresh lean pork loin, shredded

1/4 teaspoon sugar

1/4 teaspoon salt

2 quarts cold water

3/4 pound Chinese egg noodles (or vermicelli)

SAUCE

2 tablespoons hoisin sauce

2 tablespoons soy sauce

2 tablespoons dark soy sauce

21/2 teaspoons white vinegar

I teaspoon sugar

2 teaspoons Shao-Hsing wine or sherry

1/4 teaspoon sesame oil

Pinch white pepper

TO COMPLETE THE DISH

I1/2 teaspoons peanut oil

2 teaspoons minced garlic

3 Thai chilies, minced

2 teaspoons Shao-Hsing wine or sherry

4 medium Steamed Black Mushrooms (page 206)

1/2 medium red bell pepper, julienned (1/2 cup)

1/2 medium green bell pepper, julienned (1/2 cup)

Yield:
6 servings

1. Toss shredded pork with sugar and salt, allow to rest for 15 minutes.

2. In a large pot bring water to a boil over high heat. Add noodles, stir to loosen, and allow water to return to a boil. Boil for 30 seconds or until *al dente.* Turn off heat, run cold water into pot, drain. Repeat, drain thoroughly. Remove noodles to a heated serving platter.

3. Combine sauce ingredients and reserve.

4. Heat wok over high heat for 30 seconds. Add peanut oil and coat wok. When a wisp of white smoke appears, add garlic and chilies and stir briefly. Add pork, stir and cook for 30 seconds. Add wine, stir and mix well. Stir sauce, and pour in, mix well. Add the mushrooms and bell peppers to the stir-fry and cook for 1 to 1 1/2 minutes until peppers soften. Turn off heat, pour mixture over noodles and serve.

Nutrition per serving: 318 Calories; 7g Fat; 19% calories from fat; 56g Carbohydrates; 25mg Cholesterol; 407mg Sodium.

Don Don Noodles

Don Don Mien

This is a simplified and lightened variation of a well-known Sichuan noodle dish.

I ounce small dried shrimp

1/4 pound fresh lean pork loin, shredded

1/2 teaspoon dark soy sauce

I teaspoon cornstarch

1/2 ounce peanuts, dry-roasted (page 14)

21/2 cups Chicken Stock (page 37)

3 Thai chilies, minced

2 teaspoons sesame seed paste (tahini)

2 quarts cold water

3/4 pound Chinese egg noodles (or vermicelli)

3 tablespoons minced scallion greens

Yield:
6 servings

1. Soak shrimp in hot water for 15 minutes, reserve. Toss shredded pork with dark soy sauce and cornstarch, reserve. Crush dry-roasted peanuts and reserve.

2. In a large pot place chicken stock, chilies, sesame seed paste, and reserved shrimp. Cover and bring to a boil over high heat. Stir, reduce heat to low, cover pot, leaving a small opening at the lid, and simmer for 20 minutes. Raise heat back to high. Add pork mixture and stir well. Return to a boil. Boil for 1 minute. Turn off heat.

3. As the broth simmers, prepare the noodles. Place the water in a pot and bring to a boil over high heat. Add noodles, stir to separate and allow to return to a boil. Boil for 30 seconds, until *al dente*. Run cold water into pot, drain well.

4. Divide noodles into 6 individual bowls. Ladle soup atop the noodles. Sprinkle with crushed peanuts and minced scallions and serve.

Nutrition per serving: 334 Calories; 11g Fat; 24% calories from fat; 54g Carbohydrates; 32.5mg Cholesterol; 283mg Sodium.

Won Ton Soup

Won Tun Tong

Who has not eaten won ton soup? This is probably the most requested dish in any Chinese restaurant, regardless of its stature. In China, won ton are always eaten in soup, alone or in combination with other noodles. When I was a girl, the won ton vendor would come by every evening and with clicking noises, made by tapping bamboo sticks together, would announce his presence. To me it was the call to won ton soup.

5 cups Chicken Stock (page 37)
1/2 pound bok choy, cut into 1/2-inch pieces on the diagonal
24 cooked Won Ton (page 78)

Yield:
6 servings

1. Place stock in a large pot, cover and bring to a boil over high heat. Add bok choy, stir, making certain the bok choy is totally immersed in the stock. Return it to a boil. Lower heat to medium and cook for 5 minutes, or until bok choy is tender.

2. Raise heat back to high. Add won ton. Stir and immerse into soup. Return the soup to a boil. As soon as it boils, turn off the heat. Remove to a heated tureen and serve immediately.

Nutrition per serving: 156 Calories; 6g Fat; 26% calories from fat; 9g Carbohydrates; 96mg Cholesterol; 864mg Sodium.

Won Ton

Won Tun

The words for this marvelous noodle—for it is indeed a noodle—translate as "swallowing a cloud," which in China simply means light. And these tasty little packages, which the Chinese enjoy in noodle shops, are indeed light. Most Westerners have had their first won ton in soup.

The won ton is most versatile. Once it is boiled, it can be put into soup, pan-fried, deep-fried or steamed. It can be the first course of a larger meal. Best of all, if it is left over it can be frozen for use on another day.

FILLING

1/2 pound lean fresh pork loin, ground

3 ounces shrimp, shelled, deveined, washed, and cut into 1/4-inch pieces

3 scallions, both ends discarded, finely chopped

2 cloves garlic, minced

3 fresh water chestnuts, peeled, washed, finely diced

11/2 teaspoons Shao-Hsing wine or sherry

1/4 teaspoon salt

1/2 teaspoon sugar

11/2 teaspoons soy sauce

1/2 teaspoon sesame oil

2 teaspoons oyster sauce

Pinch white pepper

1 to 11/2 tablespoons cornstarch

1 medium egg

TO COMPLETE THE DISH

24 won ton skins

10 cups cold water

1 tablespoon salt

1 tablespoon peanut oil

Yield:
6 servings
or 24 won ton

1. Place all filling ingredients in a bowl and mix thoroughly, stirring clockwise, until well blended.

2. Place about 1 tablespoon of this filling in the center of a won ton skin. (Skins should be kept in plastic wrap, at room temperature, then 20 minutes before use, removed from plastic wrap. Paper coating should be peeled off, and as they are being used, the others should be kept covered with a wet towel.)

3. Keep a bowl of water at hand so that the 4 edges of the won ton can be moistened. The filling should be placed on the unfloured side of the won ton skin. The skin should be folded over the filling and squeezed along the wet edges to seal it like an envelope. Once folded and sealed, the 2 corners of the folded side should be wet and then drawn together and squeezed to create a bowlike shape. As each won ton is made, it should be placed on a floured cookie sheet to prevent sticking.

4. Repeat process until all won ton are made. Cook them in the 10 cups of water to which have been added 1 tablespoon of salt and 1 tablespoon peanut oil. The water should be boiling when won ton are added. Usual cooking time is 6 to 7 minutes, or until the skins become translucent.

5. Turn off heat. Run cold water into pot, drain. Repeat, drain thoroughly. Serve immediately.

Nutrition per serving: 129 Calories; 5g Fat; 23% calories from fat; 8g Carbohydrates; 98mg Cholesterol; 311mg Sodium.

Note: I suggest serving with a simple dipping sauce of a hot mustard and chili sauce mix. Mix 1 1/2 tablespoons of Colman's dried mustard with an equal amount of cold water, and blend. Add 1 teaspoon of chili sauce and mix well.

家鄉炒米粉

Home-Style Noodles

Gah Heung Chau Mai Fun

The words gah heung *translate as "one's region of residence," "where one lives." For example, suburban Los Angeles is a gah heung, as is Long Island. A gah heung is familiar, and in these places dishes have individual characteristics. These home-style noodles are from my gah heung of Sun Tak, outside of Canton. It is one of the more enjoyable noodle combinations of my girlhood.*

> 8 cups cold water
>
> 1/4 pound bean sprouts, washed and drained
>
> 1/2 pound rice noodles, soaked in hot water 20 minutes and
>   drained

SAUCE

> 2 tablespoons oyster sauce
>
> 2 teaspoons soy sauce
>
> I teaspoon sugar
>
> 2 teaspoons Shao-Hsing wine or sherry
>
> Pinch white pepper

TO COMPLETE THE DISH

> I1/2 teaspoons peanut oil
>
> I1/2 teaspoons minced ginger
>
> Pinch of salt
>
> 1/4 pound Barbecued Pork (page 236), thinly sliced
>
> 2 ounces snow peas, ends and strings removed, each cut into
>   3 sections on the diagonal
>
> 3 scallions, ends removed, cut into 2-inch sections, white
>   portions quartered
>
> 1/2 medium red bell pepper, julienned (1/3 cup)
>
> 2 tablespoons Chicken Stock (page 37)

Yield:
6 servings

1. In a large pot bring water to a boil over high heat. Place bean sprouts in a strainer and lower them into the water, blanch for 10 seconds. Remove sprouts, run cold water through them. Drain, reserve.

2. Allow water to return to a boil. Add the noodles and blanch for 10 seconds. Turn off heat, run cold water into pot, drain, reserve.

3. Combine sauce ingredients and set aside.

4. Heat wok over high heat for 30 seconds. Add peanut oil and coat wok. When a wisp of white smoke appears, add ginger and salt, stir briefly. Add pork, stir and cook for 30 seconds. Add snow peas, stir and cook for 20 seconds. Add white portion of scallions, stir and mix well. Add the peppers and green portions of scallions and stir well. Add chicken stock and stir to mix well. Add reserved noodles and stir all ingredients together. Stir sauce, make a well in the center of the mixture, pour in sauce and mix well. Add the bean sprouts and mix. Cook until sauce is completely absorbed and noodles are coated evenly, about 3 minutes. Turn off heat, transfer to a heated platter, and serve.

Nutrition per serving: 235 Calories; 8g Fat; 28% calories from fat; 33g Carbohydrates; 18mg Cholesterol; 333mg Sodium.

星州炒米粉 Singapore Noodles

Sing Jau Chau Mai Fon

*My guess is there exist only a very few Chinese restaurants that do not offer this noodle dish.
I have simplified it considerably and lowered its normally high-fat content considerably.*

3 quarts cold water

1/4 pound bean sprouts, washed and drained

1/2 pound rice noodles, soaked in hot water for 20 minutes
  until softened, drained

SAUCE

21/2 tablespoons oyster sauce

2 teaspoons soy sauce

1/2 teaspoon sugar

1/4 cup Chicken Stock (page 37)

CURRY

2 tablespoons curry powder

2 tablespoons Chicken Stock (page 37)

TO COMPLETE THE DISH

4 teaspoons peanut oil

2 teaspoons minced ginger

1/4 teaspoon salt

10 medium shrimp (1/4 pound), shelled, deveined, washed,
  and halved lengthwise

2 ounces Barbecued Pork (page 244), julienned

3 tablespoons Chicken Stock (page 37)

2 fresh water chestnuts, peeled, washed, and julienned

1/2 large red bell pepper, julienned (1/2 cup)

4 scallions, both ends trimmed, cut into 11/2-inch pieces

Yield:
6 servings

1. In a large pot bring water to a boil over high heat. Place bean sprouts in a strainer and lower into water, blanch for 10 seconds. Remove strainer and run cold water through bean sprouts, drain, reserve.

2. Bring water back to a boil, add rice noodles, and blanch for 10 seconds. Turn off heat, run cold water into pot, drain thoroughly, reserve.

3. Combine sauce ingredients and set aside. Combine the curry ingredients and set aside.

4. Heat wok over high heat for 30 seconds, add peanut oil and coat wok. When a wisp of white smoke appears, add ginger and salt. Cook for 15 seconds then stir in curry mixture. Cook for 30 seconds until the curry's aroma is released. Add shrimp, stir briefly. Add pork, stir briefly. Add chicken stock, stir and mix well, cook for 1 minute. Add the scallions, stir and cook briefly. Stir the sauce, make a well in the center, pour in sauce, and mix thoroughly.

5. Add reserved noodles and toss until they are well coated, and become yellow in color from the curry. Add water chestnuts and stir together for 1 minute. Add bean sprouts and peppers and mix well for 1 minute until the noodles are very hot. Turn off heat, remove to a heated platter and serve.

Nutrition per serving: 253 Calories; 6.3g Fat; 22% calories from fat; 34g Carbohydrates; 36mg Sodium; 493mg Sodium.

四
川
炒
米
粉

Rice Noodles Sichuan

Sei Chun Chau Mai Fon

In this recipe I have brought the heat and piquancy of Sichuan to cooked rice noodles. The minced chilies bring out, as they should, the other flavors in this dish. Often chilies are added simply for heat. They ought not to be; they should be integrated, and in this dish they are.

> 8 cups cold water
> 1/2 pound rice noodles, soaked in hot water for 20 minutes and drained

MARINADE

> I teaspoon ginger juice mixed with 2 teaspoons Shao-Hsing wine or sherry
> 3/4 teaspoon sugar
> 1/4 teaspoon sesame oil
> 2 teaspoons soy sauce
> 21/2 tablespoons oyster sauce
> Pinch salt
> Pinch white pepper

TO COMPLETE THE DISH

> 1/2 pound medium shrimp (20), shelled, deveined, washed, dried, and halved lengthwise
> 4 teaspoons peanut oil
> 2 teaspoons minced ginger
> 2 stalks celery, cut into matchsticks
> 3 fresh water chestnuts, peeled, washed, and julienned
> 3 tablespoons mustard pickle, finely shredded
> 2 Thai chilies, minced
> I bunch scallions, cut into 2-inch long pieces, white portions quartered lengthwise
> I teaspoon minced garlic

Yield:
10 servings

1. In a pot bring water to a boil over high heat. Add noodles and cook for 10 seconds. Turn off heat, run cold water into pot, drain thoroughly. Reserve noodles.

2. Combine marinade ingredients and add shrimp.

3. Heat wok over high heat for 30 seconds. Add 2 teaspoons peanut oil and coat wok. When a wisp of white smoke appears, add 1 teaspoon of minced ginger. Stir briefly, add celery, water chestnuts, mustard pickle, chilies, peppers, and scallions. Stir-fry for 1 to 1 1/2 minutes until scallions become bright green. Turn off heat, remove mixture, reserve. Wash wok and spatula.

4. Heat wok over high heat for 30 seconds. Add remaining 2 teaspoons peanut oil and coat wok. When a wisp of white smoke appears, add remaining minced ginger and minced garlic. Stir briefly. Add shrimp with its marinade, cook and stir until shrimp begin to turn pink. Add noodles and mix well to coat. Add reserved vegetables and mix together well for 1 1/2 minutes until very hot. Turn off heat, transfer to a heated platter and serve.

Nutrition per serving: 148 calories; 3.2g Fat; 18% calories from fat; 21g Carbohydrates; 30mg Cholesterol; 188mg Sodium.

Chapter 3

Foods From the Water

There is perhaps no food prized more at the Chinese table than fish, the freshest it can be. On the day of the lunar New Year some families, unable either by geography or circumstances to have a fresh fish as part of its New Year banquet, will place a wooden fish in the center of the dining table as a symbol of the plenty that a fish denotes. *Hoi sin*, someone will say, a phrase that stands for "ocean fresh." The words sound identical to the name of that wonderful sweet sauce made from soybeans, but there is no connection. Hoi sin, when it comes to fish and seafood, means the absolute freshest.

One of the recurring pleasures of visiting not only China and Hong Kong, but other Asian cities as well, is to wander into fish markets. If the market is a fine one, you will not find displays of crushed ice topped with mounds of lifeless shrimp, or equally lifeless fish, stacked like so many silvery logs. To the Chinese, fish are fresh when they are living. Fish are swimming, shrimp dart about in water tanks, crabs and lobsters are crawling. Hoi Sin.

It is a pleasure to watch a Chinese housewife select fish. She will come into a market and wander among the galvanized vats holding fish of all sorts, and when she sees one that she fancies she will beckon to the fishmonger and point. He will reach into the tank with a net, make certain he snares the fish wanted by the housewife and bring it up. He will remove it from the net and hold it in his hand while the housewife inspects it for the cleanness of its body, so she can make certain that there are no hook or barb marks of damage; that its gills are deep red. If the fish pleases her she will nod; the fishmonger will tap the fish on the head with a wooden mallet, stunning it. He will then quickly gut, clean, and scale it and place it in a plastic bag filled with clean sea or river water, and off the housewife will go.

That is if the meal at which that fish is to be eaten is soon. If there are to be a few hours between the purchase and the eating, the fish is taken home alive. So it is with crabs, or lobsters, or any of the mollusks. Live seafood is a virtual religion in China, particularly along its coast, in Canton, Hong Kong, and Shanghai. In Hong Kong, there is a restaurant called *Fook Lam Moon* that I consider to be the finest seafood restaurant in which I have ever eaten. In its employ is a man who is referred to, and not lightly, as the "emperor of the fish." It is his function to accept all of the fish and seafood delivered each day, to see that these fish are kept perfectly in a series of tanks. When a fish is desired by a restaurant customer, it is this "emperor of the fish" who will select it, and specify how it should be cooked.

In extended meals the dish that will close the meal is invariably a fish. Any banquet will close with a fish, not only because of custom but because of its symbolism as the close of a meal of plenty. In China, shrimp are considered happy because their name, *har*, sounds like laughter. Clams and oysters connote good fortune, and even seaweed is considered to be good luck because it is the bed from which the foods of the sea arise.

Steamed Striped Bass

Jing Lu Yue

It is said that if a master Chinese chef, a *dai see fu*, is presented with a live fish he would be able to devise more than 30 different preparations for it. I have watched masters in China, Hong Kong, and Taiwan, and I believe this to be true. We will make a modest effort here to make all of you, if not masters, then worthy apprentices.

The proper steaming of fish illustrates the Cantonese kitchen at its very best. Fish must be handled and prepared with care, and steamed to a perfect tenderness and firmness. Often chefs are recognized by how well they steam fish. What follows are first the classic steamed version from the Cantonese kitchen, then two variations that prove that identical fish, cooked with identical methods can taste markedly different with the use of different marinades and recipe additions.

I recommend striped bass for steaming, because of its firm, yet flaky, texture. However, sea bass will substitute nicely, as will snapper. Both sea bass and snapper may have to be steamed just a bit longer than specified because their heads are larger.

葱薑蒸魚

Striped Bass Steamed with Ginger and Scallions

Geung Chung Jing Hue

I whole 2-pound striped bass; have fishmonger remove scales, gills, and intestines

MARINADE

2 tablespoons soy sauce

2 tablespoons white wine

1/8 teaspoon salt

2 teaspoons white vinegar

2 teaspoons peanut oil

Generous pinch of white pepper

TO COMPLETE THE DISH

21/2 tablespoons shredded ginger

2 scallions, both ends discarded, cut into 2-inch sections, white portions lightly smashed

I teaspoon sesame oil

I scallion, greens finely sliced

I1/2 tablespoons fresh coriander (cilantro), finely sliced

Yield:
6 servings

I. To prepare fish, remove all inner fat and membranes, wash well, and dry. Place fish in a steam-proof dish. Pour in combined marinade ingredients and coat fish well, inside and out. Sprinkle I1/2 table-spoons shredded ginger and half of the sectioned scallions in the fish cavity. Lift the fish and place the remaining scallions and I tablespoon of shredded ginger in the dish and lay fish on top. Sprinkle remaining I tablespoon of shredded ginger on the fish.

2. To steam the fish, pour 8 cups of boiling water in a wok. Place the dish containing the fish in a steamer and cover. Place steamer in wok and steam for 25 minutes, until cooked (see notes).

3. Turn off heat. With the fish still in its dish, pour sesame oil over it. Then sprinkle with finely sliced scallions and coriander and serve.

Nutrition per serving: 161 Calories; less than 1g Fat; 4.7% calories from fat; 68g Carbohydrates; 58mg Cholesterol; 291mg Sodium.

Notes: As noted in the section on steaming, you may also steam the fish in a 10-inch metal cake pan. In this case, cut the fish to fit the pan and marinate as above. Place a cake rack in the wok, the cake pan on the rack, cover the wok and steam. The fish will steam quickly this way, about 12 to 15 minutes.

The cake pan with the fish may also be placed in the bed of a steamer, the steamer in the wok as noted. The steamer must be covered.

If your range does not generate very high heat, you may cut the fish into 3 sections, steam it, then before serving put the sections together on a serving platter. The steaming time in this instance will be about 12 to 15 minutes as well.

During any steaming process keep boiling water at hand to replace any that may evaporate.

With any steamed fish test the cooked flesh by gently pushing a chopstick into the most fleshy portion of the fish. If it can be easily inserted, the fish is cooked.

Steamed Striped Bass with Shredded Pork

Yuk See Jing Tue

I whole 2-pound striped bass; have fishmonger remove scales, gills, and intestines

MARINADE

2 tablespoons soy sauce

I tablespoon white wine

I 1/2 teaspoons white vinegar

4 slices fresh ginger, shredded

Pinch white pepper

TO COMPLETE THE DISH

2 tablespoons lean, fresh pork, shredded and mixed with 1/2 teaspoon sesame oil

4 Chinese black mushrooms, soaked in hot water for about 30 minutes, stems discarded, and sliced thinly

I teaspoon White Peppercorn Oil (page 41)

3 scallions, greens finely sliced

Yield:
6 servings

1. Remove all inner fat and membranes from fish, wash well and dry. Place fish in a steaming dish, pour in the combined marinade ingredients and coat fish well, inside and out. Sprinkle shredded pork on fish. Sprinkle sliced mushrooms atop this. Allow to rest for 10 minutes.

2. Steam fish until cooked. Remove from wok. Pour White Peppercorn Oil over fish, sprinkle with finely sliced scallions and serve.

Nutrition per serving: 220 Calories; 5.5g Fat; 22% calories from fat; 68g Carbohydrates; 77mg Cholesterol; 305mg Sodium.

辣椒蒸魚 Steamed Striped Bass with Chilies

Lot Jiu Jing Yue

I whole 2-pound striped bass; have fishmonger remove scales, gills, and intestines

Marinade

2 Thai chilies, minced

I 1/2 tablespoons Shao-Hsing wine or sherry

2 tablespoons soy sauce

I 1/2 teaspoons white vinegar

I teaspoon sugar

Pinch salt

Pinch white pepper

2 tablespoons fermented black beans, rinsed twice

3 tablespoons shredded ginger

To complete the dish

I teaspoon Garlic Oil (page 39)

2 tablespoons minced fresh coriander (cilantro)

Yield:
6 servings

1. To prepare the fish, remove all inner fat and membranes. Wash well and dry. Place in a steaming dish, pour in combined marinade ingredients, and coat fish well, inside and out.

2. Steam fish until cooked. Remove from wok. Pour Garlic Oil over fish and sprinkle with chopped coriander and serve.

Nutrition per serving: 166 Calories; less than Ig Fat; 4.5% calories from fat; 70g Carbohydrates; 58mg Cholesterol; 291mg Sodium.

Unicorn Fish

Kei Lun Yue

This fish swims in mythology. It is said to have been a favorite of the Ching dynasty imperial household. Its name is the Chinese representation of the unicorn, a creature with the body of a horse and the head of a dragon with a jutting horn. It is a symbol of good luck, and the dish itself is quite imaginative, as its name suggests.

> I whole 2-pound striped bass; have fishmonger remove scales, gills, and intestines (sea bass or snapper may be substituted)

MARINADE

> I teaspoon white vinegar
> I 1/2 tablespoons white wine
> I 1/2 tablespoons soy sauce
> I tablespoon shredded ginger
> Pinch salt
> Pinch white pepper

TO COMPLETE THE DISH

> 4 slices Smithfield ham, each 3 inches long, 1/2 inch wide, 1/8 inch thick (prepared for use, see page 30)
> 2 large Chinese black mushrooms, soaked in hot water for 30 minutes, stems discarded, caps cut in half
> 2 teaspoons Scallion Oil (page 39)
> 4 scallions, white portions only, shredded
> 20 strips red bell pepper
> 10 sprigs fresh coriander (cilantro)

Yield:
4 servings

I. To prepare fish, remove all inner fat and membranes, wash inside and out, drain thoroughly, and dry.

2. Score fish by making slices approximately the width of the fish, about 1 inch apart, on both sides. Cuts should be made to the bone and with the blade held at an angle. Place the fish in a steam-proof dish and pour combined marinade ingredients over it.

3. Slide a ham slice and a half mushroom cap into each of the cuts along one side, alternating the ham and the mushrooms. Place dish in a steamer and steam the fish 10 to 12 minutes, until cooked.

4. Remove dish from steamer. Drizzle Scallion Oil over fish. Sprinkle scallions and red peppers on top, garnish with coriander, and serve.

Nutrition per serving: 264 Calories; 4.1g Fat; 14% calories from fat; 104g Carbohydrates; 94mg Cholesterol; 443mg Sodium.

白水魚 White Water Fish

Bak Soi Yue

Fish cooked in this manner are referred to in China as bak soi *or "white water," because they are cooked, or poached, in boiling, bubbling "white water."*

> 3 quarts cold water

POACHING

> 4 fresh basil leaves
>
> 8 fresh mint leaves
>
> 2 garlic cloves, whole and peeled
>
> 3 scallions, ends discarded, each cut into thirds
>
> 2 teaspoons White Peppercorn Oil (page 41)
>
> 2 teaspoons salt
>
> 3 teaspoons sugar
>
> I piece ginger, I inch thick, lightly smashed

TO CONTINUE THE DISH

> I whole sea bass, I1/2 to I3/4 pounds; have fishmonger remove scales, gills and intestines

SAUCE

> 21/2 tablespoons soy sauce
>
> 21/2 tablespoons Seafood Stock (page 38)
>
> I1/2 teaspoons sugar
>
> I tablespoon Shao-Hsing wine or sherry
>
> I teaspoon white vinegar
>
> 2 teaspoons White Peppercorn Oil (page 41)
>
> 2 tablespoons shredded ginger
>
> 2 scallions, white portions only, cut into I1/2-inch lengths and shredded

Yield:
4 servings

1. To prepare fish, remove all inner fat and membranes, wash and dry thoroughly. In a fish poacher or an oval Dutch oven bring 3 quarts of water and poaching ingredients to a boil. Boil 5 minutes. Place fish in the liquid and cover. Bring back to a boil, boil for 3 minutes and turn off heat. Let fish sit for 10 minutes. Remove fish from liquid, place in a serving dish. Discard other ingredients.

2. As the fish rests, make the sauce. Place all ingredients in a saucepan, bring to a boil. Turn off heat. Pour sauce over fish and serve.

Nutrition per serving: 207 Calories; less than 1g Fat; almost 0% calories from fat; 93g Carbohydrates; 79mg Cholesterol; 440mg Sodium.

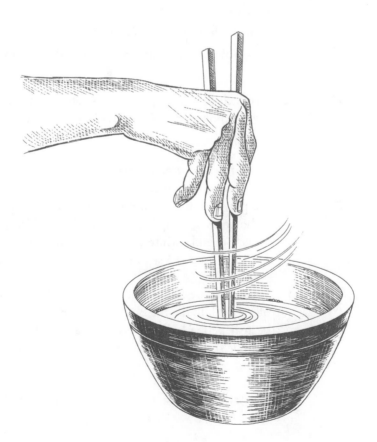

海鮮湯 Fresh Fish Soup

Hoi Sin Tong

In no other preparation do the words hoi sin *apply more. This dish is based upon fresh fish cooked in individual bowls. What makes this special is, of course, the freshness of the striped bass, sea bass, or snapper—any of which is suitable—and the stunning preparation. In China, particularly in Hong Kong, the fish is usually alive when slices are cut from it. Nothing could be fresher.*

2 fillets fresh sea bass, each 1/2 pound

4 cups cold water

Pinch of baking soda, optional

1/4 pound spinach, stems removed

1 tablespoon shredded ginger

Pinch white pepper

4 cups Chicken Stock (page 37)

1 1/2 tablespoons white portions scallions, finely sliced

Yield:
4 servings

1. Slice each fillet of fish along its side into paper thin slices, as you might slice smoked salmon. Divide slices equally into 4 portions. Reserve.

2. In a pot bring water and baking soda to a boil over high heat. Add spinach and blanch for 5 seconds. Turn off heat, run cold water into pot, and drain well. Divide spinach leaves equally and place at the bottoms of soup bowls. Sprinkle shredded ginger equally in the bowls. Sprinkle white pepper in each. Place each portion of the sliced fish atop the seasoned spinach.

3. As you prepare the bowls, the chicken stock should be heating to a rolling boil. Ladle the boiling soup into the bowls and it will cook the fish perfectly. Turn off heat after all bowls have been filled. Sprinkle the sliced scallions into each bowl and serve.

Nutrition per serving: 134 Calories; 2g Fat; 13% calories from fat; 50g Carbohydrates; 44mg Cholesterol; 660mg Sodium.

Rolled Flounder with Black Mushrooms

Dong Gu Long Lei Geun

冬
菇
龍
利
捲

There is a tradition of rolling ingredients into fish fillets that exists in Chongsan, a small district of Guangdong province that is famous for being the birthplace of Dr. Sun Yat-sen and famous as well for this gastronomic custom of rolling fish around other foods. In most cases oysters, shellfish, and other foods from the sea are rolled in fillets of flat fish, but many chefs vary their fillings to include vegetables and meats as well. In this variation I have chosen to roll those pungent Chinese black mushrooms because they complement the fish so well.

1 pound flounder (3 fish), to make 6 fillets

Marinade

2 tablespoons Shao-Hsing wine or sherry

2 tablespoons soy sauce

1 1/2 teaspoons Scallion Oil (page 39)

1/4 cup finely sliced scallions

2 teaspoons minced ginger

1 teaspoon white vinegar

1/4 teaspoon salt

1 teaspoon sugar

Pinch white pepper

1 1/2 teaspoons finely chopped fresh coriander (cilantro)

To complete the dish

6 large Chinese black mushrooms, steamed (page 206),
    julienned, and divided into 6 equal portions

1 scallion, ends trimmed, cut into 3 1/2-inch sections,
    julienned, divided into 6 equal portions

1 teaspoon Scallion Oil (page 39)

Yield:
6 servings

1. Trim each of the fish fillets into shapes roughly rectangular, about 51/2 × 31/2 inches. Mix the marinade ingredients, place in a wide, shallow dish. Add fillets, coat, and allow to rest.

2. To make the rolls, place a portion of mushrooms and scallions at one end of a fillet (if one end is wider, use it) and roll to create a cylinder. Repeat until 6 rolls are made.

3. Place the flounder rolls in a steam-proof dish, with the seam sides down, the smooth side facing up. Pour the marinade over the rolls, then steam them for 8 minutes, or until fish turns white and firm. When cooked, remove from heat, drizzle the Scallion Oil over them, and serve.

Nutrition per serving: 77 Calories; 1.6g Fat; 18% calories from fat; 2.3g Carbohydrates; 34mg Cholesterol; 350mg Sodium.

Flounder Stuffed Bean Curd

Yung Dau Fu

In China yung dau fu *always means bean curd stuffed with fish or any seafood. It is a most popular dish, particularly in southern China. This is one of the first foods fed to babies when they begin to eat solids. My babies loved it as much as their father did.*

6 ounces of flounder fillet

MARINADE

1/2 teaspoon Ginger Juice (page 43) mixed with I teaspoon Shao-Hsing wine or sherry

1/2 teaspoon soy sauce

I teaspoon White Peppercorn Oil (page 41)

2 teaspoons oyster sauce

1/4 teaspoon salt

3/4 teaspoon sugar

Pinch white pepper

I tablespoon cornstarch

3 scallions, finely chopped

TO CONTINUE THE DISH

6 cakes firm, fresh bean curd (I 1/2 pounds)

SAUCE

I tablespoon oyster sauce

I teaspoon dark soy sauce

1/2 teaspoon sugar

1/4 cup Seafood Stock (page 38)

I teaspoon White Peppercorn Oil (page 41)

Pinch white pepper

2 tablespoons minced fresh coriander (cilantro)

Yield:
6 servings

1. To prepare the fish, place on a clean chopping board. Cut into small pieces, then with a cleaver chop into a paste. Place paste in a bowl. Add the marinade ingredients and combine thoroughly. If mixture is too soft and loose, add an additional 1/2 tablespoon cornstarch. Refrigerate at least 4 hours until firm.

2. To prepare bean curd, cut each cake across diagonally and with a knife make a pocket in the diagonally cut side.

3. Place 1 tablespoon of paste in the pocket of each bean curd half, and use a butter knife to press in until smooth. Place 12 halves in a steam-proof dish. Combine the sauce ingredients, pour over bean curd, and steam for 7 minutes or until fish is cooked and firm. Remove from steamer, sprinkle with coriander, and serve.

Nutrition per serving: 130 Calories; 2g Fat; 15% calories from fat; 6g Carbohydrates; 12mg Cholesterol; 596mg Sodium.

Steamed Salmon

Jing Sah Mun Yue

Salmon once was unknown in China. Today, however, it is to be found throughout the country, particularly in the kitchens and dining rooms of the many Western hotels now in China. In Hong Kong, chefs have been cooking salmon for quite some time, and cooking it in a traditional way, with steam. Steaming any fish, including salmon, enhances its true flavor.

I pound salmon (a whole section of fish, with bone and skin intact, the closer to the more flavorful tail end, the better)

2 teaspoons white vinegar

I tablespoon soy sauce

I 1/2 tablespoons Shao-Hsing wine or sherry

Pinch salt

Pinch white pepper

I 1/2 tablespoons shredded ginger

I scallion, cut into 2-inch pieces, white portions quartered lengthwise

I teaspoon sesame oil

2 tablespoons minced fresh coriander (cilantro)

Yield:
4 servings

1. Place salmon in a steam-proof dish. Pour in vinegar, soy sauce, and wine. Add salt, pepper, ginger, and scallion. Coat fish well on both sides with mixture.

2. Steam 10 to 12 minutes, until fish is firm. It should be just slightly undercooked. Turn off heat. Drizzle sesame oil over the fish, sprinkle it with coriander, and serve.

Nutrition per serving: 153 Calories; 5g Fat; 24% calories from fat; 2g Carbohydrates; 46g Cholesterol; 291mg Sodium.

Swordfish Stir-Fried with Ginger

Geung See Chau Gim Yue

Traditionally, the Chinese cook this dish with carp, or snakehead, among other firm and meaty native fish. For my version of this classic stir-fry I use swordfish, certainly more available than those other fish, but similarly firm. Swordfish also absorbs flavors quite well.

1/2 pound swordfish steak, cut into 2 × 1-inch slices

MARINADE

> 1 teaspoon Ginger Juice (page 43) mixed with 1 tablespoon Shao-Hsing wine or sherry
>
> 1 teaspoon white vinegar
>
> 1/2 teaspoon sugar
>
> Pinch salt
>
> Pinch white pepper
>
> 1/4 teaspoon sesame oil

SAUCE

> 2 teaspoons oyster sauce
>
> 1 1/4 teaspoons sugar
>
> 2 teaspoons soy sauce
>
> Pinch white pepper
>
> 1 teaspoon cornstarch
>
> 3 tablespoons Seafood Stock (page 38)

TO COMPLETE THE DISH

> 1 teaspoon peanut oil
>
> 1 1/2 tablespoons julienned ginger
>
> 4 scallions, white portions cut into 1/4-inch pieces on the diagonal, green portions cut into 1/4-inch slices
>
> 1 tablespoon Shao-Hsing wine or sherry

Yield:
4 servings

1. Marinate swordfish in combined marinade ingredients for 10 minutes.

2. Combine sauce ingredients and set aside.

3. Heat wok over high heat for 30 seconds. Add peanut oil and coat wok with spatula. When a wisp of white smoke appears, add the ginger and white portions of scallions and stir-fry for 30 seconds. Add swordfish and marinade, stir and cook for 30 seconds more. Add Shao-Hsing wine, stir and mix well. Cook fish for 1 to 1 1/2 minutes or until fish turns white.

4. Stir sauce, pour in wok. Stir and mix well. When sauce thickens and begins to bubble, add green portions of scallions and mix thoroughly. Turn off heat, transfer to a heated dish, and serve with cooked rice.

Nutrition per serving (without rice): 171 Calories; 4g Fat; 24% calories from fat; 5.5g Carbohydrates; 41mg Cholesterol; 508mg Sodium.

Sweet and Sour Swordfish

Seun Tim Gim Yue

In China sweet and sour fish is made, depending upon individual regions, from either fresh-water or saltwater fish, from sea bass to yellow croaker, from carp to dace. A most adaptable preparation indeed, for which swordfish is perfect.

1/4 teaspoon peanut oil

1 pound swordfish steak, cut into 4 equal portions

2 slices ginger, 1/2 inch thick, lightly smashed

SAUCE

3 tablespoons white vinegar

3 tablespoons sugar

4 tablespoons ketchup

5 tablespoons cold water

1/2 teaspoon dark soy sauce

TO COMPLETE THE DISH

3 tablespoons minced carrots

3 tablespoons minced green bell pepper

2 scallions, white portions only, cut into 1/4-inch pieces

2 teaspoons cornstarch mixed with 2 teaspoons cold water

Yield:
4 servings

I. Heat wok over high heat for 40 seconds. Add peanut oil and with a paper towel coat the wok. When smoke rises, the wok is very hot. Place fish in wok, with 1 slice of ginger, lower heat to medium and cook for 2 minutes. Raise heat back to high, turn fish over, add the other piece of ginger and cook for 11/2 minutes more. Turn off heat, remove fish to a serving dish and place in a warm 275°F oven.

2. Pour all sauce ingredients into a saucepan and over medium heat, bring to a boil. Add carrots, pepper, and scallions, stir into sauce and bring back to a boil. Stir cornstarch mix and pour into saucepan, stir well and return to a boil. The sauce will thicken. Turn off heat.

3. Turn off oven heat. Remove fish. Pour sauce over fish and serve with cooked rice.

   Nutrition per serving (without rice): 154 Calories; 4g Fat; 24% calories from fat; 5g Carbohydrates; 41mg Cholesterol; 444mg Sodium.

Stir-Fried Swordfish with Tomatoes

Fan Keh Jiu Gim Yue

Swordfish becomes the fish of choice for this Cantonese preparation that would normally be made with carp, silver carp, or dace. When I was a girl I loved this summer dish, certainly for the fish, but mostly for the tanginess of the cooked fresh tomatoes.

3/4 **pound swordfish steak, cut into 4 equal pieces**

MARINADE

11/2 teaspoons white vinegar

2 teaspoons Shao-Hsing wine or sherry

Pinch of salt

Large pinch white pepper

TO COMPLETE THE DISH

13/4 teaspoons peanut oil

1 slice ginger, 1/2 inch thick, lightly smashed

2 tablespoons Shao-Hsing wine or sherry

1 teaspoon minced ginger

1 teaspoon minced garlic

1/4 teaspoon salt

1 small onion, cut into 1/4-inch dice

1 pound ripe tomatoes (2 large), cut into 1/2-inch dice

1 teaspoon sugar

1 tablespoon oyster sauce

1/4 cup Seafood Stock (page 38)

1/2 teaspoon dark soy sauce

2 scallions, cut into 1/2-inch pieces on the diagonal

2 tablespoons minced fresh coriander (cilantro)

Yield:
4 servings

1. Marinate fish in combined marinade ingredients for 15 minutes.

2. Heat wok over high heat for 20 seconds, add 1/4 teaspoon peanut oil. Use a paper towel to coat the wok. When wok is very hot, and smoke appears, add fish, marinade, and slice of ginger and cook for 1 minute. As it cooks drizzle 1 tablespoon of Shao-Hsing wine into wok and cook for another minute. Turn fish over, drizzle remaining wine over it and cook for another minute. Turn off heat, remove fish, and reserve. Wash wok and spatula.

3. Heat wok over high heat for 30 seconds. Add remaining peanut oil and coat wok. When a wisp of white smoke appears, add minced ginger, garlic, and salt and stir briefly. Add onion, stir and cook for 2 minutes. Add tomatoes, stir and mix well. Add sugar, oyster sauce, and seafood stock, stir and mix well. Cover wok and bring to a boil. Add soy sauce and mix well.

4. Lower heat, cover wok, and cook for 7 minutes or until tomatoes become soft. Add scallions, stir and mix. Add reserved fish and cover with tomato mixture. Turn heat back to high, cook for 2 minutes. Turn off heat, transfer to a heated dish, sprinkle with minced coriander and serve with cooked rice.

Nutrition per serving (without rice): 122 Calories; 3g Fat; 24% calories from fat; 5g Carbohydrates; 33mg Cholesterol; 455mg Sodium.

Garlic Steamed Shrimp

Seun Jing Har

Among the Chinese, steaming has always been the favored way of preparing shrimp. This is particularly true in those regions with access to live shrimp. Only in recent years has steamed shrimp come to be desirable in the West.

1/2 pound medium shrimp (20), shelled, but leave end portion of shell with tail on, deveined, washed and drained

1 piece of ginger, 1 inch thick, lightly smashed

2 tablespoons Crisp Garlic (page 39)

1 tablespoon Shao-Hsing wine or sherry

Pinch of white pepper

Place all ingredients in a bowl and mix, ensuring that shrimp are well coated. Pour 4 cups boiling water in a wok. Place the shrimp mixture in a steam-proof dish. Place the dish in a bamboo steamer, cover, and place in the wok. Steam for 3 or 4 minutes, or until shrimp turn pink and begin to curl. Turn off heat. Remove shrimp from steamer and serve in the steaming dish with the following dipping sauce.

DIPPING SAUCE

       2 tablespoons white wine

       2 tablespoons soy sauce

       1 teaspoon white vinegar

       3 tablespoons Seafood Stock (page 38)

       1/2 teaspoon grated ginger

       3 tablespoons finely sliced scallions

       2 teaspoons minced Thai chilies

Yield:
4 servings

Combine all ingredients in a bowl and mix well. Serve with Garlic Steamed Shrimp.

Nutrition per serving: 82 Calories; less than 1g Fat; less than 1% calories from fat; 5.1g Carbohydrates; 97mg Cholesterol; 435mg Sodium.

韭
王
炒
蝦

Yellow Chive Shrimp

Gau Wong Chau Har

Yellow chives are common throughout China, and are highly prized for their mild, delicate flavor, far more subtle than when they are green and pungent. Yellow chives are simply chives that have been deprived of sunlight as they grow. This particular combination of shrimp with yellow chives is a favorite of Canton.

SAUCE

2 teaspoons soy sauce

1 tablespoon oyster sauce

3/4 teaspoon sugar

1 1/2 teaspoon cornstarch

Pinch white pepper

1/4 cup Seafood Stock (page 38)

TO COMPLETE THE DISH

2 teaspoons peanut oil

2 teaspoons minced ginger

1 tablespoon Shao-Hsing wine or sherry

1/2 pound large shrimp (16), shelled, deveined, washed, and dried

2 fresh water chestnuts, peeled, washed, and julienned

1/4 pound yellow chives, washed, dried, trimmed at the ends, and cut into 1-inch pieces

Yield:
4 servings

1. Combine sauce ingredients and set aside.

2. Heat wok over high heat for 45 seconds. Add peanut oil, coat wok with spatula. When a wisp of white smoke appears, add ginger, stir briefly. Add shrimp and spread in a single layer, cook for 1 minute. Add Shao-Hsing wine by drizzling it into the wok along the sides. Turn shrimp over and cook for 30 seconds more, or until shrimp turn pink and begin to curl. Add water chestnuts and mix well.

3. Make a well in the center of the mixture, stir sauce and pour in. Cover with mixture and mix well. When the sauce thickens add chives and mix well. Turn off heat, transfer to a heated dish and serve.

Nutrition per serving: 118 Calories; 3.1g Fat; 23% calories from fat; 10g Carbohydrates; 97mg Cholesterol; 440mg Sodium.

蝦
龍
糊

Shrimp with Lobster Sauce

Har Lung Wu

Often it is asked of this dish, "Where is the lobster?" Well, there is none, despite its name. It is called shrimp with lobster sauce, but more correctly should be called "shrimp cooked with the same sauce that is used to cook lobsters." Which explains it all.

3/4 pound large shrimp (24), shelled, deveined, washed, and dried

MARINADE

1/2 teaspoon soy sauce

1/2 teaspoon sugar

1/4 teaspoon salt

1 1/2 teaspoons Shao-Hsing wine or sherry mixed with 1/2 teaspoon Ginger Juice (page 43)

1 tablespoon oyster sauce

Pinch white pepper

TO COMPLETE THE DISH

1 tablespoon peanut oil

1 teaspoon minced ginger

2 ounces lean pork loin, ground

2 large egg whites, beaten

1/4 cup Chicken Stock (page 37), if necessary

3 tablespoons scallions, green portions, finely sliced

Yield:
6 servings

1. Marinate shrimp in combined marinade ingredients for 20 minutes. Reserve.

2. Heat wok over high heat for 30 seconds. Add peanut oil and coat wok. When a wisp of white smoke appears, add ginger, stir briefly.

Add pork, separate and stir. When pork begins to turn color add shrimp and marinade. Mix together, spread in a thin layer, and allow to cook for 1 minute.

3. When shrimp begin to turn pink and curl, turn over and cook for another 1 to 1 1/2 minutes until shrimp become pink. Make a well in center of mixture, pour in beaten egg whites, cook for 30 seconds, then combine the mixture, cooking until the egg whites set. If mix is too thick and dry, add chicken stock and mix. Turn off heat, add scallions, and toss together. Transfer to a heated dish and serve.

Nutrition per serving: 114 Calories; 3g Fat; 23% calories from fat; 4g Carbohydrates; 97mg Cholesterol; 305mg Sodium.

原鼓炒蝦 Stir-Fried Shrimp in Bean Sauce

Yeun See Chau Har

The word yeun translates as "whole," to indicate a whole piece. Traditionally this dish was made with whole soy beans. Later the beans were ground. Still later they were fashioned into this sauce that at various times has been called "brown bean sauce" and "yellow bean sauce," as well as "ground bean sauce" and simply "bean sauce." Rest assured they are all the same sauce, all delicious.

SAUCE

I teaspoon dark soy sauce

I tablespoon oyster sauce

1/4 teaspoon sesame oil

I teaspoon sugar

TO COMPLETE THE DISH

2 teaspoons peanut oil

I1/2 teaspoons minced ginger

1/2 tablespoon bean sauce

3/4 pound large shrimp (24), shelled, deveined, washed, and dried

I tablespoon Shao-Hsing wine or sherry

I tablespoon Seafood Stock (page 38)

2 scallions, trimmed and finely sliced

Yield: 6 servings

I. Combine sauce ingredients and set aside.

2. Heat wok over high heat for 30 seconds. Add peanut oil and coat wok. When a wisp of white smoke appears, add ginger, stir briefly. Add bean sauce, mix. Add shrimp, spread in a thin layer, tipping wok from side to side to spread heat evenly. Turn shrimp over. Add wine around the edges of wok and toss together. Add stock and mix well. Cook until shrimp curl and turn pink.

3. Make a well in the center of mixture. Stir sauce, pour in and mix to coat shrimp thoroughly. Turn off heat, add sliced scallions, and toss with shrimp. Remove and transfer to a heated dish and serve.

Nutrition per serving: 84 Calories; 1.5g Fat; 16% calories from fat; 4g Carbohydrates; 86mg Cholesterol; 327mg Sodium.

葚
鼓
炒
蝦

Shrimp with Black Beans

Dau See Chau Har

This is a most familiar dish, a staple of the Cantonese kitchen. And it travels well. Wherever the Cantonese have migrated to—Singapore, Thailand, Kuala Lumpur, Jakarta, and the West—shrimp cooked with fermented black beans in the classic manner is to be found. My personal touch is using my Garlic Oil in the recipe.

SAUCE

2 teaspoons oyster sauce

I teaspoon soy sauce

3/4 teaspoon sugar

Pinch salt

I 1/2 teaspoons cornstarch

Pinch white pepper

1/4 cup Seafood Stock (page 38)

TO COMPLETE THE DISH

I 1/2 teaspoons Garlic Oil (page 39)

I teaspoon minced garlic

I tablespoon fermented black beans, washed and drained

1/2 pound large shrimp (16), shelled, deveined, washed, and dried

I tablespoon Shao-Hsing wine or sherry

I tablespoon minced fresh coriander (cilantro)

Yield:
4 servings

1. Combine sauce ingredients and set aside.

2. Heat wok over high heat for 30 seconds. Add Garlic Oil and coat wok with spatula. When a wisp of white smoke appears, add garlic and black beans. Stir for 30 seconds, add shrimp. Mix together, then spread shrimp in a thin layer. Cook for 30 seconds. Add wine by drizzling around the edges of the wok, mix well.

3. When shrimp begin to curl and turn pink, make a well in center of mixture. Stir sauce and pour in. Mix well to combine all ingredients, about 1 1/2 minutes, until sauce begins to thicken and bubble. Turn off heat, remove to a heated dish, sprinkle with minced coriander, and serve.

    Nutrition per serving: 96 Calories; 2.2g Fat; 21% calories from fat; 5g Carbohydrates; 97mg Cholesterol; 450mg Sodium.

四
川
炒
蝦

Spiced Shrimp

Sei Chun Chau Har

That spicy shrimp dishes abound is no surprise. In the course of cooking and eating most of us have had shrimp heated with hot oil, with chilies, fresh or dried, in many combinations. For this recipe I use preserved horse beans. These beans, preserved with salt and chilies, are a staple of the kitchens of western China, in Sichuan and Hunan, even to the north in Beijing. I call these shrimp sei chun, in honor of Sichuan. If you can't find horse beans with chili you can substitute hot pepper sauce, but the flavor will not be the same.

SAUCE

11/2 teaspoons preserved horse beans with chili

2 tablespoons ketchup

I teaspoon dark soy sauce

2 teaspoons white vinegar

11/2 teaspoons Shao-Hsing wine or sherry

3/4 teaspoon sugar

Pinch white pepper

21/2 teaspoons cornstarch

1/4 cup Chicken Stock (page 37)

TO COMPLETE THE DISH

2 teaspoons Garlic Oil (page 39)

11/2 teaspoons minced ginger

I small onion, 2 ounces, cut into 1/4-inch dice

3/4 pound large shrimp (24), shelled, deveined, washed, and dried

I tablespoon Shao-Hsing wine or sherry

I tablespoon Chicken Stock (page 37), if necessary

2 tablespoons scallions, green portions, finely sliced

Yield:
6 servings

1. Combine sauce ingredients and set aside.

2. Heat wok over high heat for 30 seconds. Add Garlic Oil and coat wok. When a wisp of white smoke appears, add ginger and stir briefly. Add onion, stir and cook I minute. Lower heat to medium and cook for I more minute until onion softens and becomes translucent. Raise heat back to high, add shrimp, stir and mix well with onion. Add wine and mix. (If mixture is too dry add the I tablespoon of chicken stock.) Cook until shrimp begin to curl and turn pink. Make a well in the center of the mixture, stir sauce, pour in. Cover and stir to combine well. When sauce thickens and begins to bubble, turn off heat, add scallions, transfer to a heated dish, and serve.

Nutrition per serving: 90 Calories; 2.1g Fat; 22% calories from fat; 5g Carbohydrates; 86mg Cholesterol; 492mg Sodium.

Sichuan Shrimp in Lettuce Leaves

Sei Chun Sahng Choi Bau

This custom of wrapping foods in lettuce leaves is popular throughout China. In China the lettuce most used is bor lee sahng choi, *which translates as "glass lettuce." It is fragile, its leaves snap easily, and it has a texture quite like iceberg lettuce. However, it looks like small romaine lettuce on the stalk. Iceberg, for its crispness and texture, is recommended for this wrapped preparation.*

SAUCE

> 2 teaspoons oyster sauce
>
> I tablespoon Shao-Hsing wine or sherry
>
> I tablespoon ketchup
>
> 3/4 teaspoon sugar
>
> Pinch salt
>
> Pinch white pepper
>
> 2 teaspoons cornstarch dissolved in 2 teaspoons cold water

TO COMPLETE THE DISH

> 2 teaspoons Shallot Oil (page 40)
>
> 2 teaspoons minced ginger
>
> 1/2 tablespoon Bean Sauce (page 17)
>
> 3/4 pound shrimp, shelled, deveined, washed, and cut into
>   1/2-inch pieces
>
> I small red bell pepper (3/4 cup), cut in 1/4-inch dice
>
> I small green bell pepper (3/4 cup), cut in 1/4-inch dice
>
> I jalapeño pepper, minced, with seeds
>
> 2 fresh water chestnuts, peeled, cut 1/4-inch dice
>
> 3 tablespoons Crisp Shallots (page 40)
>
> 12 iceberg lettuce leaves, about 5 inches in diameter

Yield:
6 servings
(two wrapped
bundles each)

1. Combine sauce ingredients and set aside.

2. Heat wok over high heat for 30 seconds. Add Shallot Oil and coat wok. When a wisp of white smoke appears, add ginger and bean sauce, stir briefly. Add shrimp, stir together, then add all vegetables, except the lettuce leaves. Stir-fry together for 3 minutes. Make a well in the center of the mixture, stir sauce, pour in. Mix well, stir, for about 1 to 1 1/2 minutes until very hot. Turn off heat. Remove to a heated serving plate.

3. Place 2 tablespoons of the mixture in the center of a lettuce leaf, fold to close, then serve. These should be eaten with the hands.

Nutrition per serving: 97 Calories; 2.2g Fat; 20% calories from fat; 9g Carbohydrates; 86mg Cholesterol; 296mg Sodium.

# Stuffed Scallops

Yeung Gon Bui

Dried scallops are quite common, and very expensive, in China. They are stir-fried, braised and steamed. Fresh scallops are more available these days, particularly in Hong Kong. Here is a dish I have devised using fresh scallops and steamed black mushrooms.

MARINADE

2 teaspoons Shao-Hsing wine or sherry

I tablespoon soy sauce

2 teaspoons White Peppercorn Oil (page 41)

I teaspoon white vinegar

I teaspoon sugar

2 teaspoons minced ginger

2 tablespoons minced scallions, white portions

Pinch white pepper

TO COMPLETE THE DISH

12 large sea scallops, about I 1/2 inches in diameter, I inch thick (about 3/4 pound), halved across the width

12 Steamed Black Mushrooms (page 206), about same diameter as scallops

Yield:
4 servings

1. Combine marinade ingredients and set aside.

2. Place 12 scallop halves in a steam-proof dish. Pour half the marinade over them, allow to stand 5 minutes. Place steamed mushroom atop each half, place other scallop halves on the mushrooms, sandwich fashion. Pierce each with a toothpick to secure them. Pour remaining marinade over them and steam for 3 to 4 minutes, or until scallops become firm and white. Do not oversteam. Remove steaming dish from steamer and serve.

Nutrition per serving: 170 Calories; 3g Fat; 16% calories from fat; 81g Carbohydrates; 260mg Cholesterol; 435mg Sodium.

Steamed Scallops with Yunnan Ham

Gum Wah Yuk Dai Ji

The most highly regarded hams in China come from Yunnan, west of Canton, south of Sichuan. Cooks use this strong-flavored, salty ham in many ways, alone or in combination with other foods. Because Yunnan ham is not available in the West, I suggest Smithfield ham, or one of those wonderful, dry, cured country hams from Kentucky.

> 12 sea scallops, 1 1/2 inches in diameter, 1 inch thick
>   (3/4 pound)
> 1/4 pound Smithfield Ham, prepared for use (page 30), then
>   cut into pieces 1 1/2 inches long, 1 inch wide, 1/8 inch thick

SAUCE

> 1 tablespoon Shao-Hsing wine or sherry
> 1 tablespoon soy sauce
> 2 teaspoons Scallion Oil (page 39)
> 3/4 teaspoon sugar
> Pinch white pepper

TO COMPLETE THE DISH

> 1 tablespoon minced fresh coriander (cilantro)

Yield:
4 servings

1. Using a sharp knife, make a slanting cut across the top of each scallop, about 1/2 inch deep. Place scallops in a steam-proof dish and insert a ham slice into each cut.

2. Combine sauce ingredients and pour over the scallops. Place dish in a steamer and steam for 3 to 4 minutes, or until scallops become white and firm. Do not oversteam. Turn off heat, remove dish from steamer, sprinkle with minced coriander, and serve.

   Nutrition per serving: 263 Calories; 5g Fat; 17% calories from fat; 90g Carbohydrates; 290mg Cholesterol; 460mg Sodium.

Clams

Clams are most popular in China, particularly in the southern seacoast regions, where *hoi dai gua jee*, the tiniest clams imaginable, are to be found. So small are these that to the Chinese their name translates as "watermelon seeds from the bottom of the sea." These are not available anywhere else that I know of outside of Asia. These tiny clams are famous in Shanghai where they are sautéed, in their shells, in a hot tomato-based sauce.

The Cantonese use small clams as well, just a bit larger than those found off Shanghai, in a special lunar New Year preparation. I remember as a young girl in Sun Tak we bought these small clams, already boiled. I recall that we had to get up and get out to buy them before six in the morning, otherwise they would be sold out. We would wrap these in lettuce leaves and eat them early, the "first course" of our New Year meal.

So deep is the tradition, that this dish is called *sahng choi bau*, which translates as "lettuce wrapped." There was no need to ever think about how we would eat these clams for it was always understood they were to be wrapped in lettuce.

Small clams, canned, are available in markets and are close in size to those in Canton's markets. However, for their superior taste to those in cans, I cut up fresh clams for the dishes that follow.

Minced Clams Wrapped in Lettuce

Sahng Choi Bau

4 cups cold water
8 ounces raw fresh clams (I cup)

SAUCE

I tablespoon oyster sauce
I teaspoon sugar
I teaspoon white vinegar
1/8 teaspoon white pepper
I 1/2 teaspoons cornstarch
3 tablespoons Chicken Stock (page 37)

TO COMPLETE THE DISH

I teaspoon peanut oil
2 teaspoons minced ginger
I teaspoon minced garlic
1/4 teaspoon salt
I scallion, white portions, finely sliced
1/4 cup celery, cut into 1/4-inch dice
I tablespoon Shao-Hsing wine or sherry
1/4 cup pine nuts, dry-roasted (page 14)
4 fresh water chestnuts, peeled, cut into 1/4-inch dice
8 butter lettuce leaves

Yield:
4 servings

1. Place water in a pot and bring to a boil over high heat. Add clams and blanch for 10 seconds. Run cold water into pot, drain. Allow to cool, then mince and reserve.

2. Combine sauce ingredients and set aside.

3. Heat wok over high heat for 30 seconds, add peanut oil, and coat wok. When a wisp of white smoke appears, add ginger, garlic and salt, and stir briefly. Add scallion and celery, stir for 20 seconds. Add reserved clams, stir and mix. Add the wine, mix well. Stir sauce, pour in, and mix thoroughly. When sauce thickens, turn off heat. Add the pine nuts and water chestnuts and toss well to mix. Serve immediately, wrapped in leaves of butter lettuce.

    Nutrition per serving: 90 Calories; 2.6g Fat; 24% calories from fat; 8g Carbohydrates; 30mg Cholesterol; 472mg Sodium.

豉椒炒蜆 Minced Clams with Black Beans

See Jui Chau Hin

2 cups cold water

8 ounces fresh raw clams (1 cup)

SAUCE

1/2 tablespoon oyster sauce

1 teaspoon dark soy sauce

2 teaspoons Shao-Hsing wine or sherry

1 teaspoon sugar

Pinch white pepper

2 teaspoons cornstarch

1/4 cup Chicken Stock (page 37)

TO COMPLETE THE DISH

1 1/2 teaspoons peanut oil

1 small onion, cut into 1/4-inch dice (1/2 cup)

2 teaspoons minced garlic

1 teaspoon minced ginger

2 tablespoons fermented black beans, washed, rinsed, and drained

2 medium green bell peppers (8 ounces), cut into 1/2-inch dice

1 tablespoon Shao-Hsing wine or sherry

Yield:
4 servings

1. Place water in a pot and bring to a boil over high heat. Add clams and blanch for 10 seconds. Turn off heat, run cold water into pot, drain. Repeat, mince clams and reserve.

2. Combine sauce ingredients and set aside.

3. Heat wok over high heat for 30 seconds. Add peanut oil, coat wok. When a wisp of white smoke appears, add onion, garlic, and ginger, and stir and cook for 1 minute. Add black beans and stir-fry together for 30 to 45 seconds, or until aroma of beans is released. Add clams and peppers and stir to mix. Add wine, stir and cook for 30 seconds until peppers turn bright green. Make a well in the mixture, stir sauce and pour in, mix to combine thoroughly. When sauce thickens and bubbles, turn off heat. Transfer to a heated dish and serve, with cooked rice, or as an accompaniment to Congee (page 59).

Nutrition per serving (without rice): 82 Calories; 2g Fat; 18% calories from fat; 5.2g Carbohydrates; 30mg Cholesterol; 392mg Sodium.

Steamed Crabs with Ginger

Ching Jing Hai

This is the classic Chinese method of preparing fresh crabs. The words ching jing *translate as "steamed with nothing," which means that the crabs are virtually unseasoned except for the flavor of ginger. The idea, of course, is to allow the pure, sweet taste of fresh crab to shine.*

3 quarts cold water
6 live blue crabs (2 1/2 to 3 pounds)
3 tablespoons shredded ginger

1. In a pot bring water to a boil over high heat. Place crabs in the boiling water briefly, about 10 seconds. Turn off heat, run cold water into pot, drain. Repeat twice again, until crabs cool. Discard the aprons, gills, sand sacs, mouths, and mandibles. Separate the body shells from the bodies.

2. Place the body shells on the bottom of a steam-proof dish. Sprinkle 1 tablespoon ginger on them. Place rest of crabs atop them. Sprinkle remainder of ginger on crabs. Steam for 15 minutes, or until crabs are cooked. Remove from heat and serve with the following dip, if desired.

CRAB DIP

2 tablespoons Chinkiang vinegar (or red wine vinegar)
6 tablespoons Chicken Stock (page 37)
1 tablespoon soy sauce
2 teaspoons minced ginger
3 tablespoons scallions, finely sliced
Pinch white pepper

Yield:
4 servings

Combine all ingredients.

Nutrition per serving: 43 Calories; about 0.5g Fat; about 1% calories from fat; less than 1g Carbohydrates; 12mg Cholesterol; 30mg Sodium.

焗 Wok-Baked Crabs

Guk Hai

These crabs are called guk *in China, which means "covered without air," thus "baked." In this process, a tradition of many centuries, the covered wok takes the place of an oven. In China, years ago, there were no ovens, so foods were "baked" atop the heat source.*

3 quarts cold water

6 live blue crabs (2 1/2 to 3 pounds)

2 teaspoons Garlic Oil (page 39)

6 cloves garlic, peeled and lightly smashed

4 scallions, cut into 2-inch pieces

1 slice ginger, 1 inch thick, lightly smashed

2 tablespoons Shao-Hsing wine or sherry

4 tablespoons Chicken Stock (page 37)

**Yield:
4 servings**

1. To prepare the crabs, bring water to a boil over high heat. Place crabs in water briefly, about 10 seconds. Turn off heat, run cold water into pot, drain. Repeat twice again, until they cool. Discard the aprons, gills, sand sacs, mouths, and mandibles. Separate the body shells from the bodies. Cut each crab in half.

2. Heat wok over high heat for 40 seconds, add Garlic Oil, and coat wok. When a wisp of white smoke appears, add garlic, scallions, and ginger. Stir and cook for 1 minute, until their fragrance is released. Add crabs and shells, stir to coat well, and cook for 1 1/2 minutes. Add wine and mix well. Add 2 tablespoons chicken stock and mix well.

3. Cover wok tightly (a wet towel placed at the rim where the wok cover meets the wok will keep it airtight) and "bake" for 10 minutes. Open cover, stir, and check liquid level. If dry, add remaining chicken stock. Re-cover, seal, cook for another 10 minutes until crabs are cooked. Always check for dryness. Turn heat off, remove to a heated dish, and serve.

Nutrition per serving: 67 Calories; 3g Fat; 13% calories from fat; less than 1g Carbohydrates; 12mg Cholesterol; 70 mg Sodium.

Singapore Chili Crabs

Lot Jiu Hai

This is arguably the most famous dish in Singapore, a spicy concoction to be found at its best in the big, open seacoast restaurants along Singapore's East Coast Highway. The crabs are fat and full of juice, the sauce is hot and Singaporeans love this sauce over rice after they have reduced piles of crabs cooked in it to a mound of shells. If you can't find horse beans with chili you can substitute hot pepper sauce, but the flavor won't be the same. Cornstarch can be substituted for tapioca starch, but the sauce will be cloudier.

3 quarts cold water

6 live blue crabs (2 1/2 to 3 pounds)

SAUCE

1 1/4 cups Chicken Stock (page 37)

2 tablespoons horse beans with chili

2 teaspoons fresh squeezed lemon juice

1 tablespoon sugar

2 teaspoons mushroom soy sauce

1/2 cup ketchup

2 teaspoons Shao-Hsing wine or sherry

1/4 teaspoon sesame oil

TO COMPLETE THE DISH

1 1/2 tablespoons peanut oil

5 minced shallots

1 tablespoon minced ginger

1 1/2 teaspoons minced garlic

2 Thai chilies, minced

2 tablespoons tapioca starch (or cornstarch) mixed with
    1/4 cup cold water

2 large eggs, beaten

Yield:
4 servings

1. In a pot bring water to a boil over high heat. Add crabs and boil for 2 minutes. Drain and allow to cool so they can be handled easily. Discard the aprons, gills, sand sacs, mouths, and mandibles and separate the body shells from the bodies. With a cleaver cut the crabs into quarters. Retain the top shells.

2. Combine the sauce ingredients and reserve.

3. Heat wok over high heat for 45 seconds, add peanut oil and coat wok with spatula. When a wisp of white smoke appears, add shallots, ginger, garlic, and chilies, stir and cook for 1 minute or until their aroma is released. Add the crabs, stir and mix well for 1 minute. Stir sauce and pour into crab mixture, mix thoroughly so that crabs are well coated.

4. Allow sauce to come to a boil and stir again to coat the crabs. Stir tapioca starch mixture and add to wok, stir until sauce thickens and begins to bubble. Make a well in the center of the mixture, pour in beaten eggs and stir to mix thoroughly until the eggs become cooked into small pieces in the mixture. Turn off heat, transfer to a heated dish, and serve.

Nutrition per serving: 89 Calories; 2.5g Fat; 24% calories from fat; 5g Carbohydrates; 10mg Cholesterol; 444mg Sodium.

Chapter 4

The Versatile Chicken and Other Poultry

Chicken has special significance in the Chinese kitchen. The first day of the lunar New Year, the day the Chinese call *hoi lin,* or the "opening of the year," is the day we have chicken. For chicken is the food of rebirth, symbolized by the phoenix.

All weddings must include chicken, as well as all birthdays, for this same symbolic reason. Even the day that marks the first month of a newly born infant is a day for chicken. Before weddings are celebrated families come together to eat *congee* (thickened rice soup) with chicken, again for its symbolism.

When I was growing up, our house in Sun Tak was surrounded by the homes and small farms of those who worked for us. And chickens, ducks, and geese were all about. There was no such classification as "free range." All of the poultry we eventually ate roamed as they chose. Even the ducks had only to be called each evening and they would go along to their home for the night. Chicken was our poultry of choice—so familiar, so adaptable to all cooking methods, so delicious. We ate it often. Duck was more of a festive poultry which we ate at family meals of even minor significance. Geese were reserved for very special banquets, times of celebration.

There is a restaurant in Hong Kong called *Yung Kee,* up a climbing street off Hong Kong harbor where goose is served. I remember eating it as a young girl, stuffed with cinnamon and anise, sugar, and soy then roasted until its skin was crisp as parchment. It is wonderful and I recommend it to you.

This is not to say, however, that chicken and duck were not also festive. It is just that they were more familiar at the table. It was not until I came to the United States that I learned that most of the poultry sold for cooking was not freshly killed. That is, or was, unheard of in China. Given that circumstance, let me make some suggestions that may help you when you buy poultry in the markets.

Initially let me say that there truly is no substitute for the taste of a freshly killed cooked chicken. To seek them out is worth the effort, and if possible find those that have been hand-plucked. Otherwise they probably have been plunged into boiling water in order to make their feathers easier to remove by machine. This diminishes their taste.

If buying chicken that has not been freshly killed, check the date on the packaging label. If the date is past, do not purchase the chicken. Check as well to see if the chicken has been frozen. Often frozen chickens are permitted to defrost in refrigerated display cases. A test would be to press the flesh; it could be hard, or there might be traces of crystallization on or around it. If a chicken has been in a display case for too long a time, the packaging will contain an excess of reddish, blood-colored liquid. If you are buying whole chicken breasts, have your butcher cut them from a whole chicken. If buying chicken cutlets have him do the same.

The same criteria should apply when buying ducks, turkeys, and geese. Ducks and turkeys are frozen with more frequency than chickens, so look carefully at their labels for packaging dates, and look at the birds themselves for signs of freshness. The domesticated ducks I favor are the variety known as Pekin. Their large breasts are best for Peking duck, or as that dish is called these days, Beijing Op. They are raised in confined spaces, do not run free, and grow fatter than wild ducks, with meat that is more tender. The Long Island variety of duck is an admirable substitute.

In these days of poultry in parts, breasts, thighs, legs, and other parts are sold separately. In this cookbook, where I do not prepare poultry and fowl whole, I suggest buying turkey or chicken breasts, but I caution you to buy with an eye to freshness, as I have suggested above. Turkey breasts adapt quite nicely to my recipes, particularly within the low-fat considerations of this book. I begin this portion of my book with festive chicken dishes, special preparations of which I am most fond, then go on to more simple chicken dishes. I then move on to cooking duck and turkey. The latter, once a somewhat exotic bird in China, is becoming more familiar.

乞 丐 鷄 Beggar's Chicken

Hot Yee Gai

In China this famed classic chicken recipe from Beijing is not always known as Beggar's Chicken. Simply because of its subtle tastes and its appearance, it is also called foo guai gai, *or rich and noble chicken, which I prefer. However, the story usually attached to this dish is this: A beggar, without a home, money, or food, raced away from a farm with a stolen chicken. To cook it, he covered it with mud, made a fire in a hole in the ground, and baked his chicken, peeling the feathers off before he ate.*

The dish evolved into a preparation in which chicken is stuffed with aromatics and baked in clay. I use a flour dough instead of the pond clay of China. The dough works beautifully to seal in flavors as the chicken bakes. My recipe, simplified from the classic, and lower by far in fat, requires some time and effort but the result is rewarding indeed.

> **I whole chicken, 3 to 3I/4 pounds, cleaned, fat and membranes removed**

MARINADE

> 3 tablespoons whiskey or spirits (see note page I4I)
> I cinnamon stick, broken into 4 pieces
> 2 pieces of star anise
> I teaspoon salt
> 2I/2 teaspoons sugar
> Pinch white pepper
> 2 teaspoons peanut oil

(continued)

Stuffing

21/2 teaspoons peanut oil

11/2 cups diced onions

6 Chinese black mushrooms, soaked for 30 minutes in hot
water, stems discarded, caps cut into 1/2-inch dice

1 ounce preserved mustard, washed 3 to 4 times, leaves
opened and rinsed, finely sliced

2 teaspoons Shao-Hsing wine or sherry

1 teaspoon sesame oil

1/2 teaspoon five-spice seasoning

1/2 teaspoon salt

2 teaspoons sugar

Pinch white pepper

Dough

4 cups unbleached flour

13/4 cups hot water

2 teaspoons peanut oil

To complete the dish

2 large lotus leaves, soaked in hot water for 20 minutes
until softened

2 feet of heavy-duty foil

Yield:
6 servings

1. To prepare the chicken, mix marinade ingredients and rub outside
and inside of the chicken with it. Place in a dish and set aside.

2. To prepare the stuffing, heat wok over high heat for 30 seconds.
Add peanut oil and coat wok. When a wisp of white smoke
appears, add onions and cook until soft, about 11/2 minutes. Add
mushrooms and preserved mustard and mix well. Add wine and
mix. Add sesame oil, five-spice seasoning, salt, sugar, and pepper

and stir to mix well. Remove from heat, transfer to a bowl and allow to cool.

3. To prepare the dough, place flour on a work surface and make a well in the center. Add hot water slowly with one hand, mix with the other. When water is absorbed, knead until a dough forms. Coat your hands with peanut oil and rub dough, with some pressure, to coat it. Rub hands over work surface as well. Flatten the dough until it is large enough to wrap the chicken.

4. Stuff the chicken with the prepared stuffing, packing it loosely in the cavity. Close neck and tail openings with skewers. Wrap the chicken completely in the lotus leaves, overlapping if necessary. Place wrapped chicken in center of flattened dough and wrap the chicken, sealing the edges with the fingers. Spread out the foil and place the chicken on it, breast side up. Fold foil around the chicken, closing it.

5. Preheat oven to 350°F for 15 minutes. Place chicken in a roasting pan and bake for 3 1/2 hours at 325°F. Remove from oven, allow to rest for 10 minutes. Remove foil, cut the hardened dough with kitchen shears and peel it back, cut lotus leaves and peel away, cut chicken skin and peel that back. The chicken is soft, falls away from the bone, and is best served by scooping the meat and the stuffing together to serve.

Nutrition per serving: 102 Calories; 2.3g Fat; 20% calories from fat; 4.5g Carbohydrates; 33mg Cholesterol; 622mg Sodium.

Note: The coverings insulate the chicken, so that it will remain hot enough to serve if removed from the oven 1 to 2 hours before serving.

Note: Preferred for this dish is the bottled potent grain spirit, Ng Ga Pei, from China. If you can find it in your Chinese or Asian store, by all means use it. If not, any Scotch whisky will be fine.

醉 # Shanghai Wine Chicken

Joi Gai

鶏 *The words* joi gai *are humorous. They translate as "drunken chicken," which suggests that the chicken, during the preparation becomes drunk with wine. This is a traditional dish of Shanghai, one for which the city is quite famous. It is usually served as the first course of a banquet, but of course you need not do that. It is a fine illustration of the technique of poaching. In this recipe I use breasts of chicken to illustrate how parts of chicken can be poached as easily as the whole.*

2 chicken breasts (2 pounds) with skin and bones intact

6 cups cold water

2 scallions, trimmed and cut in half

1/3 cup fresh coriander (cilantro), leaves and stems, cut into 3-inch pieces

2 small onions, cut into quarters

1 piece ginger, 1 inch thick, lightly smashed

3/4 teaspoon salt

WINE SAUCE

1/4 cup poaching liquid (see step 1)

1/2 teaspoon salt

3/4 teaspoon sugar

2 tablespoons Shao-Hsing wine or sherry

Pinch white pepper

Yield:
4 servings

1. In a large pot place water, chicken breasts, scallions, coriander, onions, ginger, and salt. Cover pot and bring to a boil over high heat. Lower heat to simmer, leave lid partially open, and simmer for 20 minutes. (Halfway through, at 10 minutes, turn chicken over.) Turn heat off, cover pot again and allow chicken to rest in liquid for 15 minutes more.

2. Combine the wine sauce ingredients with the poaching liquid from the previous step as specified above. Reserve.

3. Remove chicken from pot, allow to cool. Remove skin and bones and slice into 1 × 2-inch pieces. Place in a serving dish, stir wine sauce and pour over chicken. Allow chicken to marinate for 1 hour, refrigerated, covered with plastic wrap. Serve cool.

Nutrition per serving: 153 Calories; 3.3g Fat; 18% calories from fat; 6.5g Carbohydrates; 50mg Cholesterol; 497mg Sodium.

Chicken Poached with Chinese Celery

Heung Kon Bo Gai

Poaching chicken is a gastronomic universal in China, practiced not only in Shanghai, but in all of the country's provinces. In earlier times, most home kitchens did not include ovens. (Brick ovens existed only in restaurants and barbecue shops.) Thus, whole chickens, as well as parts of chickens, were poached or boiled in broths of different ingredients, each broth imparting its individual taste to the chicken.

These poached and boiled chickens were customarily served with dipping sauces or with accompanying vegetables that complemented the flavors of the chickens. To this day, these poached chickens are made as they always were, in restaurants which carry on the poaching traditions, occasionally in the home.

Chinese celery is quite different from the usual stalks most of us recognize. Its bright green stalks are very thin, almost like chopsticks; its leaves like those of Western celery. It is sweeter and it has a defined, strong aroma, whether raw or cooked. Chefs refer to it, with fondness, as heung kon, *which means "fragrant celery," an apt name. When it is cooking, particularly in soup or in poaching, it releases this pleasing aroma, and, in this recipe, imparts its taste to the chicken with which it is poached.*

8 cups cold water

2 heads Chinese celery, cut into 2-inch pieces (1 1/2 cups), retain leaves

1 small bunch fresh coriander (cilantro), cut into 2-inch pieces (1 cup)

8 shallots, whole, peeled

1 piece ginger, 2 inches long, lightly smashed

4 scallions, cut into 2-inch lengths

1 teaspoon salt

3 tablespoons Shao-Hsing wine or sherry

1 whole chicken, 3 1/2 pounds, all fat and membranes removed, skin left on, washed thoroughly, giblets washed and retained

DIPPING SAUCE

1 1/2 teaspoons soy sauce

1 1/2 teaspoons mushroom soy sauce

1 teaspoon white vinegar

1 teaspoon minced ginger

2 teaspoons minced garlic

2 tablespoons scallions, finely sliced

1/2 teaspoon sugar

Pinch white pepper

1/3 cup poaching liquid

Yield:
6 servings

1. In a large pot place water, celery, coriander, shallots, ginger, scallions, and salt. Cover and bring to a boil over high heat. Lower heat and simmer for 20 minutes.

2. Turn heat back to high, add wine. Turn off heat. Place chicken in the pot, breast side up. Turn heat back on to high and return to a boil. Lower heat, cover pot, and simmer for 15 minutes. Turn chicken over and simmer for another 15 minutes. Turn off heat and allow chicken to rest in the liquid for 30 minutes, with cover on.

3. While the chicken rests, combine the dipping sauce ingredients, using the poaching liquid from the pot.

4. Remove chicken from pot, and remove and discard skin. Cut chicken into bite-size pieces, place on a serving dish, and serve with dipping sauce.

Nutrition per serving: 104 Calories; 2g Fat; 18% calories from fat; 4g Carbohydrates; 33mg Cholesterol; 440mg Sodium.

Note: Strain off poaching liquid for future use. It can, of course, be eaten as a soup, as it is, or with vegetables added.

Note: As I noted earlier, some of these poached chicken dishes are complemented well with specific vegetable dishes. For this chicken I recommend Stir-Fried Broccoli Florets (see next page).

Stir-Fried Broccoli Florets

清炒玉花

Ching Chau Yuk Far

8 cups cold water

I slice ginger, 1/2 inch thick, lightly smashed

1/2 teaspoon baking soda (optional)

I bunch broccoli, cut into 2-inch-long florets, to yield
I pound

2 teaspoons Scallion Oil (page 39)

I tablespoon Shao-Hsing wine or sherry

Yield:
6 servings

I. In a large pot place water, ginger, and baking soda and bring to a boil over high heat. Add broccoli florets and blanch for 10 seconds until broccoli turns bright green. Turn off heat, run cold water into pot, and drain thoroughly.

2. Heat wok over high heat for 30 seconds, add Scallion Oil, and coat wok. When a wisp of white smoke appears, add broccoli florets. Stir-fry for I minute. Add wine and mix well, cook for I more minute. Turn off heat, remove broccoli florets and serve with poached chicken. A lovely arrangement is to place the florets around the border of the serving dish holding the chicken (previous recipe).

Nutrition per serving: II Calories; negligible Fat; negligible calories from fat; 2g Carbohydrates; 0mg Cholesterol; 4mg Sodium.

鼓油鷄 Soy Sauce Chicken

See Yau Gai

This is another unusual and festive chicken dish, one that was always made for the birthday of my Ah Paw, my grandmother. Seldom was this rich preparation made in the home, except for special occasions. Here again, I substitute chicken breasts for the whole chicken, which traditionally was the way it was made. The flavorful poaching liquid may be used to prepare the chicken again and again, enriching itself as it goes.

4 cups of Celery Chicken poaching liquid (page 144), or
    4 cups Chicken Stock (page 37)

3 pieces cinnamon stick, each 3 inches long

4 whole pieces eight-star anise

1 piece ginger, 2 inches long, lightly smashed

1 piece sugarcane, 3 inches long, or 3 tablespoons brown sugar

1/4 cup mushroom soy sauce

1/4 cup Shao-Hsing wine or sherry

2 chicken breasts (2 pounds), skin and bones left intact

Yield:
6 servings

1. In a large pot place the liquid (or stock), cinnamon, anise, ginger, and sugar and bring to a boil over high heat. Add mushroom soy sauce and bring back to a boil. Lower heat and allow to simmer for 20 minutes. Turn heat back to high, add the wine, and return to a boil. Lower chicken breasts into liquid, meat side down, and bring back to a boil. Lower heat, cover and simmer for 12 minutes. Turn chicken over and simmer for another 12 minutes. Turn off heat, leave cover on, and allow chicken to rest in liquid for 1 hour.

2. Remove chicken from pot. Remove skin and bones. Slice across into 11/2-inch pieces. Place chicken in a dish and serve.

Nutrition per serving: 121 Calories; 3.6g Fat; 18% calories from fat; 6g Carbohydrates; 33mg Cholesterol; 663mg Sodium.

Note: I recommend a specific vegetable to be served with this soy sauce chicken, Stir-Fried String Beans (see next page), because of its complementary taste and its contrasting color.

Stir-Fried String Beans

Ching Chau See Guai Dau

清炒四季豆

I teaspoon peanut oil

1/2 teaspoon minced ginger

1/2 pound string beans, ends and strings removed, cut into halves

I 1/2 tablespoons Soy Sauce Chicken liquid (previous recipe)

Yield:
6 servings

Heat wok over high heat for 30 seconds, add peanut oil and coat wok. When a wisp of white smoke appears, add ginger. Stir briefly, add string beans, and stir to mix well. Cook for 30 seconds, add liquid and mix well. When the string beans turn bright green, turn off heat. Remove the string beans and border the plate holding the Soy Sauce Chicken with them and serve.

Nutrition per serving: 11 Calories; negligible Fat; negligible calories from fat; 2.5g Carbohydrates; 0mg Cholesterol; 0mg Sodium.

Perfumed Chicken

Heung So Gai

This most flavorsome preparation illustrates a significant, but often overlooked, aspect of the Sichuan kitchen. Most people think that the cooking of Sichuan is always hot and heavily spiced. This is not so; it can be delicate and subtle as well. The customary method of preparing this dish involves chicken which has been coated with egg and flour. I have eliminated this and roasted it instead. There is no loss of flavor at all.

I whole fresh chicken, 3 1/2 pounds, fat and membranes removed

4 cups cold water

I cup white wine

I piece ginger, I 1/2 inches long, lightly smashed

3 whole pieces of eight-star anise

1/4 teaspoon Sichuan peppercorns

2 cinnamon sticks

2-inch piece dried tangerine skin

2 scallions

I teaspoon salt

2 teaspoons sugar

I tablespoon mushroom soy sauce

DIPPING SAUCE

6 tablespoons poaching liquid

I 1/2 teaspoons soy sauce

I tablespoon shredded ginger

2 tablespoons shredded scallions

Yield:
6 servings

I. In a large pot place the chicken, and all other ingredients except mushroom soy sauce and dipping sauce ingredients, and bring to a boil over high heat. Add mushroom soy sauce, cover pot, lower heat, and simmer for 15 minutes. Turn chicken over and simmer another 15 minutes. Turn off heat, remove chicken from liquid, prick skin with a fork to drain fat and allow to cool. Strain the liquid and reserve.

2. Place chicken, breast side down, on a cookie sheet. Preheat oven to 350°F for 15 minutes. Place cookie sheet in oven and roast chicken for 30 minutes. Turn over and roast another 30 minutes until golden brown.

3. Combine the dipping sauce ingredients and set aside.

3. Turn off heat. Remove chicken. Allow to cool for 5 minutes, then cut chicken into bite-size pieces and serve with the dipping sauce.

Nutrition per serving: 85 Calories; 2g Fat; 23% calories from fat; negligible Carbohydrates; 33mg Cholesterol; 643mg Sodium.

Lemon Chicken

Sai Ling Ching Gai

The name of this dish is familiar to most. Every preparation that goes by the name involves frying chicken, then pouring a lemon-flavored thick sauce over it. All except mine. I use the process of steaming chicken with fresh lemons to give this dish what I like to call style.

3/4 **pound boneless, skinless chicken cutlets, cut into 1-inch cubes**

2 **teaspoons fresh lemon juice (1/2 lemon)**

Squeezed half of lemon, cut into 4 pieces

1 **teaspoon Ginger Juice (page 43) mixed with 1 tablespoon Shao-Hsing wine or sherry**

1 1/2 **teaspoons soy sauce**

1 **tablespoon oyster sauce**

Pinch salt

1 1/2 **teaspoons sugar**

1 1/2 **teaspoons White Peppercorn Oil (page 41)**

Pinch white pepper

2 **teaspoons cornstarch**

6 **sprigs of fresh coriander (cilantro)**

Yield:
6 servings

1. Mix all ingredients, except coriander in a bowl and allow to rest and marinate for 20 minutes.

2. Place chicken and marinade in a steam-proof dish and steam for 15 minutes, or until the chicken turns white. Halfway through the steaming process, turn chicken over. (Note: If you open the cover of a steamer during any steaming process, the heat must be turned off. This will prevent a burst of steam from coming out.) Turn off heat, remove from steamer, and serve in the steaming dish, garnished with coriander sprigs. Serve with cooked rice.

Nutrition per serving (without rice): 81 Calories; 2g Fat; 22% calories from fat; less than 1g Carbohydrates; 45mg Cholesterol; 435mg Sodium.

金
針
雲
耳
蒸
鶏

My Mother's Favorite Chicken

Gum Jum Won Yee Jing Gai

In the garden of our house in Sun Tak, the suburb of Canton in which I grew up, among the trees in our courtyard was a guava tree. It was a lovely tree, but what made it important to my mother, Miu Hau, was that at its base always grew fine crops of cloud ears, or tree ears, a flower-like fungus. My mother always said that the cloud ears from her guava tree were the sweetest. She would use them and the tiger lily buds, gathered from our garden and dried, for this dish that she adored cooking and that we loved to eat.

1/2 **pound boneless, skinless chicken cutlet, cut across the grain into 2 × 1/8-inch-thick slices**

2 **tablespoons cloud ears, soaked in hot water 30 minutes, washed three times, drained**

40 **tiger lily buds, soaked in hot water 30 minutes, hard ends removed and halved**

3/4 **teaspoon Ginger Juice (page 43) mixed with 2 teaspoons Shao-Hsing wine or sherry**

1 **tablespoon oyster sauce**

2 **teaspoons soy sauce**

1 **teaspoon peanut oil**

1/2 **teaspoon sesame oil**

Pinch salt

3/4 **teaspoon sugar**

2 **teaspoons cornstarch**

4 **tablespoons cold water**

Pinch white pepper

6 **sprigs of fresh coriander (cilantro)**

Yield: .
4 servings

1. Combine all ingredients, except coriander, in a bowl. Mix well. Allow to marinate for 20 minutes. Place mixture in a steam-proof dish, then in steamer, and steam for 10 to 12 minutes until the chicken turns white. Halfway through the steaming process turn the mixture.

2. Turn off heat, remove dish from steamer, garnish with coriander sprigs, and serve with cooked rice.

Nutrition per serving (without rice): 96 Calories; 3g Fat; 27% calories from fat; 2g Carbohydrates; 48mg Cholesterol; 253mg Sodium.

Steamed Chicken with Chinese Mushrooms

Dong Gu Jing Gai

This is my version of another chicken preparation that I remember from my childhood. Usually it was made with a whole chicken, cut up, bones and all. For this interpretation I use chicken cutlets once again. Again, the flavor is preserved and the fat content reduced considerably.

MARINADE

1/2 teaspoon Ginger Juice (page 43) mixed with 1/2 teaspoon white wine

1/2 teaspoon white vinegar

I teaspoon soy sauce

2 teaspoons oyster sauce

1/4 teaspoon salt

I teaspoon sugar

I teaspoon Shallot Oil (page 40)

Pinch white pepper

I teaspoon cornstarch

2 tablespoons Chicken Stock (page 37)

TO COMPLETE THE DISH

1/2 pound boneless, skinless chicken cutlets, cut into I-inch cubes

7 large Chinese black mushrooms (1/2 cup), soaked in hot water for 30 minutes, washed, stems removed, mushrooms cut into 1/2-inch pieces

1/2 cup scallions, white portions cut into I-inch pieces

I 1/2 tablespoons shredded red bell peppers

I 1/2 tablespoons shredded green bell peppers

Yield:
4 servings

1. Combine marinade ingredients in a large bowl and mix thoroughly to blend. Add chicken, mushrooms, and scallions to marinade. Mix well, allow to stand for 1 hour, covered, refrigerated.

2. Place all ingredients in a steam-proof dish, then in steamer, and steam for 20 minutes. Halfway through steaming process turn chicken pieces over. Turn off heat, remove steaming dish, sprinkle with shredded red and green peppers, and serve.

Nutrition per serving: 87 Calories; 3g Fat; 28% calories from fat; 5.5g Carbohydrates; 48mg Cholesterol; 424mg Sodium.

Steamed Chicken with Black Beans

See Jup Jing Gai

This traditional dish is from the Cantonese kitchen. Usually this would be prepared with a whole chicken, cut up and braised in a pot. I steam chicken cutlets instead, with my Crisp Garlic and Garlic Oil, to ensure its flavor, but with a significant decrease in fat and oil.

3/4 **pound boneless, skinless chicken cutlets, cut into 1-inch cubes**

1 **tablespoon tapioca starch**

11/2 **tablespoons fermented black beans, washed to remove salt and drained**

11/2 **teaspoons Garlic Oil (page 39)**

1 **tablespoon Crisp Garlic (page 39)**

1/2 **teaspoon Ginger Juice (page 43)**

1 **tablespoon Shao-Hsing wine or sherry**

2 **teaspoons oyster sauce**

1 **teaspoon dark soy sauce**

3/4 **teaspoon sugar**

Pinch white pepper

11/2 **tablespoons minced fresh coriander (cilantro)**

Yield:
6 servings

1. Place all ingredients, except coriander, in a bowl and toss to mix and coat chicken thoroughly and evenly. Place chicken and marinade in a steam-proof dish, then in steamer, and steam for 25 minutes. Halfway through the steaming process turn the chicken mixture.

2. Turn off heat. Remove dish from steamer, sprinkle with minced coriander, and serve with cooked rice.

Nutrition per serving (without rice); 64 Calories: 2g Fat; 28% calories from fat; 2g Carbohydrates; 45mg Cholesterol; 31mg Sodium.

Steamed Chicken with Leeks

Dai Seun Jing Gai

大蒜蒸鷄

In China, leeks are somewhat different from those with which most of us are familiar. They resemble fat, oversized scallions, with reddish-tinged rounded bulbs. The leaves are long, flat, and green like those of the usual sort. The Chinese call them, with some humor, dai seun, or "big garlic." The tastes of both varieties are quite similar, however, so enjoy your chicken with whichever dai seun you fancy.

1/2 **pound boneless, skinless chicken cutlets, cut into I-inch cubes**

I **cup of leeks, white portions, washed well and cut into** 1/4-**inch pieces on the diagonal**

3/4 **teaspoon Ginger Juice (page 43) mixed with** I1/2 **teaspoons Shao-Hsing wine or sherry**

I1/4 **teaspoons White Peppercorn Oil (page 41)**

2 **teaspoons oyster sauce**

Pinch salt

1/2 **teaspoon sugar**

I1/4 **teaspoons cornstarch**

3 **tablespoons Chicken Stock (page 37)**

2 **tablespoons shredded scallions, white portions**

Yield:
4 servings

I. Place chicken and all other ingredients, except scallions, in a bowl. Toss to mix and coat well. Allow to marinate for 30 minutes.

2. Place chicken and marinade in a steam-proof dish, then in a steamer, and steam for 20 minutes, or until chicken turns white. Halfway through the steaming process turn the chicken mixture over. Turn off heat, remove steaming dish, sprinkle with shredded scallions, and serve.

Nutrition per serving: I09 Calories; 4g Fat; 28% calories from fat; I.5g Carbohydrates; 48mg Cholesterol; 355mg Sodium.

Steamed Hunan Chicken

Jing Lot Gai

In Hunan, this traditional dish is made with chicken legs that are oil blanched and fried. Once again, the steaming process preserves flavor without the excessive amounts of oil used in the original recipe.

1/2 pound boneless, skinless chicken cutlets, cut into 1-inch cubes

2 teaspoons cornstarch

1 tablespoon soy sauce

1 tablespoon julienned ginger

2 teaspoons hoisin sauce

1 teaspoon sugar

1 teaspoon white vinegar

1 tablespoon Shao-Hsing wine or sherry

1 1/2 teaspoons White Peppercorn Oil (page 41)

1/2 cup scallions, white portions, cut into 1/2-inch slices on the diagonal

1/2 teaspoon Hot Pepper Flakes (page 42)

2 tablespoons minced red bell pepper

Yield:
4 servings

Place chicken and all other ingredients, except minced bell pepper, in a bowl, toss to mix and coat chicken thoroughly. Place in a steam-proof dish, then in a steamer, and steam for 15 minutes, or until chicken turns white. Halfway through the steaming process turn over chicken mixture. Turn off heat and serve in the steaming dish, sprinkled with minced red bell peppers.

Nutrition per serving: 71 Calories; 2g Fat; 28% calories from fat; 6g Carbohydrates; 48mg Cholesterol; 435mg Sodium.

Roast Chicken

Guk Gai

When I was a child in China, most household kitchens did not have ovens, so poultry and meats were prepared atop stoves, in a variety of ways as I have demonstrated. Or one could buy roasted chicken in barbecue shops. Thus, when we made our poultry-based salads, for example, we usually poached our chickens and other poultry, then shredded the meat for the mixtures. In the dishes that follow, the usual, authentic method of preparing chicken for such use is to poach it. But you may wish to use roasted chicken for these recipes, which is fine. Here is a very simple roast, which will provide a supply of chicken for several salads. On the other hand, you may simply like the roast chicken itself. Enjoy.

2 large chicken breasts, 1 1/2 pounds each, with skin and bones retained, washed, fat and membranes removed

1 tablespoon rice vinegar

2 tablespoons Shao-Hsing wine or sherry

1 teaspoon salt

1/8 teaspoon white pepper

6 cloves garlic, thinly sliced

1 cup water

Yield:
About 20 to 24 ounces of lean roasted chicken meat, which, when divided in half, will be sufficient for the two salads that begin on the next page

1. Place chicken breasts in a roasting pan. Rub chicken on both sides with rice vinegar, then with the wine. Sprinkle with salt, then with white pepper. Place breasts on a rack, meat side up, slip slices of garlic under the skin, between skin and meat. Add 1 cup of water to bottom of roasting pan.

2. Place in a preheated 375°F oven and roast for 30 minutes. Turn chicken over, lower heat to 350°F and roast another 30 minutes. Turn over again, lower heat to 325°F, and roast for another 15 minutes, until cooked. Make a cut in the meatiest portion of the breast to see if it is white and cooked.

3. Turn off heat, remove chicken, and allow to cool to room temperature. Then you may work with it. Discard skin and bones.

雙
桃
沙
律

Two Peach Chicken Salad

Seung Toh Sah Lut

This is the ultimate dish for a summer day. Fresh peaches are abundant, for eating, for stewing, for combining with other foods in imaginative ways, and for salads. How very adaptable is the sweet peach. In this recipe I have combined the sweetness of the fresh with the tartness of the pickled, both so complementary to the chicken.

7 to 8 ounces of roasted chicken meat (page 159), hand-shredded

I medium fresh peach, halved, pitted, skin left on, and julienned (I cup)

1/2 medium Pickled Peach (page 46), julienned (1/2 cup)

I medium yellow bell pepper, julienned (I cup)

I large carrot, peeled and julienned (I cup)

2 scallions, white portions, julienned (1/4 cup)

4 tablespoons Crisp Shallots (page 40)

1/4 teaspoon salt (optional)

1/4 cup My Rice Wine Vinaigrette (page 44)

Yield:
6 servings

Place chicken and all other ingredients in a bowl and toss together until all are well combined and coated. Transfer to a platter and serve.

Nutrition per serving: 101 Calories; 2g Fat; 14% calories from fat; 4.5g Carbohydrates; 32mg Cholesterol; 166mg Sodium.

杜
菜
鶏
少
律

Chicken and Mango Salad

Mong Gua Gai Sah Lut

Mango is at its best throughout Asia in the summer months, even in late spring. It, like many other fruits, melds well with flavored, cooked chicken.

7 to 8 ounces roasted chicken meat (page 159), hand-shredded

1/2 medium mango, ripe but firm, peeled and julienned (I cup)

I small cucumber, peeled, seeded, and julienned (I cup)

I red bell pepper, julienned (I cup)

I stalk celery, cut into 2-inch lengths and julienned (I cup)

2 fresh water chestnuts, peeled and julienned (1/4 cup)

2 scallions, white portions, halved and julienned (1/4 cup)

2 tablespoons Ginger Pickle (page 45)

1/4 teaspoon salt (optional)

1/4 cup My Rice Wine Vinaigrette (page 44)

Yield:
6 servings

Place chicken and all other ingredients in a bowl and toss well to combine so that all are well coated. Transfer to a platter and serve.

Nutrition per serving: 124 Calories; 2.5g Fat; 18% calories from fat; 6.5g Carbohydrates; 15mg Cholesterol; 270mg Sodium.

Chicken with Snow Peas

Seut Dau Chau Gai Pin

These most familiar Chinese culinary components, snow peas, are referred to by the Chinese as hoh lan dau, *or "Holland peas," which recognizes their lineage. They combine well with many different ingredients.*

I cup plus 2 tablespoon Chicken Stock (page 37)

I slice ginger, 1/2 inch thick, lightly smashed

1/2 pound boneless, skinless chicken cutlets, thinly sliced against the grain into 2 × I-inch pieces

SAUCE

I1/2 tablespoons oyster sauce

1/2 tablespoon soy sauce

I teaspoon Shao-Hsing wine or sherry

1/2 teaspoon sesame oil

I teaspoon sugar

2 teaspoons tapioca starch

Pinch white pepper

1/4 cup Chicken Stock (page 37)

TO COMPLETE THE DISH

2 teaspoons peanut oil

I teaspoon minced ginger

2 teaspoons minced garlic

1/4 teaspoon salt

6 ounces snow peas, ends and strings removed, each cut into thirds on the diagonal

3 scallions, ends removed, cut into 1/2-inch pieces on the diagonal, white portions lightly smashed

4 freshwater chestnuts, peeled and thinly sliced

I tablespoon Shao-Hsing wine or sherry

Yield:
6 servings

1. In a wok bring 1 cup of chicken stock and slice of ginger to a boil over high heat. Add chicken and blanch until chicken turns white, about 1 minute. Turn off heat, remove chicken, strain, and reserve.

2. Combine sauce ingredients and set aside.

3. Heat wok over high heat for 30 seconds. Add peanut oil and coat wok. When a wisp of white smoke appears, add ginger, garlic, and salt, stir briefly. Add snow peas, scallions, and water chestnuts. Stir to mix for 45 seconds. Add reserved chicken and stir-fry for 30 seconds. Add wine and mix well. Add 2 tablespoons chicken stock, mix, and cook for 1 minute. Make a well in the mixture, stir sauce, pour in, stir to combine thoroughly. When sauce begins to thicken and bubble, turn off heat, transfer to a heated dish and serve.

Nutrition per serving: 77 Calories; 2.5g Fat; 28% calories from fat; 4.5g Carbohydrates; 32mg Cholesterol; 446mg Sodium.

鶏 Chicken Ding
丁
Gai Ding

The Chinese word ding *translates as "small squares," an apt description for this dish. This is a classic, in which the nuts combined with the chicken can be cashews, peanuts, walnuts, or pecans. I chose cashews, whose taste I prefer. When I was a little girl I used to volunteer to roast the cashews for this dish, so I could taste them on the sly. If you substitute cornstarch for tapioca starch, the sauce will be cloudier.*

I cup plus 2 tablespoons Chicken Stock (page 37)

I slice ginger, 1/2 inch thick, lightly smashed

1/2 pound boneless, skinless chicken cutlet, cut into 1/2-inch cubes

SAUCE

I1/2 tablespoons oyster sauce

I1/2 teaspoons soy sauce

I teaspoon sugar

1/4 teaspoon sesame oil

2 teaspoons tapioca starch (or cornstarch)

Pinch white pepper

2 tablespoons Chicken Stock (page 37)

TO COMPLETE THE DISH

2 teaspoons peanut oil

I teaspoon minced ginger

I1/2 teaspoons minced garlic

I tablespoon hoisin sauce

I tablespoon Shao-Hsing wine or sherry

1/4 pound snow peas, cut into 1/2-inch pieces

I ounce cashews (1/4 cup), dry roasted (page 14)

3 large fresh water chestnuts, peeled, cut into 1/4-inch dice

1/2 cup bamboo shoots, cut into 1/4-inch dice

Yield:
4 servings

1. Place I cup chicken stock in pot with slice of ginger, bring to a boil over high heat. Blanch the chicken for I1/2 minutes until chicken turns white. Remove, drain, and reserve.

2. Combine sauce ingredients and set aside.

3. Heat wok over high heat for 30 seconds. Add peanut oil and coat wok. When a wisp of white smoke appears, add minced ginger and garlic, stir briefly. Add hoisin sauce, stir to mix. Add reserved chicken, stir to coat. Add wine, stir briefly. Add snow peas, stir them briefly, then add water chestnuts, and bamboo shoots. Add I tablespoon chicken stock. Stir-fry for 2 minutes. If needed, add the remaining tablespoon of chicken stock. Make a well in the mixture, stir sauce, pour in, stir to mix thoroughly. When sauce darkens and thickens turn off heat, transfer to a heated dish, sprinkle with cashews and serve.

Nutrition per serving: 143 Calories; 7g Fat; 22% calories from fat; 9.3g Carbohydrates; 51mg Cholesterol; 693mg Sodium.

榨菜鷄絲 Chicken with Sichuan Mustard Pickle

Ja Choi Gai See

Sichuan mustard pickle, once rare but now widely available, loose or canned, is a fine ingredient in combination with other foods. It is virtually never eaten by itself.

I cup plus 3 tablespoons Chicken Stock (page 37)
I slice ginger, 1/2 inch thick, lightly smashed
1/2 pound boneless, skinless chicken cutlet, julienned

SAUCE

I 1/2 tablespoons oyster sauce

I teaspoon soy sauce

I teaspoon white vinegar

I teaspoon Shao-Hsing wine or sherry

I teaspoon sugar

1/4 teaspoon sesame oil

2 1/2 teaspoons tapioca starch

Pinch white pepper

1/4 cup Chicken Stock (page 37)

TO COMPLETE THE DISH

I 1/2 teaspoons peanut oil

I teaspoon minced ginger

I 1/2 teaspoons minced garlic

2 Thai chilies, minced

I 1/2 tablespoons Sichuan mustard pickle, shredded

I medium carrot, julienned

I large stalk celery (3/4 cup), julienned

3 scallions, cut into 1/2-inch pieces on the diagonal, white
    portions lightly smashed

I tablespoon Shao-Hsing wine or sherry

Yield:
4 servings

1. In a pot place I cup chicken stock with slice of ginger and bring to a boil over high heat. Blanch the chicken for 45 seconds. Remove, drain, reserve.

2. Combine sauce ingredients and set aside.

3. Heat wok over high heat for 30 seconds, add peanut oil and coat wok. When a wisp of white smoke appears, add minced ginger and garlic and stir briefly. Add reserved chicken and stir to mix. Add all vegetables and stir-fry to mix well. Add wine and stir and mix for 45 seconds. Add 2 tablespoons chicken stock and stir together for 1 1/2 minutes. If mixture is dry, add remaining tablespoon of stock. Make a well in the mixture, stir sauce, pour in. Mix well. When sauce darkens and begins to bubble, turn off heat. Transfer to a heated dish and serve.

Nutrition per serving: 124 Calories; 3g Fat; 21% calories from fat; 8g Carbohydrates; 48mg Cholesterol; 796mg Sodium.

Mango Chicken Stir-Fry

Mong Gua Chau Gai Yuk

In Canton and Hong Kong the use of fruit stir-fried with meats or fish and seafood is quite common. It was with some amazement that I read one day that Western chefs had "discovered" that fruit was quite marvelous when cooked with other ingredients. Better late than never, I suppose. I have re-created this dish from the repertoire of one of my aunts in Hong Kong.

3/4 cup Chicken Stock (page 37)

6 ounces chicken cutlet, cut into thin slices, 1 1/2 inches long

2 large broccoli stems, cut in half lengthwise, then cut into
1/4-inch pieces (1 1/4 cups)

SAUCE

1 1/2 tablespoons oyster sauce

2 teaspoons soy sauce

2 teaspoons Shao-Hsing wine or sherry

3/4 teaspoon sugar

1/4 teaspoon sesame oil

1 tablespoon cornstarch

Pinch white pepper

1/4 cup Chicken Stock (page 37)

TO COMPLETE THE DISH

1 1/2 teaspoons peanut oil

1/4 teaspoon salt

1 1/2 teaspoons minced ginger

1 1/2 teaspoons minced garlic

1 small mango, peeled, cut into 1 × 1/2-inch slices (1 cup)

1 medium red bell pepper, cut into 1/2-inch dice (1 cup)

2 scallions, trimmed and cut into 1/2-inch pieces on the
diagonal

1 tablespoon Shao-Hsing wine or sherry

Yield:
6 servings

1. In a wok bring chicken stock to a boil over high heat. Add chicken slices, stir to separate. When chicken turns white, I to I1/2 minutes, pick up chicken with strainer and allow to drain. Bring stock back to a boil, add broccoli stems, and cook for I minute. Remove and drain. Empty stock, reserve for another use. Wash wok and spatula.

2. Combine sauce ingredients and set aside.

3. Heat wok over high heat for 30 seconds, add peanut oil and coat wok. When a wisp of white smoke appears, add salt, ginger, and garlic, stir. When garlic turns light brown, add chicken and stir briefly. Add broccoli and stir to mix. Add mango, bell pepper, and scallions and stir to mix well. Cook for I minute. Drizzle the wine into the wok at the edges, stir and mix well, cook for I1/2 minutes. Make a well in the mixture, stir sauce, and pour in. Stir-fry, mixing all ingredients thoroughly. When sauce thickens and begins to bubble, turn off heat. Transfer to a heated dish and serve.

Nutrition per serving: 68 Calories; 2g Fat; 22% calories from fat; 4.5g Carbohydrates; 24mg Cholesterol; 499mg Sodium.

Chicken Stir-Fried with Melon

Mut Gua Chau Gai Yuk

Any melon will do for this dish—cantaloupe, as I use, or honeydew, or that very special melon of south China, the hami, *a very crisp cantaloupe.*

3/4 cup plus 2 tablespoons Chicken Stock (page 37)

6 ounces boneless, skinless chicken cutlet, cut into 2 × 1-inch slices

2 ounces string beans, cut into 1/2-inch pieces on the diagonal (1/2 cup)

SAUCE

1 1/2 tablespoons oyster sauce

2 teaspoons soy sauce

1/2 teaspoon sesame oil

2 teaspoons Shao-Hsing wine or sherry

1/2 teaspoon sugar

Pinch white pepper

1 tablespoon cornstarch

3 tablespoons Chicken Stock (page 37)

TO COMPLETE THE DISH

1 1/2 teaspoons peanut oil

Pinch salt

2 teaspoons minced ginger

2 scallions, cut into 1/2-inch pieces on the diagonal

3 fresh water chestnuts, peeled, cut into 1/8-inch slices (1/2 cup)

1 medium red bell pepper, cut into 1/2-inch dice

1/2 small cantaloupe, peeled, cut into thirds lengthwise, then into 1/3-inch slices (1 1/2 cups)

1 tablespoon Shao-Hsing wine or sherry

Yield:
6 servings

1. Heat wok over high heat for 30 seconds. Add 3/4 cup chicken stock and bring to a boil. Add chicken, stir to loosen it, cook for 1 to 11/2 minutes or until chicken turns white. Remove chicken with strainer and allow to drain. Bring stock back to a boil, add string beans and blanch for 30 seconds, or until they turn bright green. Turn off heat, remove string beans to the strainer, and allow them to drain with the chicken. Pour off stock for another use. Wash wok and spatula.

2. Combine sauce ingredients and set aside.

3. Heat wok over high heat for 30 seconds. Add peanut oil and salt and coat wok. When a wisp of white smoke appears, add ginger to wok and stir. Add scallions, stir and cook for 30 seconds. Add chicken and string beans, stir and cook for 1 minute. Add water chestnuts and bell pepper and mix well. Add the cantaloupe and mix, then add the wine and mix again. Add 2 tablespoons chicken stock, stir to mix. Make a well in the mixture, stir sauce, and pour in. Stir to combine, making certain all ingredients are well coated. When sauce thickens and begins to bubble, turn off heat, transfer chicken to a heated dish and serve.

Nutrition per serving: 84 Calories; 2g Fat; 19% calories from fat; 7.5g Carbohydrates; 24mg Cholesterol; 465mg Sodium.

Shredded Chicken with Sesame Mustard Sauce

Mah Lot Sau See Gai

This dish is in the tradition of the Hakka people of southern China, and illustrates a traditional method of preparing chicken for inclusion in a salad.

3/4 pound boneless, skinless chicken cutlets

I tablespoon Shao-Hsing wine or sherry

I teaspoon soy sauce

3/4 teaspoon sugar

1/2 teaspoon White Peppercorn Oil (page 41)

2 scallions, ends discarded, cut into 2-inch sections

I slice fresh ginger, 1/2 inch thick, lightly smashed

DRESSING

2 teaspoons sesame seed paste (tahini)

I 1/2 tablespoons minced shallots

1/4 teaspoon salt

I 1/2 teaspoons sugar

2 1/2 tablespoons steaming liquid, hot

I tablespoon oyster sauce

I teaspoon White Peppercorn Oil (page 41)

I teaspoon mushroom soy sauce

I 1/2 tablespoons Shao-Hsing wine or sherry

I tablespoon Colman's dry mustard mixed with
    I tablespoon of steaming liquid

TO COMPLETE THE DISH

Red lettuce leaves

I 1/2 teaspoons white sesame seeds, dry-roasted (page 14)

Yield:
6 servings

1. Place chicken in a steam-proof dish. Add wine, soy sauce, sugar, White Peppercorn Oil, scallions, and ginger, and toss well to coat the chicken. Steam for 20 minutes, or until chicken is cooked. Turn off heat, remove chicken, and allow to cool. Reserve steaming liquid for use in next step.

2. To make the dressing, place sesame seed paste, shallots, salt, and sugar in a bowl. Add the hot steaming liquid, and mix until sesame paste dissolves. Add oyster sauce, oil, mushroom soy sauce, and wine and combine until mixture is smooth. Add mustard mixture and combine until well blended.

3. Hand shred the chicken into pieces 1/2 inch thick and add to the dressing. Mix thoroughly, making certain chicken is well coated. Place in a serving platter atop a bed of red lettuce leaves, sprinkle with roasted sesame seeds and serve.

Nutrition per serving: 70 Calories; 2g Fat; 25% calories from fat; 2.5g Carbohydrates; 45mg Cholesterol; 404mg Sodium.

Tea-Smoked Duck

Long Jing Op

Necessary for this fragrant and flavorful preparation is Dragon Well Tea, a green tea native to Hangzhou, near Shanghai. Packages of it are labeled Long Jing, *or* Lung Ching, *or* Loong Tsing, *but no matter the intonation they are all Dragon Well. The same tea is also grown, processed, and packaged in Taiwan as well, and its quality is equally as good. Fine to drink and wonderful to smell, it is a marvelous ingredient with which to cook.*

This preparation, which requires several steps, is another of those festive poultry dishes that would be served on a special occasion. It is also a dish unlikely to be found in restaurants. So enjoy the effort, and the result.

I whole duck, 5 pounds (freshly killed preferred), washed, cavity cleaned with running water, membranes and fat removed, drained, and dried thoroughly

2 tablespoons Shao-Hsing wine or sherry

2 teaspoons sugar

2 teaspoons salt

3 cinnamon sticks

3 pieces eight-star anise

3 slices ginger, each I 1/2 inches long

6 cups boiling water

2/3 cup Dragon Well Tea leaves

2 tomatoes, sliced

Yield:
8 servings

1. To prepare the duck, place in a large steam-proof dish. Rub duck well with wine, outside and in, then with sugar and salt, outside and in. Place I stick of cinnamon, I piece of anise, and I slice of ginger in the cavity. Place remaining spices on both sides of duck.

2. To steam the duck, place dish with duck in a wok by setting it on a cake rack above 6 cups of boiling water. Cover wok. Steam for I 1/4 hours. During the process check water in wok; if it evaporates, replace with boiling water at hand. After steaming, remove dish with duck and allow to cool to room temperature. Do not touch duck while it is hot, since you may damage the skin.

3. To smoke the duck, place tea leaves in a dry wok; roast until smoking. Remove duck from steaming dish, place on a rack over the leaves, and cover with wok cover. Place wet cloth around the rim where it meets wok to seal it tightly. Lower heat to medium and smoke the duck for 7 to 10 minutes.

4. To roast the duck, preheat oven to 375°F for 20 minutes. Prick the duck all over the body with a fork. This will allow fat beneath the skin to drain. Place duck on a foil-lined cookie sheet on a rack and roast, breast side down for 30 minutes. Turn over and roast for another 30 minutes. Turn off heat. Remove duck from oven and allow to rest for 5 minutes.

5. To serve, remove skin, discard cavity ingredients, cut duck into bite-size pieces. Place sliced tomatoes around the edge of a serving platter, place duck pieces in the center, and serve.

Nutrition per serving: 102 Calories; 3g Fat; 24% calories from fat; 1.5g Carbohydrates; 24mg Cholesterol; 468mg Sodium.

Note: An advantage to cooking Tea-Smoked Duck is that it can be partially prepared in advance. All steps through smoking and up until the final roasting can be done a day in advance. A benefit of cooking duck in this fashion, whether in advance, or the same day, is that the steps involved allow a great amount of the fat in the duck to drain away.

Steamed Duck with Pickled Peaches

Toh Jee Jing Op

This duck is a festive dish, rarely cooked in restaurants, and then only by special arrangement. It was a dish cooked in our family kitchen as a special event. The preparation is pure Cantonese in origin, traditionally made stuffed with sour preserved plums. These jarred plums are extremely sour and I prefer to use my own pickled peaches instead, for a more pleasant adaptation.

> I whole duck, 5 pounds (freshly killed preferred), washed, cavity cleaned with running water, fat and membranes removed, drained, and dried thoroughly

STUFFING

> I Pickled Peach (page 46), pitted and minced
>
> 5 cloves garlic, minced
>
> 2 teaspoons bean sauce
>
> 1/4 teaspoon salt
>
> I tablespoon rice vinegar
>
> 3 tablespoons brown sugar

TO CONTINUE THE DISH

> 6 cups boiling water
>
> I 1/2 tablespoons dark soy sauce
>
> I orange, cut into thin half-moon slices

Yield:
8 servings

1. To prepare the duck, mix stuffing ingredients and fill duck cavity. Close body openings with skewers.

2. To steam, place stuffed duck in a steam-proof dish, and place the dish in a wok on a rack above 6 cups boiling water. Steam precisely as done in Tea-Smoked Duck recipe (page 174).

3. To roast the duck, coat the steamed duck with the soy sauce. Prick it all over with a fork, place on a foil-lined cookie sheet, and roast. Roast precisely as done in Tea-Smoked Duck recipe.

4. To serve the duck, remove the skin. Cut duck into bite-size pieces. Place orange slices around the edge of a platter, place duck in center and serve.

   Nutrition per serving: 102 Calories; 3g Fat; 23% calories from fat; 1.5g Carbohydrates; 24mg Cholesterol; 253mg Sodium.

Note: I suggest the pickled peach stuffing may be served as an accompaniment to the duck. As with the previous recipe, the pricking of the duck skin and its removal after roasting reduces the fat and salt contents considerably.

Turkey

For Gai

Turkey is known in China as *for gai*, which translates as "fire chicken," an allusion to its variegated feathers and red wattle. When I was living with my aunt in Hong Kong, I recall turkey being regarded as a somewhat exotic bird, and we would wonder about its taste. My first taste of it was at a Christmas dinner cooked by my cousin, who had married an Englishman, and was visiting with us at the time. We found that it was something like chicken, but it was delicious. From that time on we ate "fire chicken" on many special occasions. To this day I love turkey and cook it in many ways, both in Western and Chinese fashions.

 # Turkey Stir-Fried with Snow Peas

Seut Dau Chau For Gai

Traditionally this stir-fry is an all-purpose dish. Cooking meats with snow peas is not uncommon in China, where the dish can be made with chicken, beef, pork, even veal, and in this case, turkey.

> 1/2 cup Chicken Stock (page 37)
>
> 6 ounces boneless, skinless turkey cutlets, cut thinly into
>   1 × 2-inch slices
>
> 6 ounces snow peas, ends and strings removed, each halved on
>   the diagonal

SAUCE

> 1 1/2 tablespoons oyster sauce
>
> 2 teaspoons Shao-Hsing wine or sherry
>
> 1 1/2 teaspoons soy sauce
>
> 1 teaspoon sugar
>
> 1/4 teaspoon sesame oil
>
> 2 teaspoons cornstarch
>
> 1/4 cup Chicken Stock (page 37)

To complete the dish

I 1/4 teaspoons peanut oil

I teaspoon minced ginger

Pinch salt

6 scallions, white portions, cut into 1/4-inch pieces on diagonal

I tablespoon Shao-Hsing wine or sherry

Yield:
4 servings

1. Heat wok over high heat. Add 1/2 cup chicken stock and bring to a boil. Add turkey slices and stir and poach for I minute, or until turkey turns white. Turn off heat, place turkey in a strainer to drain. Turn heat back to high, bring liquid to a boil. Add snow peas, stir and cook for 45 seconds or until they turn bright green. Turn off heat, remove to the strainer with the turkey and drain. Reserve liquid for future use. Wash and dry wok and spatula.

2. Combine sauce ingredients and set aside.

3. Heat wok over high heat for 30 seconds. Add peanut oil and coat wok. When a wisp of white smoke appears, add ginger and salt and stir briefly. Add scallions, stir and cook 45 seconds or until their aroma is released. Add turkey and snow peas, stir and cook for 30 seconds. Add wine, mix well, cook for I minute. Make a well in the mixture, stir sauce, pour in. Mix well. When sauce thickens and begins to bubble turn off heat. Transfer to a heated dish and serve.

Nutrition per serving: 143 Calories; 2.8g Fat; 17% calories from fat; 6g Carbohydrates; 45mg Cholesterol; 439mg Sodium.

Turkey Stir-Fried with Onions and Peppers

Chung Jiu Chau For Gai

Here turkey traditionally becomes a stand-in for chicken. However, as I made such dishes, I began to reconsider; let us have turkey on its own terms, with its distinct flavor. Why not indeed.

3/4 cup plus 3 tablespoons Chicken Stock (page 37)
6 ounces boneless, skinless turkey cutlet, cut into 1 × 2-inch slices

SAUCE

2 tablespoons oyster sauce
2 teaspoons dark soy sauce
1 teaspoon sugar
2 teaspoons Shao-Hsing wine or sherry
2 teaspoons cornstarch
Pinch white pepper
1/4 cup Chicken Stock (page 37)

TO COMPLETE THE DISH

1 teaspoon Onion Oil (page 40)
1 teaspoon minced ginger
1 teaspoon minced garlic
1/4 teaspoon salt
1/2 pound onions, thinly sliced (11/2 cups)
2 medium green bell peppers, thinly sliced (8 ounces)
1 tablespoon Shao-Hsing wine or sherry

Yield:
4 servings

1. Heat wok over high heat, add 3/4 cup chicken stock, and bring to a boil. Add turkey and poach for 1 1/2 minutes or until turkey turns white. Turn off heat, remove turkey to strainer and drain. Wash and dry wok and spatula.

2. Combine sauce ingredients and set aside.

3. Heat wok over high heat for 30 seconds, add Onion Oil and coat wok. When a wisp of white smoke appears, add ginger, garlic, and salt, stir briefly. Add onions and peppers, stir-fry for 1 minute. Add 2 tablespoons chicken stock and stir-fry for 1 minute. Add turkey and mix for 1 minute. Add wine and stir 30 seconds. If mixture is dry add remaining tablespoon chicken stock, stir and cook 30 seconds. Make a well in mixture, stir sauce, and pour in. Stir and cook well for 1 to 1 1/2 minutes. When sauce thickens and bubbles, turn off heat. Transfer to a heated dish and serve.

Nutrition per serving: 156 Calories; 2.5g Fat; 14% calories from fat; 6.6g Carbohydrates; 45mg Cholesterol; 589mg Sodium.

Turkey with Preserved Bean Curd

Wu Yue Chau For Gai

In China, preserved bean curd is eaten alone, with rice, with Congee (page 59), or in combination with virtually any meat, seafood, or vegetable. It blends well with anything with which it is cooked, including turkey.

3/4 cup Chicken Stock (page 37)

6 ounces boneless, skinless turkey cutlet, cut into 1 × 2-inch slices

1/2 pound fresh mushrooms, cut into 1/4-inch slices

SAUCE

1 1/2 tablespoons oyster sauce

1 teaspoon dark soy sauce

1 1/4 teaspoons sugar

1 tablespoon cornstarch

Pinch white pepper

1/4 cup Chicken Stock (page 37)

TO COMPLETE THE DISH

1 1/2 teaspoons Shallot Oil (page 40)

2 shallots, cut into 1/4-inch dice (2 tablespoons)

1 1/2 teaspoons minced ginger

3 cakes preserved bean curd, mashed in a bit of its own liquid

1 carrot, julienned (1 cup)

1 stalk celery, julienned (1 cup)

2 tablespoons Shao-Hsing wine or sherry

Yield:
4 servings

1. Heat wok over high heat, add chicken stock, and bring to a boil. Add turkey, and poach for 1 minute or until turkey turns white. Turn off heat, remove turkey with strainer and allow to drain. Turn heat back to high, bring back to a boil, and add mushrooms. Stir

and cook for 1 minute. Turn off heat, place mushrooms in strainer with turkey, and drain. Reserve stock for future use. Wash and dry wok and spatula.

2. Combine sauce ingredients and set aside.

3. Heat wok over high heat for 30 seconds, add Shallot Oil and coat wok. When a wisp of white smoke appears, add shallots and ginger, stir and cook for 1 1/2 minutes. Add preserved bean curd, mix and cook for 30 seconds. Add carrots and celery and cook for 1 1/2 to 2 minutes or until carrots soften. Add turkey and mushrooms, mix well, then add wine and cook for 1 minute. Make a well in the mixture, stir sauce, pour in, stir to mix. When sauce thickens and bubbles, turn off heat, transfer to a heated dish, and serve.

Nutrition per serving: 163 Calories; 2.5g Fat; 13% calories from fat; 6g Carbohydrates; 45mg Cholesterol; 462mg Sodium.

酸
辣
火
鶏

Hot and Tart Turkey

Seun Lot For Gai

This is a recipe with its roots in Sichuan, where it would, in all probability, be made with chicken. Despite its roots, it lacks the excessive oiliness that often characterizes the food of China's west.

3/4 cup plus I tablespoon Chicken Stock (page 37)
6 ounces boneless, skinless turkey cutlet, cut into I × 2-inch slices

SAUCE

I 1/2 teaspoons white vinegar
3 tablespoons ketchup
I 1/2 teaspoons sugar
1/4 teaspoon salt
2 teaspoons Shao-Hsing wine or sherry
2 teaspoons cornstarch
1/4 cup Chicken Stock (page 37)
Pinch white pepper

TO COMPLETE THE DISH

I teaspoon Sichuan Peppercorn Oil (page 42)
I teaspoon minced ginger
I 1/2 teaspoons minced garlic
1/4 teaspoon salt
6 scallions, white portions, cut into 1/4-inch pieces on the diagonal (3/4 cup)
3 Thai chilies, thinly sliced, with seeds
2 stalks celery, cut into matchsticks (I 3/4 cups).
1/2 cucumber, peeled, seeded, cut into matchsticks (I 1/4 cups)
1/2 red bell pepper, julienned (1/2 cup)
I tablespoon Shao-Hsing wine or sherry

Yield:
4 servings

1. Heat wok over high heat, add 3/4 cup chicken stock, and bring to a boil. Poach the turkey for 1 1/2 minutes or until turkey turns white. Turn off heat, remove turkey to a strainer, and drain. Reserve stock for future use. Wash and dry wok and spatula.

2. Combine sauce ingredients and set aside.

3. Heat wok over high heat for 30 seconds, add Sichuan Peppercorn Oil, and coat wok. When a wisp of white smoke appears, add ginger, garlic, and salt, stir briefly. Add scallions and chilies, stir for 30 seconds. Add remaining vegetables and stir-fry for 1 minute. Add the 1 tablespoon of chicken stock, stir and mix. Add turkey and stir for 1 minute. Add wine, stir and mix for 30 seconds. Make a well in the mixture, stir sauce, pour in. Cook about 1 to 1 1/2 minutes or until sauce thickens and bubbles. Turn off heat, transfer to a heated dish, and serve.

Nutrition per serving: 172 Calories; 2.8g Fat; 12% calories from fat; 8g Carbohydrates; 45mg Cholesterol; 615mg Sodium.

薑
蔥
焗
火
雞

Wok-Baked Turkey with Shallots

Gawn Chung Guk For Gai

When the wok is covered during cooking, traditionally the food being cooked is referred to in China as "baked." This goes back to the days of few ovens, when "baking" occurred atop the stop. Another aspect of this method of cooking is the fact that little liquid is used.

SAUCE

2 tablespoons oyster sauce

2 tablespoons ketchup

I teaspoon dark soy sauce

I1/2 teaspoons sugar

Pinch white pepper

TO COMPLETE THE DISH

I1/2 teaspoons peanut oil

1/4 teaspoon salt

2 ounces shallots, cut into 1/4-inch dice (1/3 cup)

I1/2 teaspoons minced garlic

1/2 pound boneless, skinless turkey cutlet, cut into 3/4-inch dice

I tablespoon Shao-Hsing wine or sherry

2 medium red bell peppers, cut into 1/2-inch dice (8 ounces)

5 tablespoons Chicken Stock (page 37)

1/4 teaspoon sesame oil

Yield:
4 servings

I. Combine sauce ingredients and set aside.

2. Heat wok over high heat for 30 seconds, add peanut oil and salt and coat wok. When a wisp of white smoke appears, add shallots and garlic and stir to mix for I minute, or until their aromas are released. Add turkey and stir well. Cook for 30 seconds. Add wine and mix. Add sauce mixture, stir, making certain the turkey is evenly coated. Add peppers, stir, and mix well.

3. Add 3 tablespoons chicken stock and stir in. Cover wok and allow mixture to come to a boil. Remove cover and stir the mixture. Lower heat to medium. If mixture is dry add remaining stock. Cover wok again and cook for 5 minutes. Turn off heat, remove cover, stir in sesame oil, and blend well. Transfer to a heated dish and serve.

Nutrition per serving: 179 Calories; 4g Fat; 16% calories from fat; 4g Carbohydrates; 60mg Cholesterol; 517mg Sodium.

雪耳蒸火鷄

Steamed Turkey with Cloud Ears

Wan Yee Jing For Gai

Turkey can be steamed like its cousin the chicken. This preparation with cloud ears, that flowery, delicately flavored fungus, is my alteration of that steamed chicken dish, my mother's favorite.

1/2 pound boneless, skinless turkey cutlet, cut into 1 × 2-inch slices

3/4 cup scallions, white portions, cut into 1/2-inch pieces on the diagonal

2 tablespoons cloud ears, soaked in hot water for 30 minutes, washed three times to remove grit, and drained

1 teaspoon Ginger Juice (page 43) mixed with 1 tablespoon Shao-Hsing wine or sherry

1 1/2 tablespoons oyster sauce

1/2 teaspoon white vinegar

1 teaspoon soy sauce

1/2 teaspoon sesame oil

1/2 teaspoon peanut oil

Pinch white pepper

2 teaspoons cornstarch

1/2 cup Chicken Stock (page 37)

Yield:
4 servings

Place turkey and all other ingredients in a bowl and toss thoroughly to combine and coat. Place mixture in a steam-proof dish and steam for 15 to 20 minutes, or until turkey turns white and is cooked. Halfway through the steaming process, turn the mixture. Turn off heat and serve in the steaming dish with cooked rice.

Nutrition per serving (without rice): 145 Calories; 2g Fat; 14% calories from fat; 2.8g Carbohydrates; 60mg Cholesterol; 422mg Sodium.

棒
棒
火
鶏

Hacked Turkey

Pong Pong For Gai

This is an adaptation of a familiar Sichuan dish called hacked chicken. Its Chinese name, pong pong, *translates as "pound, pound" to indicate that the chicken, when cooked, is pounded to break its fiber, for shredding.*

1/2 pound boneless, skinless turkey cutlets

3 cups cold water

I scallion, ends discarded, shredded

1/4 teaspoon salt

I teaspoon sugar

I slice ginger, 1/4 inch thick, lightly smashed

SAUCE

2 teaspoons sesame seed paste

I tablespoon mushroom soy sauce

3 tablespoons Chicken Stock (page 37)

I 1/2 teaspoons sugar

I 1/2 teaspoons white vinegar

I teaspoon minced garlic

3/4 teaspoon Hot Pepper Oil (page 42)

I 1/2 teaspoons Shao-Hsing wine or sherry

I tablespoon finely sliced scallions

I 1/2 cups shredded lettuce

Yield:
4 servings

1. In a large pot place turkey, water, scallions, salt, sugar, and ginger, and bring to a boil over high heat. Lower heat and partially cover the pot. Cook for about 7 minutes. Turn off heat, allow turkey to rest in liquid for 20 minutes.

2. Remove from liquid, place on a chopping board, and pound the cutlet with a rolling pin or wooden dowel to break its fiber. Shred the meat with your fingers. Refrigerate turkey for 4 hours, until cold.

3. Combine sauce ingredients and set aside. Remove turkey from refrigerator. Spread lettuce on a serving platter. Place shredded turkey atop it, pour sauce over it, and serve.

Nutrition per serving: 161 Calories; 2.5g Fat; 14% calories from fat; 2.5g Carbohydrates; 60mg Cholesterol; 369mg Sodium.

蜜
瓜
火
鷄
少
律

Turkey and Melon Salad

Mut Gua For Gai Sah Lut

Turkey is poached for this warm-weather salad with melon. In Hong Kong, where I first tasted it, it's usually made with roasted duck. I enjoyed the mixture of flavors so much, that I devised my version with poached turkey.

1/2 pound turkey cutlet

3 cups cold water

I scallion, ends discarded, shredded

1/4 teaspoon salt

I teaspoon sugar

I slice ginger, 1/4 inch thick, lightly smashed

2 tablespoons pine nuts, dry roasted (page 14)

3/4 cup cantaloupe, julienned

1/4 cup celery, julienned

1/4 cup red bell pepper, julienned

1/4 cup scallions, white portions, julienned

1/2 teaspoon salt

I teaspoon sugar

3/4 teaspoon soy sauce

I teaspoon White Peppercorn Oil (page 41)

I 1/4 teaspoons white vinegar

I teaspoon Shao-Hsing wine or sherry

I orange, thinly sliced into half-moons

Yield:
4 servings

I. In a pot place turkey, water, scallions, salt, sugar, and ginger and bring to a boil over high heat. Lower heat, partially cover pot, and cook for about 7 minutes. Turn off heat, allow turkey to rest in poaching liquid for 20 minutes.

2. Remove turkey from liquid, place on a chopping board, pound with a rolling pin or wooden dowel to break its fiber. Shred the meat with your fingers.

3. Place the shredded turkey and all remaining ingredients, except orange slices, in a bowl and mix together thoroughly to blend. Cover bowl and refrigerate for 4 hours. Serve cool in a platter garnished with orange half-moons around the platter's edge.

Nutrition per serving: 177 Calories; 2.8g Fat; 14% calories from fat; 4g Carbohydrates; 60mg Cholesterol; 442mg Sodium.

Chapter 5

Foods From the Land

Perhaps in no other culture is there such respect for vegetables as there is in China. Unlike the cooking of many other countries where vegetables are merely add-ons, Chinese cuisine often focuses on the vegetable. It is the platter of bok choy or *choi sum*, cooked alone, perhaps with some oyster sauce, that is important. It is any of many varieties and forms of bean curd, *dau fu* to the Chinese, that becomes the core not only of a family meal, but of the daily diet of observant Buddhists and Taoists.

Throughout most of China, often it is the vegetable that is the star, with meat or fowl or seafood as the supporting player, selected for its compatibility with that particular vegetable. This is particularly true in the southern part of China, a tropical land where vegetables, fruits, beans, and nuts abound, where two crops each year is not an unusual phenomenon.

It has been with pleasure that I have seen more and more Chinese vegetables appear on market shelves, not only in vegetable markets in traditional Chinese immigrant enclaves, but in supermarkets and neighborhood groceries. Bok choy and its tiny sweet cousin, Shanghai bok choy, thin fingerlike eggplants; water spinach; taro root; winter melon; *choi sum*, cabbage from Tianjin, which has come to be known as Napa cabbage; lotus root; bitter melon; silk squash; the kumquat; even the kiwi, are quite common, not at all mysterious. Perhaps you were not aware that the kiwi was native to China, even though New Zealand, with some help in the United States, has successfully claimed and marketed it as its own. Are you aware that the ubiquitous white radish, called *daikon* by the Japanese, and by nearly everybody else, is Chinese in origin? That the shiitake mushroom is the Chinese black mushroom? It was with some amusement that I recently read that snow pea shoots, the tender tips of the snow pea vine, had been "discovered" by Western chefs. In fact it was suggested that one Swiss fellow had made the "discovery." Well, I and others have been cooking with these *dau miu* for many, many years, unaware, I suppose, that they had not yet been "discovered." Many of us have been, over the years, amused, occasionally irked by such "discoveries," and by countless misidentifications of Chinese vegetables.

I grew up surrounded by vegetables and fruits. In the region of Sun Tak, the suburb of Canton in which I was raised, small, flattened tomatoes—called *gum chin gut,* or "gold coin tangerines," because of their color—grew wild. Pumpkins and other squashes were to be found growing without formal cultivation around the borders of the farms that surrounded our home. Water spinach grew wild as well in the small water-filled rivulets that bordered the rice fields of Sun Tak. My grandmother, my Ah Paw, had a garden of delights. She insisted that there be a never-ending supply of *choi sum* and bok choy, lettuce, scallions, and leeks for her to enjoy. There was a pomegranate tree behind her house from which I would pick fruit, and trees on which grew those sweet kumquats, *loquat,* and *longans.*

In my book *From the Earth: Chinese Vegetarian Cooking,* I have recounted my childhood love of fruits and vegetables; and a reverence for them was instilled in me by Ah Paw. I have never forgotten what she told me; that food that comes from the earth is deserving of care and respect.

In this chapter I provide a cross-section of the world of Chinese vegetables, from the soybean with its sprouts and its curd to the various stemmed and stalked vegetables. There are steamed dishes, stir-fries, and salads. Most of the vegetables will be familiar to you; some will be found in Chinese or Asian markets. All are worth any effort needed to seek them out.

Four Season Beans

Sei Guai Dau

In China, particularly in Canton, the string bean is known as sei guai, or the "four season" bean, simply because it was available throughout the year.

8 cups cold water

1/2 teaspoon baking soda (optional)

12 ounces string beans, ends removed

SAUCE

I tablespoon dark soy sauce

I teaspoon sugar

1/4 teaspoon sesame oil

I teaspoon white vinegar

I teaspoon Shao-Hsing wine or sherry

I teaspoon cornstarch

3 tablespoons Chicken Stock (page 37)

TO COMPLETE THE DISH

2 teaspoons White Peppercorn Oil (page 41)

2 teaspoons minced fresh ginger

2 teaspoons minced garlic

2 ounces lean fresh pork, coarsely ground

2 teaspoons Shao-Hsing wine or sherry

Yield:
6 servings

1. In a large pot place water and baking soda, cover and bring to a boil over high heat. Add string beans, immerse, and stir. Cook for 2 minutes. Turn off heat, run cold water into pot, drain; repeat. Reserve string beans.

2. Combine the sauce ingredients in a bowl and set aside.

3. Heat wok over high heat for 30 seconds. Add White Peppercorn Oil to coat wok. When a wisp of white smoke appears, add ginger and garlic and stir briefly. Add pork and mix well. Add wine and stir in. When pork turns white add string beans, stir and cook for 3 minutes. Make a well in the mixture, stir sauce, pour in. Mix thoroughly. When sauce thickens, turn off heat. Transfer to a heated dish and serve.

Nutrition per serving: 66 Calories; 2g Fat; 26% calories from fat; 4g Carbohydrates; 9mg Cholesterol; 216mg Sodium.

String Beans with Preserved Bean Curd

腐
乳
炒
荳
仔

Wu Yu Chau Dau Jai

Occasionally the Chinese refer, with humor, to string beans as dau jai, *or "baby beans," to distinguish them from the more familiar long beans, which must presumably be adult. This dish is traditionally made with these long beans, but string beans adapt admirably.*

6 cups cold water

1/2 teaspoon baking soda (optional)

12 ounces string beans, ends removed, broken into halves

3 cakes preserved bean curd

1 1/2 teaspoons Onion Oil (page 40)

1 1/2 teaspoons minced garlic

1 teaspoon minced ginger

2 tablespoons Vegetable Stock (page 36)

Yield:
4 servings

1. In a pot bring water with baking soda to a boil over high heat. Add string beans, stir and immerse and blanch for 1 minute. Turn off heat, run cold water into pot, drain. Repeat, drain thoroughly, and reserve.

2. Mash preserved bean curd with a bit of the liquid from its jar, just enough to make it smooth. Set aside.

3. Heat wok over high heat for 30 seconds, add Onion Oil to coat wok. When a wisp of white smoke appears, add garlic and ginger. Stir until garlic aroma is released, about 30 seconds. Add preserved bean curd and stir well, cook for about 20 seconds, or until its fragrance is released. Add string beans and stir-fry together for 30 seconds. Add 1 tablespoon of vegetable stock and mix well. If mixture is dry, add another tablespoon of stock. Turn off heat, transfer to a heated dish and serve.

Nutrition per serving: 54 Calories; 1.5g Fat; 24% calories from fat; 3g Carbohydrates; 0mg Cholesterol; 13mg Sodium.

Steamed Bean Curd with Scallions

Jing Dau Fu

For this dish I like the bean curd cakes whole. Dau fu is eaten in many fashions, whole or cut up. I believe that my Scallion Sauce contrasts best with the bean curd steamed whole.

4 cakes fresh bean curd (1 pound)

SAUCE

1 tablespoon oyster sauce

1 tablespoon cornstarch

1 teaspoon dark soy sauce

1/4 teaspoon salt

1/2 teaspoon sugar

3/4 cup Vegetable Stock (page 36)

TO COMPLETE THE DISH

2 teaspoons peanut oil

4 scallions, ends discarded, cut into 11/2-inch pieces, white portions quartered lengthwise

Yield:
4 servings

1. Place bean curd in a steam-proof dish, then in a steamer. Steam for 10 minutes. As the bean curd steams, combine the sauce ingredients in a bowl and set aside.

2. To prepare the scallions, heat wok over high heat for 30 seconds. Add peanut oil to coat wok. When a wisp of white smoke appears, add scallions. Stir-fry for 30 seconds or until they become bright green. Remove from wok, transfer to a heated dish.

3. Stir sauce and pour into wok over low heat. Continue stirring clockwise until sauce thickens and becomes dark brown. Add scallions and mix well. Pour over bean curd and serve.

Nutrition per serving: 123 Calories; 3g Fat; 22% calories from fat; 6g Carbohydrates; 0mg Cholesterol; 320mg Sodium.

Steamed Bean Curd with Shrimp

Dau Fu Jing Har

This is an excellent example of Cantonese home cooking. Rarely found in restaurants, this dish is referred to with fondness as lo siu ping on, or "suitable for the young and the old." And so it is, and for everyone else in between. It is striking for its appearance as well; it looks quite like a simple scrambled or shirred egg. This dish is at its best when served hot.

2 cakes fresh bean curd (8 ounces)

3 ounces shrimp, shelled, deveined, washed, drained, cut into 1/4-inch pieces

1 scallion, green and white parts, finely sliced

1 teaspoon minced fresh ginger

1 extra large egg white, beaten

1 tablespoon oyster sauce

2 tablespoons Chicken Stock (page 37)

2 teaspoons Shao-Hsing wine or sherry

1 teaspoon sugar

Pinch salt

Pinch white pepper

2 tablespoons minced fresh coriander (cilantro)

1/2 teaspoon Garlic Oil (page 39)

Yield:
4 servings

1. Mash the bean curd in a mixing bowl. Add all remaining ingredients, except minced coriander and 1/4 teaspoon of Garlic Oil, and mix well until all ingredients are smoothly blended.

2. Place in a steam-proof dish in a steamer and steam for 8 to 10 minutes or until the mixture firms and the shrimp become pink. Turn off heat, remove dish from steamer, sprinkle first with minced coriander then with remaining 1/4 teaspoon of Garlic Oil, and serve immediately.

Nutrition per serving: 85 Calories; 2.5g Fat; 25% calories from fat; 2.5g Carbohydrates; 32mg Cholesterol; 197mg Sodium.

美容荳腐

Steamed Bean Curd with Ham

Fu Yung Dau Fu

The words fu yung *translate as "light," "beautiful," and "elegant," all of which describe this subtle steamed preparation. The Chinese suggest that, as you eat it, you must feel as if you are devouring a cloud. This dish is traditionally made with the salty ham from Yunnan. I recommend Smithfield ham, prepared as I outline in the introduction. If Smithfield ham is not available, use baked Virginia ham or a country ham. The taste will be slightly different. If you substitute cornstarch for tapioca starch, the sauce will be cloudier.*

> 2 cakes fresh bean curd (8 ounces)
>
> 3 large egg whites, beaten
>
> 2 ounces Smithfield ham, soaked, desalted (page 30) and cut into 1/8-inch dice
>
> 1/4 teaspoon salt (optional)
>
> 1 1/2 tablespoons tapioca starch (or cornstarch)
>
> 1 1/2 tablespoons oyster sauce
>
> Pinch white pepper
>
> 1/2 cup Chicken Stock (page 37)
>
> 1/2 cup green peas, fresh or frozen

Yield:
4 servings

1. Mash the bean curd in a mixing bowl. Add egg whites, ham, salt, tapioca starch, oyster sauce, white pepper, and chicken stock and mix to blend all ingredients smoothly.

2. Transfer the mixture to a steam-proof dish, pat into an even layer, sprinkle peas on top. Steam for 20 minutes, until the mixture sets. Turn off heat, serve in its steaming dish, with cooked rice or Congee (page 59).

   Nutrition per serving (without rice): 77 Calories; 2g Fat; 23% calories from fat; 1g Carbohydrates; 5mg Cholesterol; 270mg Sodium.

Water Spinach with Preserved Bean Curd

腐乳炒通心菜

Wu Yue Chau Ong Choi

A most traditional dish. There are two varieties of this hollow-stemmed vegetable known as water spinach, one grown in water, the other on land; the latter is more commonly available here. As children we would simply go out and pick it wild, along streams and riverbanks. Regular spinach can be substituted if necessary, but the taste will be different.

I 1/2 teaspoons peanut oil

I 1/2 teaspoons minced garlic

Pinch salt

3 tablespoons Vegetable Stock (page 36)

I pound water spinach, washed, hard ends removed, broken into 3-inch pieces, drained well (yield 3/4 pound)

2 cakes (about 2 teaspoons) preserved bean curd, mashed with a bit of their liquid

Yield:
4 servings

Heat wok over high heat for 30 seconds, add peanut oil, coat wok. When a wisp of white smoke appears, add garlic and salt, stir until garlic releases its aroma, about 30 seconds. Add 2 tablespoons vegetable stock and stir-fry until the liquid in wok boils. Add water spinach and stir-fry to ensure the spinach is well coated. If the mixture is dry, add remaining stock. Stir until the water spinach softens, about I to I 1/2 minutes. Add the bean curd and cook I 1/2 minutes. Turn off heat, transfer to a heated dish, and serve.

Nutrition per serving: 82 Calories; 2g Fat; 28% calories from fat; 2g Carbohydrates; 0mg Cholesterol; 23mg Sodium.

Hunan Bean Curd

Mah Paw Dau Fu

This is an oddly named dish. In Hunan the words mah paw *mean "older lady," and refer to a real, older woman with a pocked face. The dish was named for her, for she created it spiced with horse beans and chilies. It is one of the most famous dishes of Hunan, one with a long tradition. I call it Hunan Bean Curd, but in China it is known by its familiar "older woman" name.*

    11/4 teaspoons peanut oil
    I teaspoon minced garlic
    I ounce lean ground beef, mixed well with 1/4 teaspoon
        cornstarch

SAUCE

    11/2 teaspoons Shao-Hsing wine or sherry
    11/2 teaspoons preserved horse beans with chili
    11/2 tablespoons ketchup
    21/2 teaspoons oyster sauce
    1/2 teaspoon white vinegar
    I teaspoon sugar
    3/4 teaspoon dark soy sauce
    6 Sichuan peppercorns, crushed
    2 teaspoons cornstarch
    2 tablespoons Chicken Stock (page 37)

TO COMPLETE THE DISH

    I teaspoon minced ginger
    2 scallions, both ends discarded, cut into 1/2-inch pieces on the
        diagonal (separate green and white portions)
    I large tomato, cut into 1/4-inch dice
    2 tablespoons Chicken Stock (page 37)
    2 cakes fresh bean curd (8 ounces), cut into 1/2-inch cubes

Yield:
6 servings

1. Heat wok over high heat for 30 seconds, add 1/2 teaspoon peanut oil to coat wok. When a wisp of white smoke appears, add garlic and stir briefly. Add beef, lower heat to medium, stir and break the beef apart. Cook for 45 seconds until beef changes color. Turn off heat, remove from wok, set aside.

2. Combine the sauce ingredients in a bowl and set aside.

3. Turn heat back to high for 15 seconds. Add remaining 3/4 teaspoon peanut oil to coat wok. Immediately add the ginger and the white portions of scallions, stir and cook for 45 seconds. Add tomatoes, stir and mix well, cook for 1 minute. Add stock and mix well. Bring to a boil, lower heat, cover wok and allow to simmer for 5 minutes.

4. Raise heat back to high, add reserved beef mixture, and mix well. Add bean curd and stir to mix well. Bring back to a boil. Make a well in the mixture, stir sauce, pour in. Stir-fry thoroughly and allow to return to a boil. Add green portions of scallions and stir in. Turn off heat, transfer to a heated dish and serve with cooked rice.

Nutrition per serving (without rice): 68 Calories; 2g Fat; 28% calories from fat; 3.3g Carbohydrates; 4.5mg Cholesterol; 240mg Sodium.

山
水
莲
腐

Bean Curd with Fresh Mushrooms

San Soi Dau Fu

In this preparation the words san soi *translate as "water which runs down the mountain," a reference to the high quality of fresh bean curd made with pure water. This summer recipe by one of Canton's most revered cooks, Chun Wing, who was also one of Hong Kong's great cooking teachers, is a renowned dish in China.*

> **8 cups cold water**
> **2 1/4 teaspoons salt**
> **1/2 pound broccoli florets (I head)**
> **4 ounces medium fresh white mushrooms, cut into quarters**

SAUCE

> **2 1/2 tablespoons oyster sauce**
> **I 1/2 teaspoons sugar**
> **I teaspoon dark soy sauce**
> **I teaspoon soy sauce**
> **Pinch white pepper**

TO COMPLETE THE DISH

> **I 1/2 teaspoons peanut oil**
> **I 1/2 teaspoons minced ginger**
> **4 cakes (I pound) fresh bean curd, cut into 1/2-inch dice**
> **I tablespoon Shao-Hsing wine or sherry**
> **I tablespoon cornstarch mixed with 6 tablespoons Vegetable Stock (page 36)**
> **1/4 teaspoon sesame oil**

Yield:
6 servings

I. In a pot bring water and salt to a boil over high heat. Add broccoli, stir and blanch for 30 seconds. Add fresh mushrooms, stir and blanch for 30 seconds more. Turn off heat, run cold water into pot, drain. Repeat, allow broccoli and mushrooms to drain thoroughly.

2. Combine the sauce ingredients and set aside.

3. Heat wok over high heat for 30 seconds, add 1 1/2 teaspoons peanut oil, coat wok. When a wisp of white smoke appears, add minced ginger and remaining 1/4 teaspoon salt, stir together for 30 seconds. Add broccoli and mushrooms, stir-fry for 1 1/2 minutes. Add bean curd and stir to mix well. Add wine and mix. Add the cornstarch-vegetable stock mixture, stir to coat all ingredients evenly. Cook for 2 minutes. Make a well in the mixture, stir sauce, pour in, mix thoroughly. When sauce thickens and bubbles, turn off heat. Pour in sesame oil and blend well. Transfer to a heated dish and serve with cooked rice.

Nutrition per serving (without rice): 66 Calories; 1g Fat; 14% calories from fat; 5g Carbohydrates; 0mg Cholesterol; 327mg Sodium.

Steamed Black Mushrooms

Jing Dong Gu

I always include this recipe in my cookbooks, not only because they are tasty, but because once prepared they become ingredients in many other dishes, as you will note in this book. They can be eaten just as they are cooked here, warm, at room temperature, even cold as an appetizer or side dish.

24 dried Chinese black mushrooms, each cap about the size of a silver dollar

1/2 teaspoon salt

1 1/2 teaspoons sugar

4 teaspoons dark soy sauce

2 tablespoons Shao-Hsing wine or sherry

1/2 cup Chicken Stock (page 37)

2 scallions, ends removed, green and white parts cut into 2-inch pieces

1 slice fresh ginger, 1 inch thick, lightly smashed

Yield:
6 servings

1. Soak mushrooms in hot water for 1 hour. Wash thoroughly, squeeze out excess water. Remove stems, place mushrooms in a steamproof dish. Add salt, sugar, soy sauce, wine, and stock and toss with mushrooms. Sprinkle scallions on top, add ginger to the dish, and steam the mushrooms for 30 minutes.

2. Turn off heat, remove from steamer. Discard scallions and ginger and gently toss mushrooms in remaining liquid. Serve immediately, hot, or allow to cool before serving. They may be kept, refrigerated, covered with plastic wrap for 4 to 5 days.

Nutrition per serving: 20 Calories; negligible fat grams; 0 calories from fat; 3.5g Carbohydrates; 0mg Cholesterol; 250mg Sodium.

雙菇沙律 Two Mushroom Salad

Seung Gu Sah Lut

I have created this salad using steamed black mushrooms as a base. The flavors of the steamed mushrooms carry over into the mix of a dish that is perfect for a summer day.

4 ounces fresh mushrooms, washed, dried and thinly sliced (I 1/4 cups)

6 medium Chinese black mushrooms, steamed (see previous recipe) and julienned (1/2 cup)

I scallion, white portion, shredded

1/2 medium red bell pepper, julienned (1/2 cup)

2 teaspoons freshly squeezed lemon juice

1/4 teaspoon salt

1/2 teaspoon sugar

1/8 teaspoon white pepper

**Yield:
4 servings**

Mix all ingredients thoroughly in a bowl, so that all become well coated. Allow to rest, refrigerated, at least I hour before serving, so that the flavors blend. Transfer to a dish and serve.

Nutrition per serving: 20 Calories; 0g Fat; 0% calories from fat; 3.5g Carbohydrates; 0mg Cholesterol; 152mg Sodium.

Bean Sprouts with Scallions

Chung Chau Nga Choi

This is one of my favorite vegetable combinations, colorful, with subtle though defined comple-mentary flavors. The words for bean sprouts, nga choi, translate as "tooth vegetable," indicating their crispness when bitten into. When I refer to bean sprouts, I mean mung bean sprouts, the most common variety. I specify when soybean sprouts are to be used.

4 cups cold water

1/2 pound bean sprouts, washed and drained

I 1/2 teaspoons Scallion Oil (page 39)

1/4 teaspoon salt

2 teaspoons minced ginger

6 scallions, cut into I 1/2-inch sections, white portions
    quartered lengthwise

I tablespoon Vegetable Stock (page 36)

Yield:
4 servings

1. In a pot bring water to a boil over high heat. Add bean sprouts, stir and blanch for no more than 20 seconds. Turn off heat, run cold water into pot, drain. Repeat, drain thoroughly. Set bean sprouts aside.

2. Heat wok over high heat for 30 seconds, add Scallion Oil and coat wok. When a wisp of white smoke appears, add salt and ginger, stir briefly. Add scallions, stir. Add stock, stir-fry for 45 seconds, or until scallions turn bright green. Add bean sprouts, stir, cook for I minute. Turn off heat, transfer to a heated dish, and serve.

Nutrition per serving: 51 Calories; less than Ig Fat; 13% calories from fat; 3.5g Carbohydrates; 0mg Cholesterol; 169mg Sodium.

Bean Sprouts with Browned Onions

Chung Yau Chau Nga Choi

I created this dish by accident. I was cooking one afternoon at the Stags' Leap Winery in the Napa Valley, and found I had an unplanned mound of fresh bean sprouts on hand. What to do? I had some Browned Onions left over from making Onion Oil. Aha! Why not a mix? And it turned out just fine. I use a little salt at the end of cooking to prevent the pure white bean sprouts from becoming dull or gray, which can happen if you add salt too early.

6 cups cold water

3/4 pound bean sprouts

1 teaspoon Onion Oil (page 40)

1 teaspoon minced garlic

2 teaspoons minced ginger

2 scallions, trimmed, cut into 2-inch sections, white portions
  quartered lengthwise

2 tablespoons Browned Onions (page 40)

1/4 teaspoon salt

Yield:
4 servings

1. In a pot bring water to a boil over high heat. Add bean sprouts and blanch for 10 seconds. Run cold water into pot, drain. Repeat, drain thoroughly. Set aside bean sprouts.

2. Heat wok over high heat for 30 seconds, and add Onion Oil to coat wok. When a wisp of white smoke appears, add garlic and ginger, stir briefly. Add scallions, stir and cook for 30 seconds. Add Browned Onions and stir to mix well. Add bean sprouts and stir-fry for 1 minute, until the mixture is very hot, and all ingredients are well coated. Turn off heat, add salt and toss to mix well. Transfer to a heated dish and serve. This may be served at room temperature as well, or cold.

Nutrition per serving: 37 Calories; 1g Fat; 25% calories from fat; 3g Carbohydrates; 0mg Cholesterol; 155mg Sodium.

Bean Sprouts with Barbecued Pork

Nga Choi Chau Char Siu

This is an example of a simple home-cooked dish, one seldom found in restaurants. The widely cultivated bean sprouts are eaten in Chinese homes almost daily. They are easily digested and believed to be among those foods that cool one's system.

4 cups cold water

I slice ginger, 1/2 inch thick, lightly smashed

3/4 pound bean sprouts, washed and drained

SAUCE

2 teaspoons oyster sauce

I teaspoon soy sauce

1/2 teaspoon Shao-Hsing wine or sherry

1/2 teaspoon sesame oil

1/2 teaspoon sugar

2 teaspoons cornstarch

1/4 cup Chicken Stock (page 37)

TO COMPLETE THE DISH

I teaspoon Sichuan Peppercorn Oil (page 42)

I tablespoon ginger, julienned

3 ounces Barbecued Pork (page 236), julienned

6 scallions, trimmed, cut into 2-inch sections, white portions quartered lengthwise

2 tablespoons Chicken Stock (page 37)

Yield:
6 servings

I. In a pot bring water and slice of ginger to a boil over high heat. Add bean sprouts, stir, immerse and blanch for 15 seconds. Turn off heat, run cold water into the pot, drain well. Toss the sprouts until all water is removed. Reserve.

2. Combine sauce ingredients and set aside.

3. Heat wok over high heat for 30 seconds, add Sichuan Peppercorn Oil and coat wok. When a wisp of white smoke appears, add julienned ginger, stir briefly. Add pork, stir-fry for 30 seconds. Add scallions and mix. Add stock and stir for about 1 to 1 1/2 minutes, or until scallions turn bright green. Add bean sprouts and stir-fry for 1 minute, or until very hot. Make a well in the mixture, stir reserved sauce, pour in, mix well. When sauce begins to thicken and bubble turn off heat, transfer to a heated dish, and serve.

Nutrition per serving: 73 Calories; 1g Fat; 14% calories from fat; 4.5g Carbohydrates; 12mg Cholesterol; 234mg Sodium.

大薑菜炒牛肉

Soybean Sprouts with Beef

Dai Dau Choi Chau Ngau Yuk

This dish is a prize of the home kitchen. I remember the sweetness of the sprouts and the strength of the beef, and each time I cook this dish, a favorite of my aunt in Hong Kong, the memory of my years in her home come back to me.

6 cups cold water

I slice ginger, 1/2 inch thick, lightly smashed

3/4 pound soybean sprouts, washed, drained

Beef Marinade

1/4 teaspoon sesame oil

1/2 teaspoon Ginger Juice (page 43) mixed with I teaspoon Shao-Hsing wine or sherry

I teaspoon oyster sauce

1/4 teaspoon sugar

1/4 teaspoon dark soy sauce

Pinch white pepper

1/2 teaspoon cornstarch

To continue the dish

1/4 pound lean London broil, thinly sliced

Sauce

I tablespoon oyster sauce

1/2 teaspoon dark soy sauce

I1/2 teaspoons Shao-Hsing wine or sherry

1/2 teaspoon sugar

Pinch white pepper

2 teaspoons cornstarch

2 tablespoons Chicken Stock (page 37)

To complete the dish

I teaspoon peanut oil

I teaspoon minced garlic

I teaspoon minced ginger

I tablespoon Shao-Hsing wine or sherry

2 tablespoons Chicken Stock (page 37)

2 scallions, trimmed, cut into 2-inch sections, white portions quartered lengthwise

Yield:
6 servings

1. In a pot bring water and slice of ginger to a boil over high heat. Add soybean sprouts, stir and immerse, blanch for 10 seconds. Turn off heat, run cold water into the pot, drain well. Reserve sprouts.

2. Combine beef marinade ingredients and add beef. Set aside.

3. Combine the sauce ingredients and reserve.

4. Heat wok over high heat for 30 seconds, add peanut oil, coat wok. When a wisp of white smoke appears, add minced garlic and ginger, stir until garlic turns light brown. Add beef and marinade, stir and cook for 30 seconds. Add sprouts, mix well, and cook for 40 seconds. Add wine, stir to mix. Add stock, cook for 1 minute. Make well in the mixture, stir sauce, pour in. Stir-fry and mix. When sauce begins to bubble, add scallions and mix well. Turn off heat, transfer to a heated dish and serve.

Nutrition per serving: 93 Calories; 2.6g Fat; 23% calories from fat; 5g Carbohydrates; 16mg Cholesterol; 435mg Sodium.

Soybean Sprouts and Purple Asparagus Salad

Jee Lo Dai Dau Sah Lut

This could easily be a simple salad of two ingredients, but often the color of a food becomes intriguing. So I specify that lovely, purple asparagus, simply because of its color. Its taste is identical to its more familiar green cousin, which you may use if you are unable to find it.

6 cups cold water

1 slice ginger, 1/2 inch thick, lightly smashed

6 stalks purple asparagus, washed and hard ends removed

3/4 pound soybean sprouts, washed and drained

2 tablespoons Ginger Pickle (page 45)

1 1/2 tablespoons white vinegar

1/2 teaspoon Garlic Oil (page 39)

1/4 teaspoon salt

Yield:
6 servings

1. In a large pot bring water and slice of ginger to a boil over high heat. Add asparagus and blanch for 15 seconds. Remove with tongs and place in a bowl of ice water to halt the cooking. Allow to stand for 2 minutes, then remove, drain, cut into 2-inch julienne. Reserve.

2. While asparagus is in the ice water, return the water in the pot to a boil. Blanch soybean sprouts for 15 seconds. Turn off heat, run cold water into pot, drain thoroughly.

3. Place asparagus, sprouts, Ginger Pickle, vinegar, Garlic Oil, and salt in a bowl. Toss together to combine the ingredients until they are well coated. Serve at room temperature, or cold, after refrigeration.

Nutrition per serving: 30 Calories; 0.5g Fat; 14% calories from fat; 4g Carbohydrates; 0mg Cholesterol; 103mg Sodium.

Asparagus Steamed with Garlic and Ginger

Jing Lo Sun

With each passing season asparagus becomes more familiar, more desirable, and more widely cooked. I have placed asparagus into soups, stir-fried it with meats or with other vegetables, even wrapped it in fish. Here is a simple and different way of preparing asparagus.

I pound asparagus, washed, hard ends removed, and sliced
 into 1/2-inch widths on the diagonal

1/4 teaspoon salt

2 teaspoons Shao-Hsing wine or sherry

I tablespoon shredded ginger

4 cloves garlic, finely sliced

I tablespoon oyster sauce

I teaspoon Garlic Oil (page 39)

I 1/2 tablespoons shredded red bell pepper

I tablespoon pine nuts, dry-roasted (page 14)

Yield:
4 servings

I. Place asparagus and all other ingredients, except shredded bell pepper and roasted pine nuts, in a steam-proof dish. Mix well to coat the asparagus, place dish in steamer and steam for 7 to 8 minutes, until asparagus is tender. Turn off heat, remove dish from steamer, sprinkle with bell pepper and roasted pine nuts and serve.

Nutrition per serving: 55 Calories; 1.5g Fat; 24% calories from fat; 9g Carbohydrates; 0mg Cholesterol; 340mg Sodium.

上
海
白
菜

Shanghai Bok Choy

Seung Hoy Bok Choy

This stalked vegetable is very sweet. It is called seung hoy, *a pronunciation of Shanghai, because it is so popular there. It's also called* siu bok choy, *or "little bok choy," even though its bulb and green leaves resemble its bigger cousin. These heads are so tasty, and often so tiny, that they are frequently used as garnishes. Some are larger, and sold by weight rather than by the stalk. I generally choose to cook them alone, without accompaniment, to savor their taste.*

> 4 cups cold water
>
> I slice ginger, 1/2 inch thick, lightly smashed
>
> 1/4 teaspoon baking soda (optional)
>
> I 1/4 pounds Shanghai bok choy (about 4 heads), outer leaves and stalks trimmed, heads quartered

SAUCE

> I tablespoon oyster sauce
>
> I teaspoon mushroom soy sauce
>
> 1/2 teaspoon sugar
>
> 1/2 teaspoon Shao-Hsing wine or sherry
>
> I teaspoon cornstarch
>
> I tablespoon Chicken Stock (page 37)

TO COMPLETE THE DISH

> I teaspoon Sichuan Peppercorn Oil (page 42)
>
> 2 teaspoons shredded ginger (young preferred)
>
> 2 tablespoons Chicken Stock (page 37)

Yield:
4 servings

I. In a large pot bring water, slice of ginger, and baking soda to a boil over high heat. Add bok choy and return to a boil. Turn off heat, run cold water into pot, drain. Repeat, drain thoroughly, reserve.

2. Combine sauce ingredients and reserve.

3. Heat wok over high heat for 30 seconds, add Sichuan Peppercorn Oil, coat wok. When a wisp of white smoke appears, add shredded ginger, stir briefly. Add bok choy and stir-fry for 1 minute. If mixture is too dry add 1 tablespoon of stock, stir. If necessary, add remaining stock. Cook for 1 minute. Make a well in the mixture, stir sauce, pour in. Stir and mix until sauce turns dark brown. Turn off heat, transfer to a heated dish, and serve.

Nutrition per serving: 52 Calories; 1g Fat; 21% calories from fat; 6g Carbohydrates; 0mg Cholesterol; 360mg Sodium.

Choi Sum with Oyster Sauce

Ho Yau Choi Sum

Choi Sum resembles Chinese broccoli or broccoli rabe, but has small, yellow flower buds, and is not bitter at all. Rather it is quite sweet and mild, and widely available in Chinese and Asian markets.

I 1/2 pounds choi sum
8 cups cold water
I slice ginger, 1/2 inch thick, lightly smashed
1/2 teaspoon baking soda (optional)

SAUCE

I 1/2 tablespoons oyster sauce
2 tablespoons Vegetable Stock (page 36)
I teaspoon dark soy sauce
Pinch salt
Pinch white pepper
I 1/2 teaspoons Garlic Oil (page 39)

Yield:
4 servings

1. Prepare choi sum. Use the tender inside leaves of the choi sum bunch. Stick your fingernail in the bottom end of each stalk; it should be crisp, but the nail should penetrate. This indicates tenderness. Wash, drain, and dry the stalks.

2. Bring the water, ginger, and baking soda to a boil over high heat. Add choi sum, immerse and blanch for I minute, until it becomes bright green. Turn off heat, run cold water into the pot, drain thoroughly. Place choi sum stalks in a serving dish.

3. Place all sauce ingredients in a saucepan and bring to a boil. Turn off heat, pour over choi sum and serve.

   Nutrition per serving: 64 Calories; less than Ig Fat; just over 1% calories from fat; 9.5g Carbohydrates; 0mg Cholesterol; 362mg Sodium.

Stir-Fried Broccoli with Shallots

Chung Tau Chau Yuk Far

I like to think of this as a bit of an advancement over a basic stir-fry. In Chinese yuk far translates as "jade flower." So I stir the "jade" with my fragrant Shallot Oil, then add the residue of Crisp Shallots to create a different dish.

1 1/2 teaspoons Shallot Oil (page 40)

1 slice ginger, 1/2 inch thick, lightly smashed

1/4 teaspoon salt

2 cups broccoli florets (1 small bunch), each floret about
    1 1/2 × 1 1/2 inches

1 tablespoon Shao-Hsing wine or sherry

1 tablespoon Vegetable Stock (page 36)

2 tablespoons Crisp Shallots (page 40)

**Yield:
6 servings**

Heat wok over high heat for 30 seconds, add Shallot Oil and coat wok. When a wisp of white smoke appears, add ginger and salt, stir until ginger browns. Add broccoli and stir-fry for 30 seconds. Add wine and mix well. Stir-fry for 1 minute and add stock. Stir and cook for 3 minutes, or until the broccoli turns bright green. Add Crisp Shallots and mix well. Turn off heat, transfer to a heated dish, and serve.

Nutrition per serving: 36 Calories; less than 1g Fat; 19% calories from fat; 3g Carbohydrates; 0mg Cholesterol; 108mg Sodium.

Stir-Fried Chinese Broccoli

Chau Gai Lon

Chinese broccoli differs from the broccoli with which most of us are familiar. It comes in stalks, rather than in fat bunches. It is deep green, with small white flowers that are not eaten. In fact, when the flowers begin to form on the stalks of Chinese broccoli, it is a sign that the vegetable is too mature and is losing its tenderness. It is best to eat just at the point when buds are about to form. Its slightly bitter taste sweetens as it cooks.

6 cups cold water

1/2 teaspoon baking soda (optional)

I slice ginger, 1/2 inch thick, lightly smashed

I 1/4 pounds Chinese broccoli, leaves removed, tough bottom stems removed, cut into I-inch pieces on the diagonal

SAUCE

I tablespoon oyster sauce

I teaspoon dark soy sauce

1/2 teaspoon sugar

1/4 teaspoon sesame oil

I teaspoon cornstarch

1/4 cup Chicken Stock (page 37)

Pinch salt

Pinch white pepper

TO COMPLETE THE DISH

I teaspoon Sichuan Peppercorn Oil (page 42)

1/2 teaspoon salt

2 teaspoons minced garlic

Yield:
4 servings

1. In a pot bring water, baking soda, and ginger to a boil over high heat. Add broccoli and blanch for 45 seconds. Turn off heat, run cold water into the pot, drain. Repeat, drain thoroughly, and reserve.

2. Combine sauce ingredients and reserve.

3. Heat wok over high heat for 30 seconds, add Sichuan Peppercorn Oil and coat wok. When a wisp of white smoke appears, add salt and garlic and stir briefly. Add reserved broccoli, stir to mix. Cook for about 1 1/2 minutes until very hot. Make a well in the mixture, stir sauce and pour in. Stir-fry to cook until sauce thickens and begins to bubble. Turn off heat, transfer to a heated dish, and serve.

Nutrition per serving: 47 Calories; 1.2g Fat; 16% calories from fat; 9g Carbohydrates; 0mg Cholesterol; 425mg Sodium.

Two Cabbage Stir-Fry

炒香肉椰菜

Chau Hung Yuk Yeh Choi

The Chinese name for this dish translates as "red and green cabbage," which properly describes it. The colors are complementary, as are the nuances in taste of the different cabbages. This is a dish that is fine on its own, or as a side dish for a meat or fish main course.

11/2 teaspoons Shallot Oil (page 40)

I tablespoon shredded ginger

1/2 teaspoon salt, to taste

1/2 pound green cabbage, inner white portions only, cut into pieces 3 × 1/4 inches

1/2 pound red cabbage, tough outer leaves removed, inner portion cut into pieces 3 × 1/4 inches

I tablespoon white wine

3 tablespoons Vegetable Stock (page 36)

I tablespoon Crisp Shallots (page 40)

Yield:
6 servings

Heat wok over high heat for 30 seconds and add Shallot Oil to coat wok. When a wisp of white smoke appears, add ginger and salt and stir briefly. Add cabbage, stir-fry for 30 seconds. Add white wine by drizzling it down the edges of wok, mix well. Add 2 tablespoons stock and stir to mix. Cook for 7 minutes, stirring frequently. If liquid if absorbed too quickly, add remaining tablespoon of stock, but only if needed. Cook until cabbage is tender. Add Crisp Shallots and toss well to mix. Turn off heat, transfer to a heated dish, and serve.

Nutrition per serving: 30 Calories; less than Ig Fat; 25% calories from fat; 3g Carbohydrates; 0mg Cholesterol; 120mg Sodium.

Hot Shredded Cabbage

Lot Yeh Choi See

Here is a salad of yeh choi, or "grandfather vegetable," as it is known in China. It is cold and hot—cold to the mouth, hot on the tongue; a good summer dish much favored in Beijing and Shanghai.

1 1/4 **pounds green cabbage, trimmed and shredded to yield 6 cups**

2 **tablespoons white vinegar**

2 **tablespoons sugar**

3/4 **teaspoon salt**

2 **green Thai chilies, minced**

2 **tablespoons red bell pepper, julienned**

Yield:
6 servings

1. Mix all ingredients, except bell pepper, in a bowl to combine and coat well. Place in refrigerator, cover, and allow to rest at least 4 hours, preferably overnight.

2. Before serving, add bell pepper, toss to mix. Transfer to a platter and serve.

Nutrition per serving: 27 Calories; 0g Fat; 0% calories from fat; 7g Carbohydrates; 0mg Cholesterol; 251mg Sodium.

Romaine Lettuce with Browned Onions

Sahng Choi Chau Gum Chung

All lettuce in China is sahng choi, *and so these long, green, crisp stalks are just another variety, without a special name. This is a simple preparation, but the flavor of onions imparts a different cast to a common stir-fried lettuce dish.* Gum chung *translates as "golden onions."*

8 cups cold water

I slice ginger, 1/2 inch thick, lightly smashed

1/4 teaspoon baking soda (optional)

I1/4 pounds romaine lettuce, cut into I1/2-inch sections

SAUCE

I1/2 tablespoons oyster sauce

I teaspoon dark soy sauce

2 teaspoons Shao-Hsing wine or sherry

1/2 teaspoon sugar

I tablespoon cornstarch

Pinch white pepper

1/4 cup Vegetable Stock (page 36)

1/8 teaspoon salt

TO COMPLETE THE DISH

1/2 teaspoon Onion Oil (page 40)

I teaspoon minced ginger

2 tablespoons Vegetable Stock (page 36)

3 tablespoons Browned Onions (page 40)

Yield:
4 servings

I. In a pot bring water, slice of ginger, and baking soda to a boil over high heat. Add lettuce, immerse and blanch for 10 seconds. Turn off heat, run cold water into pot, drain. Repeat, drain thoroughly. Reserve lettuce.

2. Combine sauce ingredients and reserve.

3. Heat wok over high heat for 30 seconds, add Onion Oil and coat wok. When a wisp of white smoke appears, add minced ginger, stir briefly. Add lettuce, stir and cook for 1 minute. Add 1 tablespoon of stock, mix well. If dry, add remaining stock. Add Browned Onions and stir to combine. Make a well in the mixture, stir sauce, pour in. Stir-fry until sauce thickens and begins to bubble. Turn off heat, transfer to a heated dish, and serve.

Nutrition per serving: 52 Calories; 1g Fat; 17% calories from fat; 8.5g Carbohydrates; 0mg Cholesterol; 332mg Sodium.

Stir-Fried Chives with Eggs

Gau Choi Chau Don

This simple, yet marvelous, dish comes from Shanghai, from my good friends, the Wong family. San Yan Wong has done the calligraphy for this as well as my other books; he is also an extraordinarily fine chef.

6 extra-large eggs

2 pinches salt

Pinch white pepper

2 teaspoons peanut oil

2 1/2 cups Chinese chives, washed, dried, cut into 1/2-inch
    pieces

1 tablespoon Vegetable Stock (page 36)

Yield:
4 servings

1. Beat eggs with 1 pinch of salt and pinch of white pepper. Reserve.

2. Heat wok over high heat for 30 seconds, add peanut oil and the other pinch of salt, coat wok. When a wisp of white smoke appears, add chives and stir-fry for 45 seconds. Add stock and stir and mix until chives become bright green, about 30 seconds. Stir eggs, pour into wok, and scramble, softly, with chives. Transfer immediately to a heated dish and serve, with cooked rice.

Nutrition per serving: 156 Calories; 7.5g Fat; 28% calories from fat; 16g Carbohydrates; 319mg Cholesterol; 163mg Sodium.

Pickled Pear and Jicama Salad

和味梨沙律

Wor Mei Lei Sah Lut

I find this salad a fascinating mixture, combining my own pickled pear with that current darling of the American Southwest kitchen, jícama. Of course jícama, known as sah gut *in China, has been familiar there for some time. It was a favorite snack of mine as a child, cool, crisp and sweet.*

1/2 **cup Pickled Pear (page 46), julienned**

3/4 **pound jícama, peeled, washed, julienned**

1 1/2 **tablespoons white vinegar**

1 1/2 **tablespoons sugar**

1/2 **teaspoon salt**

Yield:
8 servings

Toss all ingredients together thoroughly, to combine and to coat well. Refrigerate, covered, at least 4 hours before serving, preferably overnight. Serve cold.

Nutrition per serving: 40 Calories; less than 1g Fat; less than 1% calories from fat; 9g Carbohydrates; 0mg Cholesterol; 227mg Sodium.

Note: Serve as a first course, as a condiment, or as an accompaniment to other foods. I suggest that it would blend well with chicken and with barbecued pork dishes.

蒜茸茄子 Steamed Eggplant with Garlic Sauce

Sun Yung Ai Guah

This dish has its roots in Sichuan and Hunan. As it is customarily prepared, the eggplant is deep-fried, then stir-fried. I have lessened the fat content considerably by steaming the eggplant instead. However, the flavors remain defined and intense.

I pound eggplant, peeled and sliced lengthwise into 1/2-inch strips

SAUCE

I tablespoon dark soy sauce

1/2 teaspoon Hot Pepper Flakes (page 42)

2 teaspoons sugar

2 teaspoons oyster sauce

I teaspoon white vinegar

1/4 teaspoon salt

I teaspoon cornstarch mixed with I tablespoon Vegetable Stock (page 36)

1/2 teaspoon Shao-Hsing wine or sherry

TO COMPLETE THE DISH

I1/2 teaspoons peanut oil

2 teaspoons minced garlic

I1/2 tablespoons Vegetable Stock (page 36)

Yield:
4 servings

I. Lay strips of eggplant in a steam-proof dish. Steam for 12 to 15 minutes until very soft. Turn off heat. Remove from steamer and reserve.

2. Combine sauce ingredients and reserve.

3. Heat wok over high heat for 30 seconds. Add peanut oil to coat wok. When a wisp of white smoke appears, add garlic, stir until garlic turns light brown, about 10 seconds. Add eggplant and mix well. Add stock and stir to mix, cooking until eggplant begins to come apart. Make a well in the mixture, stir sauce, pour in. Cook and mix until sauce begins to bubble. Turn off heat, transfer to a heated dish, and serve.

Nutrition per serving: 58 Calories; 1.5g Fat; 23% calories from fat; 9g Carbohydrates; 0mg Cholesterol; 440mg Sodium.

蕃
茄
煑
茄
子

Braised Tomatoes with Eggplant

Fon Keh Jiu Ai Gua

In China, eggplant is called ai gua, or "short squash," another of the many perfect descriptions of foods that emanate from my native country. Some eggplants are indeed short and squat, others are fingerlike. The eggplant lends itself to braising, because as it cooks to softness, its flavor intensifies. In this recipe I braise eggplant, then combine it with tomatoes and bean curd to make a vegetable stew. If you can't find horse beans with chili, you may substitute hot pepper sauce, but the taste will not be the same.

I 1/2 teaspoons peanut oil

I slice ginger, 1/2 inch thick, lightly smashed

I 1/2 teaspoons minced garlic

1/4 teaspoon salt

2 medium tomatoes, cut into 1/2-inch dice

1/2 pound eggplant, unpeeled and cut into 1/2-inch dice

1/2 cup Vegetable Stock (page 36)

SAUCE

I teaspoon white vinegar

2 teaspoons Shao-Hsing wine or sherry

2 tablespoons ketchup

1/2 teaspoon dark soy sauce

I teaspoon sugar

I teaspoon preserved horse beans with chilies

Pinch white pepper

TO COMPLETE THE DISH

1/4 cup Vegetable Stock (page 36)

I cake (4 ounces) fresh bean curd, cut into 1/2-inch dice

2 scallions, trimmed, cut into 1/2-inch pieces on the diagonal

Yield:
4 servings

1. Heat wok over high heat for 30 seconds, add peanut oil, coat wok. When a wisp of white smoke appears, add ginger and cook for 10 seconds. Add minced garlic and salt, stir. When garlic turns light brown, add tomatoes, stir and mix, cook for 10 seconds. Add eggplant, stir and mix, cook for 20 seconds. Add 1/2 cup stock and stir to mix well. Bring to a boil, then lower heat, cover wok, and allow to cook for 15 to 20 minutes.

2. Meanwhile, combine the sauce ingredients and reserve.

3. When the eggplant is tender, turn the heat back to high, add bean curd, stir. Add scallions, stir to mix well. Bring back to a boil. Make a well in the mixture, stir sauce, pour in, stir to mix. Allow the mixture to return to a boil. Turn off heat, transfer to a heated dish, and serve.

   Nutrition per serving: 86 Calories; 2.5g Fat; 26% calories from fat; 9.6g Carbohydrates; 0mg Cholesterol; 544mg Sodium.

木瓜沙律

Green Papaya Salad

Muk Gua Sah Lut

Papaya is a most familiar fruit, particularly throughout Southeast Asia, and in southern China. Usually it is eaten fresh and raw. Occasionally it is steamed as a dessert. But this most versatile of fruits is also excellent pickled, as a soup ingredient, or stir-fried. I recall eating this simple crisp salad as a child. If green papaya is not available, you may use an unripe, very firm papaya and prepare it identically. The green papaya, however, is quite hard, very crisp, and preferred. You will note that this salad, while it uses the green papaya, differs greatly from the Green Papaya Pickle early in this book.

I small green papaya (I pound) peeled, seeded, cut into
  quarters lengthwise, then julienned

2 tablespoons rice vinegar

2 tablespoons sugar

I teaspoon salt

Yield:
8 servings

Mix all ingredients together thoroughly, to coat the papaya. Refrigerate for at least 4 hours, preferably overnight. Serve cold, either as an appetizer, as an accompaniment, or as a salad to close a meal.

Nutrition per serving: 28 Calories; less than Ig Fat; less than 1% calories from fat; 7.5g Carbohydrates; 0mg Cholesterol; 283mg Sodium.

Chapter 6

肉 To Confucius Meat Was Pork

Traditionally in China, the term *meat* referred to pork, and in many parts of the country, this is still true. In the north and west of China there is more consumption of lamb and mutton than in the center and south of the country, and only recently have the Chinese begun to eat veal, which is referred to as *ngau jai yuk,* or "meat of the suckling cow."

Every area had, and still has, access to pigs, and it is said that the Chinese make use of every bit of this valuable animal. Its bristles go into brushes, its organs form the basis for rich braising stocks, its legs are pickled and steamed, its liver is the basis for several varieties of those marvelous *lop cheung* sausages. Pork is stir-fried, braised, roasted, barbecued, steamed, and fried. It is a ubiquitous ingredient in all manner of dim sum. When meat is mentioned in those two-thousand-year-old cookbooks of China, pork is meant. When Confucius wrote in great detail about the proper ways to cut up foods, including meat, he meant pork.

Beef has always existed in the Chinese kitchen, but has always been less popular, except in the west, in Sichuan and Hunan, where the stronger aroma and taste of beef marries well with the more intense flavors of the cooking in those regions. Most Buddhists, of course, eat little meat, and when they do, they usually eat pork, never beef.

An observant Buddhist such as my grandmother, Ah Paw, refrained from all meat, including pork, on the first and fifteenth of each month, and for the first fifteen days of the lunar New Year. At other times, she would insist that family gatherings, birthdays, and feasts be marked with dishes of pork. A wedding feast always had to include a roasted suckling pig, as did an engagement feast and the traditional banquet that celebrated the first month birthday of the family's first child. The Dragon Boat festivals held in the spring in many Chinese cities are occasions for roast suckling pig.

Pork is regarded by the Chinese as an ideal food for the benefit of one's system. Its meat, it is said, lubricates the interior, and because of this is favored by the elderly. Big chunks of fresh pork form the bases for soups especially geared for the elderly, who drink the soup, then eat the boiled pork with flavored dips. When I was a child in Sun Tak, such a soup was always prepared for my grandmother. But it was a soup I loved, and I would always be sure to be around her when it was served to her, so that I might have some.

There was little beef on the hoof in the region of Canton in which I was raised. What beef we ate always came from the market, and we regarded it as a special meat, one difficult to come to like because of its strong aroma. When we ate it, in most cases we marinated it first in ginger juice and wine to soften its aromas and taste, and when we stir-fried it, it was always with pungent vegetables. Most often we steamed beef. It was our preferred way of eating it, a method that to me then, even today, makes beef an elegant meat. Never did we have anything like a broiled steak. Only in Hong Kong was beef served in that fashion, and it was there that I had my first taste of beef cooked that way. I must tell you, I loved it, and do to this day.

Nor is it unusual any longer for beef to be roasted, grilled, or broiled in the Chinese kitchen. Gradually the same thing is happening to veal. Initially veal was encountered only in Hong Kong, usually in Western-style restaurants, but these days this lovely, clean meat is admired by the chefs of Hong Kong's Chinese kitchens as well. And it is being adapted to Chinese cooking techniques with great success. I cook with it, in the Chinese manner, very often. I have even made dim sum dumplings with veal.

But veal is still not eaten widely in China, nor in Taiwan. It remains a special meat. Pork is still the meat of choice in China. In this section of my book are some of the traditional, and familiar, ways of cooking pork, as well as some fresh approaches. The beef recipes are my adaptations of this strong meat to the Chinese kitchen, and you will find veal preparations as well in recipes that are surely Chinese in character, but preserve the essence of this meat, so new to the Chinese methods of cooking.

Pork, as you are aware, is a meat with a large amount of fat content. You will note that my preparations, while true to Chinese cooking techniques, considerably lessen the fat content of this meat; equally for beef. Enjoy them.

又 Barbecued Pork

Char Siu

 This is commonly known as barbecued pork even though it is not really barbecued. When it is cooked in Chinese restaurants it is usually roasted, over fire. Or it is broiled. Traditionally, after the pork has been roasted it is dipped in a wash of honey. Instead I use honey as an integral part of the cooking process, which sweetens and intensifies the taste of the pork.

I lean pork loin, 3 pounds

I 1/2 tablespoons dark soy sauce

I 1/2 tablespoons soy sauce

3 tablespoons honey

I 1/2 tablespoons oyster sauce

2 tablespoons Shao-Hsing wine or sherry

I 1/2 tablespoons hoisin sauce

Pinch white pepper

I teaspoon five-spice seasoning

Yield:
4 servings
per strip

1. To prepare the pork, cut loin lengthwise into 4 equal strips. Use a small knife to pierce the meat at intervals, to tenderize it. Line a roasting pan with foil. Place strips of meat in pan. Mix all ingredients and pour over pork strips. Allow to marinate in the refrigerator at least 4 hours, or overnight. Allow the pork to return to room temperature before broiling.

2. Preheat oven to broil for 20 minutes. Place roasting pan inside and broil 30 to 50 minutes. To test, remove one piece of pork after 30 minutes, slice to see if it is cooked. During the broiling period pork should be basted about 5 times, turned over 4 times. If sauce dries, add water to roasting pan.

3. When cooked, remove pork, slice, and serve hot. It can also be served cold as a first course or appetizer. One strip will serve 4 people; note however that during broiling, almost one-half of the weight will be lost; thus a cooked strip will consist of about 6 ounces.

Nutrition per serving: 171 Calories; 6g Fat; 29% calories from fat; 13g Carbohydrates; 52mg Cholesterol; 490mg Sodium.

Note: This basic recipe can also be used in many others, as you will see. The marinade may also be used as a sauce ingredient, or in stocks. It will keep, refrigerated in a sealed jar, for 2 to 3 months.

If you wish to make a greater portion of barbecued pork, perhaps for a party, you may simply double the recipe in every respect. Or you may wish to eat some of it at one meal, saving the rest for future use. The cooked pork may be frozen, double-wrapped in plastic and foil. It will keep up to 3 months.

Barbecued Spare Ribs

Siu Pai Guat

This is another of those preparations with which most people are familiar. It happens to be one of my family's favorite dishes, perhaps one of the few things about which they agree.

I rack of pork ribs, about 3 pounds
I 1/2 tablespoons oyster sauce
2 tablespoons hoisin sauce
I tablespoon soy sauce
I tablespoon dark soy sauce
2 tablespoons honey
I 1/2 tablespoons Shao-Hsing wine or sherry
Pinch white pepper
2 tablespoons cold water

Yield:
4 servings

1. To prepare the ribs, with a sharp knife remove the flap from the rack as well as any extra fat, then score the ribs all over. Line a roasting pan with foil, place rack of ribs in pan. Combine all remaining ingredients, pour over ribs, and with your hands rub the marinade into the rack. It must marinate in the refrigerator at least 4 hours, preferably overnight. Allow the rack to return to room temperature before broiling.

2. Preheat oven to broil for 20 minutes. Place pan in broiler and broil for 30 to 50 minutes. You may have to add water if sauce begins to evaporate. During the broiling process baste the ribs several times and turn over rack several times as well. After 30 minutes cut between two ribs to see if meat is cooked.

3. When cooked remove from broiler. Cut between individual ribs to serve. Usually a I-pound rack will yield 6 ounces of meat around the bones.

Nutrition per serving: 171 Calories; 6g Fat; 29% calories from fat; 13g Carbohydrates; 52mg Cholesterol; 490mg Sodium.

又燒炒葱 Barbecued Pork Stir-Fried with Scallions

Char Siu Chau Chung

This is one excellent use for barbecued pork, perhaps pork that you have cooked earlier. Our family eats this dish on a more or less regular basis. This pork, which I call all-purpose, goes well with so many other foods.

1 strip of Barbecued Pork (page 236) thinly sliced

4 bunches scallions, trimmed, cut into 2-inch lengths, quarter white portions lengthwise, separate white and green portions

2 tablespoons Barbecued Pork Marinade (page 236) mixed with 1/4 cup Chicken Stock (page 37)

2 teaspoons peanut oil

Yield:
6 servings

Heat wok over high heat for 30 seconds, add peanut oil and coat wok. When a wisp of white smoke appears, add white portions of scallions, stir for 20 seconds. Add pork, stir and mix briefly. Add green portions of scallions, stir, add marinade-stock mix and stir to mix. Cook until scallions turn bright green and sauce begins to bubble. Turn off heat, transfer to a heated dish, and serve.

Nutrition per serving: 106 Calories; 4g Fat; 29% calories from fat; 10g Carbohydrates; 34mg Cholesterol; 420mg Sodium.

Barbecued Pork with Soybean Sprouts

Char Siu Chau Dai Dau Choi

You will see elsewhere in this book a recipe for bean sprouts and barbecued pork. This recipe is different, because it uses soybean sprouts. These differ markedly in size, texture, and taste from mung bean sprouts, which are referred to generically as bean sprouts. Soybean sprouts are longer, with a yellow bean bud at the tip, which is eaten, and it has a crisper bite. And do not break off that bud; it is a prime reason for eating this sprout.

6 cups cold water

3/4 pound soybean sprouts, with bud beans left on

SAUCE

I1/2 tablespoons oyster sauce

I teaspoon dark soy sauce

2 teaspoons Shao-Hsing wine or sherry

1/2 teaspoon sugar

Pinch salt

Pinch white pepper

I tablespoon cornstarch

1/4 cup Chicken Stock (page 37)

TO COMPLETE THE DISH

I1/2 teaspoons peanut oil

I teaspoon minced ginger

I teaspoon minced garlic

1/2 strip Barbecued Pork (page 236), thinly sliced

2 ounces garlic chives (or regular chives), cut into 1-inch
pieces (I cup)

I tablespoon Shao-Hsing wine or sherry

Yield:
6 servings

1. In a pot bring water to a boil over high heat. Add sprouts and blanch for 15 seconds. Run cold water into pot, drain. Repeat twice more, drain thoroughly, reserve.

2. Combine sauce ingredients. Reserve.

3. Heat wok over high heat for 30 seconds, add peanut oil and coat wok. When a wisp of white smoke appears, add ginger and garlic, stir briefly. Add pork and stir to mix, cook for 30 seconds. Add chives, stir for 45 seconds. Add wine and mix well for another 30 seconds. Add bean sprouts, stir-fry for 1 minute. Make a well in the mixture, stir sauce, pour in and stir-fry to mix. When the sauce thickens and bubbles, turn off heat, transfer to a heated dish, and serve.

   Nutrition per serving: 102 Calories; 2g Fat; 17% calories from fat; 14g Carbohydrates; 17mg Cholesterol; 435mg Sodium.

炒
又
燒
絲 Barbecued Pork with Carrots and Celery

Chau Char Siu See

Here is still another stir-fry combination with barbecued pork. I hope that these recipes will spur you to create your own dishes. The secret of course is compatibility.

SAUCE

I tablespoon oyster sauce

I teaspoon dark soy sauce

2 teaspoons Shao-Hsing wine or sherry

1/2 teaspoon sugar

Pinch white pepper

I 1/2 teaspoons cornstarch

1/4 cup Chicken Stock (page 37)

TO COMPLETE THE DISH

I 1/2 teaspoons peanut oil

I teaspoon minced ginger

I teaspoon minced garlic

1/2 strip Barbecued Pork (page 236), julienned

I large carrot, julienned (I cup)

I large stalk celery, julienned (I cup)

3 tablespoons Chicken Stock (page 37)

2 water chestnuts, peeled, julienned

Yield:
6 servings

I. Combine the sauce ingredients, reserve.

2. Heat wok over high heat for 30 seconds, add peanut oil and coat wok. When a wisp of white smoke appears, add ginger and garlic, stir briefly. Add pork, stir to mix for 30 seconds. Add I tablespoon of stock, stir and mix, cook for 30 seconds. Add carrots and celery.

Stir-fry for I minute, add second tablespoon of stock, mix. Cook for 30 seconds, add remaining stock and mix thoroughly. Cook until the carrots wilt slightly, about I minute. Make a well in the mixture, stir sauce, pour in. Mix and cook. When sauce thickens and bubbles, turn off heat. Add water chestnuts and toss until combined and well coated. Transfer to a heated dish and serve with cooked rice or Congee (page 59).

Nutrition per serving (without rice): I06 Calories; 3g Fat; 25% calories from fat; 3g Carbohydrates; I8mg Cholesterol; 219mg Sodium.

又 Diced Barbecued Pork with
烧 Mixed Vegetables
菘

Char Siu Sung

The word sung *translates as "small pieces," and that is what this barbecued pork and vegetable dish is, a mix of diced meat and vegetables. So many tastes, in small bites, another of the fond memories of my girlhood.*

1 1/2 teaspoons peanut oil

1 teaspoon minced ginger

1 teaspoon minced garlic

1/2 strip Barbecued Pork (page 236), cut into 1/4-inch dice

1 medium stalk celery, cut into 1/4-inch dice (1/2 cup)

3 water chestnuts, peeled, cut into 1/4-inch dice (1/3 cup)

2 medium Steamed Black Mushrooms (page 206) cut into
    1/4-inch dice

1/4 cup bamboo shoots, cut into 1/4-inch dice

1 red bell pepper, cut into 1/4-inch dice (1/2 cup)

1 tablespoon Shao-Hsing wine or sherry

2 tablespoons Barbecued Pork marinade (page 236)

**Yield:
4 servings**

Heat wok over high heat for 30 seconds, add peanut oil and coat wok. When a wisp of white smoke appears, add ginger and garlic, stir briefly. Add pork, stir and cook for 30 seconds. Add all the vegetables, stir to mix, cook for 1 minute. Add wine, mix well, cook for 30 seconds. Add marinade, stir together, cooking for 1 more minute. Turn off heat, transfer to a heated dish, and serve with cooked rice.

Nutrition per serving (without rice): 159 Calories; 5g Fat; 28% calories from fat; 6.5g Carbohydrates; 4.5mg Cholesterol; 117mg Sodium.

Steamed Pork with Preserved Vegetables

梅菜蒸猪肉

Mui Choi Deuk Jee Yuk

This dish is from the Cantonese home kitchen. It was always cooked while we were recovering from an illness. I recall having it after measles, fevers, and bad colds. It helped our recovery, it was said, because it gave us appetites. I have been making it for my children since my oldest was six months old. They have never stopped loving it, and neither have I.

4 ounces Preserved Mustard (page 26)

8 ounces lean ground pork

3/4 teaspoon Ginger Juice (page 43) mixed with I tablespoon Shao-Hsing wine or sherry

I tablespoon oyster sauce

I1/2 teaspoons dark soy sauce

I1/2 teaspoons sugar

I teaspoon White Peppercorn Oil (page 41)

Pinch white pepper

3 tablespoons cold water

2 teaspoons cornstarch

Yield:
4 servings

1. Wash and rinse the preserved mustard to remove salt and sand, several times if necessary. Squeeze off excess water, slice finely to yield 3/4 cup.

2. Place preserved mustard, pork, and all other ingredients in a bowl and mix until combined well. Place in a steam-proof dish and steam for 15 to 20 minutes. The dish is cooked when the texture is firm. Turn off heat, remove dish from steamer and serve with cooked rice or Congee (page 59).

   Nutrition per serving (without rice): 269 Calories; 8g Fat; 26% calories from fat; 4.6g Carbohydrates; 56mg Cholesterol; 352mg Sodium.

Stir-Fried Sichuan Pork

Sei Cheun Chau Yuk See

There is a mistaken belief that all Sichuan cooking is excessively oily. It is true that a good deal of oil is used, and that some dishes are quite high in oil, but the key word is some. It is possible to maintain true Sichuan tastes by blanching in water instead of in oil.

3/4 cup Chicken Stock (page 37)

8 ounces lean pork loin, julienned

I small carrot, julienned

SAUCE

1/2 teaspoon Hot Pepper Flakes (page 42)

I teaspoon soy sauce

2 teaspoons oyster sauce

3/4 teaspoon sugar

2 teaspoons Shao-Hsing wine or sherry

1/8 teaspoon salt

Pinch white pepper

2 teaspoons cornstarch

1/4 cup Chicken Stock (page 37)

TO COMPLETE THE DISH

2 teaspoons Garlic Oil (page 39)

I teaspoon minced ginger

I teaspoon minced garlic

1/2 medium red bell pepper, julienned

1/2 medium green bell pepper, julienned

3 scallions, trimmed, cut into 2-inch lengths, white portions quartered lengthwise

1/4 cup bamboo shoots, julienned

Yield:
6 servings

1. Heat wok over high heat. Add stock, bring to a boil. Add pork and carrot, stir to separate. Cook for 30 to 40 seconds, or until pork turns white. Turn off heat, remove pork and carrot, reserve. Remove poaching stock from wok, reserve.

2. Combine the sauce ingredients. Reserve.

2. Wipe off wok and spatula. Heat wok over high heat for 30 seconds, add Garlic Oil and coat wok. When a wisp of white smoke appears, add ginger and garlic, stir briefly. Add peppers, scallions, and bamboo shoots and stir-fry together for 1 minute. Add 2 tablespoons of poaching stock and stir-fry for 1 more minute. Add pork and carrot, stir together thoroughly, for 1 more minute until very hot. Make a well in the mixture, stir sauce, pour in. Mix well. When sauce begins to bubble, turn off heat, transfer to a heated dish, and serve.

Nutrition per serving: 163 Calories; 5.5g Fat; 28% calories from fat; 2.5g Carbohydrates; 37mg Cholesterol; 202mg Sodium.

白
切
肉

White Cut Pork

Bok Chit Yuk

The "white" in this famous Sichuan preparation refers to the plain water in which the yuk, *or meat, is cooked. The sauce makes this traditional preparation special. White Cut Pork is always served cold, as an appetizer.*

8 cups cold water

I 1/2 pounds lean pork loin

I teaspoon salt

I large onion, peeled, cut into quarters

I slice ginger, I inch thick, lightly smashed

2 cloves garlic

2 teaspoons sugar

DIPPING SAUCE

I tablespoon soy sauce

I tablespoon dark soy sauce

1/4 teaspoon Hot Pepper Oil (page 42)

1/4 teaspoon Hot Pepper Flakes (page 42)

2 teaspoons white vinegar

2 teaspoons Shao-Hsing wine or sherry

2 teaspoons sugar

I 1/2 teaspoons minced garlic

3 tablespoons minced scallions (white and light green parts)

1/4 cup of the liquid used to boil pork

Yield:
8 servings

I. In a large pot bring water to a boil over high heat. Add the pork and all other ingredients, but not dipping sauce ingredients. Lower heat, cover pot partially, and simmer for I 1/2 to 2 hours. The pork is cooked when a chopstick can be inserted into it easily. During the cooking process turn the pork 4 or 5 times.

2. Remove pork from pot and place in a bowl of cold water. Allow to rest there for 5 minutes. Remove and allow it to cool further. (Be sure to reserve 1/4 cup of the boiling liquid for use in the dipping sauce.) Wrap in plastic wrap and refrigerate. When ready to serve, slice pork paper thin and arrange on a platter. Meanwhile, combine the sauce ingredients in a bowl. Set in the middle of the platter surrounded by the sliced pork. Serve as an appetizer or first course.

Nutrition per serving: 210 Calories; 4g Fat; 25% calories from fat; 24g Carbohydrates; 84mg Cholesterol; 60mg Sodium.

Steamed Pork with Two Pickles

木瓜酸蒸猪肉

Muk Gua Seun Jing Jiuk

This is my variation on the Chinese theme of steamed pork. I have prepared steamed pork accompanied by several of my pickles, but I had never cooked them together. One afternoon I decided to try them in combination, and this is the result.

8 ounces lean pork loin cut into thin I × 2-inch slices

I 1/2 tablespoons shredded Ginger Pickle (page 45)

1/4 cup julienned Pickled Green Papaya (page 47)

2 tablespoons Ginger Pickle liquid (page 45)

I 1/2 tablespoons oyster sauce

I teaspoon dark soy sauce

I tablespoon Shao-Hsing wine or sherry

I teaspoon Shallot Oil (page 40)

2 teaspoons cornstarch

Pinch white pepper

Yield:
4 servings

Place all ingredients in a bowl and mix thoroughly until all are coated evenly. Transfer to a steam-proof dish and steam for 20 minutes, or until pork mixture is firm. Remove dish from steamer and serve with cooked rice.

Nutrition per serving (without rice): 262 Calories; 8g Fat; 27% calories from fat; 9g Carbohydrates; 56mg Cholesterol; 355mg Sodium.

Curry Roasted Beef

咖喱燒牛柳

Gah Lei Siu Ngau Lau

This is a perfect example of how the Chinese kitchen absorbs the taste of another cuisine and with subtle changes makes it part of its own repertoire. Beef cooked with curry is widely enjoyed in India, Singapore, Thailand, and Indonesia, and was brought to China by spice traders. In both Canton and Hong Kong there are many versions of curry-enhanced preparations; I have several of my own. This is one of them.

2 pounds lean beef tenderloin, a single piece, 9 to 10 inches long

1/3 cup mushroom soy sauce or double dark soy sauce

2 1/2 tablespoons spicy curry powder (preferably Madras brand)

Pinch white pepper

1/4 cup honey

2 teaspoons Coriander Oil (page 41)

2 tablespoons water, or more as needed

Yield:
6 servings

1. With the back of a knife make 6 marks, equally spaced, across the beef to divide it into portions. With a cleaver cut two-thirds of the way through the meat at the markings.

2. In a bowl mix the soy sauce, curry powder, white pepper, and honey. Place the beef in a shallow roasting pan lined with foil. Pour marinade over it and rub the meat inside the cuts and out, thoroughly, to coat. Cover with plastic wrap and refrigerate overnight.

3. About an hour before cooking, remove beef from refrigerator and allow to stand, basting frequently with the marinade, as it comes to room temperature.

4. Preheat oven to 500°F. Rub the beef with the Coriander Oil and roast, depending on your preference, 10 minutes for rare, 15 minutes for medium, and 25 minutes for well-done beef. Baste with the marinade in the pan every 5 minutes. Add 2 tablespoons of water (or more) to pan if the curry sauce begins to dry out.

5. When cooked, remove from oven. Cut the meat through at the indicated slice marks and serve, with a bit of the sauce poured on top. Serve remaining curry sauce in a boat on the side. This curry roasted beef is perfect with cooked rice because of its sauce. In the cooking process the beef will be reduced in size and weight by a third.

Nutrition per serving (without rice): 292 Calories; 8g Fat; 24% calories from fat; 0g Carbohydrates; 128mg Cholesterol; 56mg Sodium.

少奉牛肉 Beef Satay

Sah Deh Ngau Yuk

This is my version of the beef satay of Southeast Asia. Customarily satays are marinated in sauce flavored with ground peanuts and coconut milk, and served with peanut-based sauces. My version is lighter and makes no use of peanuts, but I add whiskey to the marinade for its aroma and the emphasis is on curry.

2 pounds beef tenderloin, a single piece, 8 inches long

1/3 cup dark soy sauce

21/2 tablespoons spicy curry powder (Madras brand preferred)

1/4 teaspoon white pepper

2 tablespoons blended whiskey

1/4 cup honey

2 teaspoons peanut oil

Yield:
8 servings

1. Cut tenderloin into 8 equal slices, then each slice into quarters. You will have 32 cubes of beef.

2. Combine the remaining ingredients in a large bowl to make a marinade. Add beef cubes to it and mix thoroughly to coat the beef. Allow the beef and marinade to rest at least 8 hours, or overnight, covered with plastic wrap, in the refrigerator.

3. Remove from refrigerator, allow to rest for 30 minutes, then place the cubes of beef on metal skewers, 4 per skewer. The beef is ready for cooking. This may be done in different ways.

   - To grill: Grill over a charcoal fire, turning the skewers as the beef grills until cooked to the doneness preferred—rare, medium, or well done. Brush with marinade during grilling. Remove from grill and serve on skewers.

- To broil: Place skewers in a foil-lined roasting pan with marinade and broil in a preheated broiler, 4 to 8 minutes, according to your preference—rare, medium, or well done. Turn skewers during broiling. Remove from broiler and serve on skewers.

- Alternately, you may broil these beef cubes without skewering them. Place the cubes of beef in a foil-lined roasting pan and broil in a preheated broiler, for 4 to 8 minutes, according to the doneness desired—rare, medium, or well done. Turn cubes over once during the broiling. When done, remove from broiler and serve over cooked rice, with the sauce. Whichever method you choose, the beef will be reduced in size and weight by a third during the cooking.

Nutrition per serving (without rice): 201 Calories; 5g Fat; 24% calories from fat; 0g Carbohydrates; 74mg Cholesterol; 38mg Sodium.

鼓椒炒牛 Pepper Steak

See Jiu Chau Ngau

Nothing complements tender, sliced beef so well as do green peppers, garlic, and black beans. Blended and cooked together over high heat, or as the Cantonese say, "wok hei," they provide enticing aromas and taste. When my daughter was young she claimed that as she was coming home from school one day, she was able to smell this dish from two blocks away.

4 ounces lean London broil, thinly sliced across the grain

MARINADE

I teaspoon Shao-Hsing wine or sherry mixed with
1/2 teaspoon Ginger Juice (page 43)
I teaspoon cornstarch
Pinch white pepper

TO CONTINUE THE DISH

2 teaspoons peanut oil
I teaspoon minced ginger
3/4 pound green bell peppers (2 medium), thinly sliced
2 tablespoons Chicken Stock (page 37)

SAUCE

I tablespoon oyster sauce
2 teaspoons cornstarch
3/4 teaspoon dark soy sauce
1/2 teaspoon sugar
1/4 teaspoon sesame oil
Pinch white pepper
1/4 cup Chicken Stock (page 37)
2 teaspoons Shao-Hsing wine or sherry

To complete the dish

I teaspoon minced garlic
I 1/2 tablespoons fermented black beans, washed and drained
Pinch salt

Yield:
6 servings

1. Place beef in a bowl with combined marinade ingredients. Allow to rest for 20 minutes.

2. Heat wok over high heat for 30 seconds. Add I teaspoon peanut oil, coat wok. When a wisp of white smoke appears, add minced ginger, stir briefly. Add peppers, stir and cook for 45 seconds, then add I tablespoon of stock and mix well. When peppers turn bright green, turn off heat, remove from wok, reserve.

3. Combine the sauce ingredients in a bowl. Reserve.

4. Wipe off wok and spatula with paper towel. Turn heat back to high, add remaining teaspoon peanut oil, coat wok. When a wisp of white smoke appears, add garlic and black beans. Stir and cook for 45 seconds, or until their aroma is released. Add beef and marinade, spread in a thin layer. Cook for 30 seconds, turn over and stir together. Add wine and mix well. Add remaining stock and mix well. Add reserved peppers, stir-fry together for I minute, until very hot. Make a well in the mixture, stir sauce, pour in. Cook until sauce thickens and begins to bubble. Turn off heat, transfer to a heated dish, and serve with cooked rice.

Nutrition per serving (without rice): 100 Calories; 2g Fat; 18% calories from fat; 7g Carbohydrates; 18mg Cholesterol; 271mg Sodium.

四
川
炒
牛
肉

Sichuan Beef

Sei Chun Chau Ngau Yuk

This is surely one of the best known of all of China's dishes. There are however, many versions of it, most of them oversweetened, many with an overabundance of oil (Westernized adaptations of this Sichuan classic). What follows is most traditional, with less fat. If you can't find horse beans with chili, you may substitute hot pepper sauce, but the taste will not be the same. You can also substitute two Thai chili peppers for the Sichuan mustard pickle, if unavailable, but this will also change the flavor.

4 ounces lean London broil, julienned

Marinade

I teaspoon Shao-Hsing wine or sherry mixed with
      1/2 teaspoon Ginger Juice (page 43)
I teaspoon cornstarch
Pinch white pepper

Sauce

2 teaspoons preserved horse beans with chili
2 teaspoons oyster sauce
I teaspoon white vinegar
I teaspoon sugar
1/2 teaspoon dark soy sauce
2 teaspoons cornstarch
Pinch white pepper
1/4 cup Chicken Stock (page 37)

To complete the dish

2 teaspoons peanut oil

1 teaspoon minced ginger

1 medium carrot, cut into matchsticks (3/4 cup)

2 medium stalks celery, cut into matchsticks (3/4 cup)

6 scallions, cut into 2-inch sections, white portions julienned

1/3 cup bamboo shoots, julienned

2 tablespoons Sichuan mustard pickle, julienned

3 tablespoons Chicken Stock (page 37)

1 teaspoon minced garlic

2 teaspoons Shao-Hsing wine or sherry

Yield:
6 servings

1. Place beef in a bowl with combined marinade ingredients. Allow to rest for 20 minutes.

2. Combine sauce ingredients. Reserve.

3. Heat wok over high heat for 30 seconds, add 1 teaspoon peanut oil and coat wok. When a wisp of white smoke appears, add ginger, stir briefly. Add carrot, celery, scallions, bamboo shoots, and Sichuan mustard pickle, and stir-fry for 1 minute. Add 1 tablespoon stock, mix well. If mixture is dry, add another tablespoon of stock. Stir to mix well. Turn off heat, remove vegetables, and reserve.

4. Wipe off wok and spatula. Turn heat back to high, add remaining teaspoon of peanut oil and coat wok. When a wisp of white smoke appears, add garlic, stir, add beef and marinade and spread in a thin layer. Cook for 30 seconds, turn beef over, stir. Add wine, mix well. Add remaining stock, mix well. Add reserved vegetables and stir-fry all together for 1 minute. Make a well in the mixture, stir sauce, pour in. Stir to combine thoroughly. When the sauce thickens and begins to bubble, turn off heat, transfer to a heated dish, and serve with cooked rice.

Nutrition per serving (without rice): 93 Calories; 2g Fat; 20% calories from fat; 6g Carbohydrates; 18mg Cholesterol; 242mg Sodium.

酸菜炒牛肉 Stir-Fried Beef with Sour Mustard Pickle

Seun Choi Chau Ngau Yuk

These mustard greens are quite popular in China, because it is believed that they increase one's appetite. It is a dish favored in the summer. When it is hot one has little appetite; so cooking a dish with these greens will create an appetite for what will follow.

6 tablespoons Chicken Stock (page 37)
4 ounces lean London broil, cut into 1 × 2-inch thin slices

SAUCE

1 1/2 tablespoons oyster sauce

2 teaspoons Shao-Hsing wine or sherry

1 1/2 teaspoons dark soy sauce

1 1/4 teaspoons sugar

2 1/2 teaspoons cornstarch

Pinch white pepper

1/4 cup Chicken Stock (page 37)

TO COMPLETE THE DISH

1 1/2 teaspoons peanut oil

1 tablespoon shredded ginger

2 medium stalks celery, cut into matchsticks (1 cup)

6 ounces sour mustard pickle, sliced thinly across (1 cup)

3 tablespoons red bell pepper, julienned

1 tablespoon Shao-Hsing wine or sherry

Yield:
4 servings

1. Heat wok over high heat, add 4 tablespoons stock and bring to a boil. Add beef, stir and cook for 45 seconds, or until beef turns color. Turn off heat, remove to a strainer to drain, reserve. Wash and dry wok and spatula.

2. Combine sauce ingredients, reserve.

3. Heat wok over high heat for 30 seconds, add peanut oil and coat wok. When a wisp of white smoke appears, add ginger, stir briefly. Add celery and mustard pickle, stir-fry for 45 seconds. Add remaining 2 tablespoons of stock, stir to mix. Add beef and peppers, stir-fry for 1 minute. Add wine, stir and mix. Make a well in the mixture, stir sauce and pour in. Stir to mix thoroughly. When sauce thickens and bubbles, turn off heat. Transfer to a heated dish and serve with cooked rice.

Nutrition per serving (without rice): 125 Calories; 3g Fat; 23% calories from fat; 5g Carbohydrates; 27mg Cholesterol; 410mg Sodium.

五
香
牛
肉

Five-Spice Beef

Ng Heung Hgau Yuk

This dish, with its origins in Beijing, will be familiar to many. The beef is usually served cold, thinly sliced, as part of an array of appetizers that precedes banquets. You may wish to serve it as an introduction to a meal, but it is perfect as a course by itself, or as one of many dishes on a buffet table. In Asian groceries you will see packages labeled "five-spice powder." Do not use this mixture for this dish because it will not impart the defined flavors of my recipe.

> 2 pounds lean shin of beef; request a round piece, rather than a flat one
>
> 4 cups cold water
>
> 2 ounces sugarcane sugar (or 4 tablespoons brown sugar)
>
> 1/4 cup Shao-Hsing wine or sherry
>
> 2 cloves garlic, whole
>
> 1 slice ginger, 1/2 inch thick, lightly smashed
>
> 2 sticks cinnamon
>
> 2 pieces eight-star anise (whole flower)
>
> 6 Sichuan peppercorns, whole
>
> 1/4 cup dark soy sauce

Yield:
6 servings

1. In a large pot place all ingredients, except soy sauce. Cover and bring to a boil over high heat. Add soy sauce, bring back to a boil. Lower heat to simmer, leave a small opening at the lid of the pot, and cook at a simmer for 21/2 hours. Turn the beef frequently. The beef is cooked when a chopstick can be inserted into it easily.

2. Turn off heat. Cover pot, remove to a cooler surface, and allow beef to rest in its liquid until it comes to room temperature. Put the meat and liquid in separate bowls and refrigerate, preferably overnight. Serve the beef, cold, thinly sliced. Reserve the liquid for another use (see note to follow).

From the time the cooking process begins, until the meat has cooled and is ready for slicing, the beef will have been reduced to 11/2 pounds.

Nutrition per serving: 219 Calories; 6g Fat; 25% calories from fat; negligible Carbohydrates; 224mg Cholesterol; 168mg Sodium.

Note: The sauce, which becomes aspiclike, may be used in other recipes, or as an addition to stocks. If left at room temperature, or briefly heated, it will liquefy. It may be used in place of soy sauce in a recipe, or to stir-fried vegetables, if you wish.

Home-Style Steamed Beef

家鄉蒸牛肉

Gar Heung Jing Ngau Yuk

This is Cantonese home cooking at its best. Rarely is this preparation to be found in restaurants. In my home in Hong Kong this fragrant dish would come to the table where we would be anxiously waiting to spoon it over rice. It is regarded as a winter dish, since the elderly believe that beef cooked in this manner will keep the body warm.

8 ounces lean ground beef sirloin

I large scallion, finely sliced (1/2 cup)

2 water chestnuts, peeled, cut into 1/8-inch dice (1/4 cup)

2 teaspoons grated ginger mixed with I tablespoon
    Shao-Hsing wine or sherry

I tablespoon oyster sauce

1/2 teaspoon rice vinegar

I teaspoon Onion Oil (page 40)

I tablespoon mushroom soy sauce or double dark soy sauce

I teaspoon sugar

I tablespoon cornstarch

1/4 cup Chicken Stock (page 37)

Pinch salt

Pinch white pepper

1/4 cup green peas, fresh or frozen (thawed)

Yield:
4 servings

Place all ingredients, except green peas, in a bowl and mix, stirring continuously in one direction, to combine thoroughly. Place contents in a steam-proof dish and steam about 15 minutes, or until the beef is cooked. Turn off heat, sprinkle green peas on top, and serve in steaming dish with cooked rice.

Nutrition per serving (without rice): 109 Calories; 2.5g Fat; 20% calories from fat; 4.5g Carbohydrates; 27mg Cholesterol; 423mg Sodium.

Steamed Orange Beef

Jing Chong Pei Ngau Yuk

This variation of the previous recipe is my creation. Many people know orange beef as a sugar-laden, twice-fried dish. How different is mine! It gives all of the defined flavor of the familiar preparation but without any of its heaviness.

8 ounces lean ground beef sirloin

2 teaspoons grated orange zest

3 water chestnuts, peeled, cut into 1/8-inch dice (1/3 cup)

I large scallion, white and light green parts finely sliced
    (1/2 cup)

2 teaspoons grated ginger mixed with I tablespoon
    Shao-Hsing wine or sherry

I tablespoon oyster sauce

I tablespoon dark soy sauce

I teaspoon Shallot Oil (page 40)

I teaspoon sugar

1/2 teaspoon white vinegar

I tablespoon cornstarch

Pinch salt

Pinch white pepper

1/4 cup Chicken Stock (page 37)

1/4 cup minced red bell pepper

2 tablespoons minced fresh coriander (cilantro)

8 iceberg lettuce leaves, about 5 inches in diameter

Yield:
4 servings

Place all ingredients, except peppers, coriander, and lettuce leaves, in a bowl and mix, stirring continuously in one direction, to combine thoroughly. Place contents in a steam-proof dish and steam for about 15 minutes, or until beef is cooked. Turn off heat, remove beef from steamer, sprinkle first with peppers, then with coriander, and spoon the mixture into lettuce leaves to serve.

Nutrition per serving: 182 Calories; 4.5g Fat; 23% calories from fat; 5g Carbohydrates; 54mg Cholesterol; 437mg Sodium.

Beef Steamed with Pickled Peaches

Seun Toh Jing Ngau Yuk

In Canton this dish is traditionally cooked with preserved plums that are so sour they must be counteracted with a good deal of sugar. I have replaced this sourness and excessive sweetness with my own Pickled Peaches. What has emerged has become a recurring delight in my family.

8 ounces lean London broil, sliced thinly across the grain

3 tablespoons minced Pickled Peaches (page 46)

I tablespoon Ginger Pickle (page 45)

I teaspoon White Peppercorn Oil (page 41)

I teaspoon white vinegar

3/4 teaspoon sugar

2 teaspoons mushroom soy sauce

I tablespoon tapioca starch mixed with 3 tablespoons Pickled Peach liquid (page 46)

5 scallions, separate white and green portions (whites sliced into 1/2-inch pieces on the diagonal [1/2 cup], greens sliced finely [1/4 cup])

**Yield:
4 servings**

Place all ingredients, except scallion greens, in a bowl and mix well to combine and coat. Transfer to a steam-proof dish and place in a bamboo steamer in a wok over 4 cups boiling water. Steam for 10 to 12 minutes, or until beef is cooked. Turn off heat, remove from steamer, sprinkle with green portions of scallions, and serve with cooked rice.

Nutrition per serving (without rice): 180 Calories; 4.5g Fat; 22% calories from fat; 5g Carbohydrates; 54mg Cholesterol; 235mg Sodium.

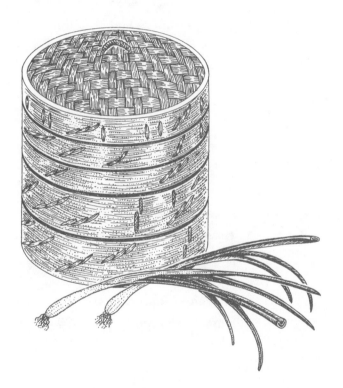

雪
豆
炒
牛
仔
肉 # Stir-Fried Veal with Snow Peas

Seut Dau Chau Ngau Jai Yuk

Veal is not at all common in China. It is to be found usually on the menus of Hong Kong and in the restaurants of the Western hotels in China. Nevertheless, this marvelous meat, which as I have previously noted is called by the Chinese ngau jai yuk, *or "meat of the suckling cow," is working its way into the Chinese kitchen. I find it most adaptable to Chinese techniques.*

I cup plus 2 tablespoons Chicken Stock (page 37)

8 ounces veal loin, thinly sliced into I × 21/2-inch pieces

6 ounces snow peas, ends and strings removed, each sliced
    into three pieces on the diagonal

SAUCE

2 teaspoons soy sauce

2 teaspoons Shao-Hsing wine or sherry

I teaspoon sugar

I1/2 tablespoons oyster sauce

1/2 teaspoon white vinegar

I tablespoon cornstarch

Pinch salt

Pinch white pepper

1/4 cup Chicken Stock (page 37)

TO COMPLETE THE DISH

I1/2 teaspoons peanut oil

I1/2 teaspoons minced ginger

I teaspoon minced garlic

1/4 teaspoon salt

1/2 medium red bell pepper, cut into 1/2-inch dice (1/2 cup)

I tablespoon Shao-Hsing wine or sherry

Yield:
4 servings

1. Heat wok over high heat, add 1 cup of chicken stock and bring to a boil. Add veal and poach for 30 seconds. Remove with a strainer and drain, reserve.

2. Bring stock back to a boil, add snow peas, stir and cook for 30 seconds until they turn bright green. Turn off heat, remove to the strainer holding the veal. Remove stock, reserve for future use. Wash and dry wok and spatula.

3. Combine sauce ingredients. Reserve.

4. Heat wok over high heat for 30 seconds, add peanut oil and coat wok. When a wisp of white smoke appears, add ginger, garlic, and salt, stir briefly. Add veal, snow peas, and pepper and stir-fry for 30 seconds. Add wine and mix well, cook for 30 seconds. Add remaining 2 tablespoons of stock, and mix and cook for 30 seconds more. Make a well in the mixture, stir sauce and pour in. Stir-fry together until sauce thickens and begins to bubble. Turn off heat, transfer to a heated dish, and serve.

Nutrition per serving: 179 Calories; 2g Fat; 10% calories from fat; 6g Carbohydrates; 54mg Cholesterol; 652mg Sodium.

子蘆炒牛仔肉

Veal with Ginger Pickle and Asparagus

Ji Loh Chau Ngau Jai Yuk

This is an easy balance of textures and tastes, the mildness of the veal contrasting with the tart pickle and the crispness of fresh asparagus. How fine in spring!

I cup Chicken Stock (page 37)

8 ounces veal loin, sliced across the grain into I × 2-inch pieces

1/2 pound asparagus, using tender shoots and tips, cut into 1/2-inch pieces on the diagonal (I cup)

SAUCE

2 teaspoons Shao-Hsing wine or sherry

1/2 teaspoon sesame oil

I tablespoon oyster sauce

1/2 teaspoon dark soy sauce

I tablespoon cornstarch

3/4 teaspoon sugar

Pinch salt

Pinch white pepper

1/4 cup Chicken Stock (page 37)

TO COMPLETE THE DISH

I1/2 teaspoons peanut oil

I teaspoon minced garlic

1/2 medium red bell pepper, cut into diagonal 1/2 × I-inch pieces

2 tablespoons Ginger Pickle (page 45)

1/4 cup scallions, white portions, cut into 1/2-inch pieces on the diagonal

I tablespoon Shao-Hsing wine or sherry

Yield:
4 servings

1. Heat wok over high heat, add chicken stock and bring to a boil. Add veal and poach for 45 seconds. Turn off heat, remove veal with strainer, and drain.

2. Turn heat back to high, return stock to a boil. Add asparagus and cook for 30 seconds until they turn bright green. Remove and add to strainer holding veal. Remove stock for future use. Wash and dry wok and spatula.

3. Combine the sauce ingredients. Reserve.

4. Heat wok over high heat for 30 seconds, add peanut oil and coat wok. When a wisp of white smoke appears, add garlic, stir briefly. Add veal and asparagus, stir to mix. Add scallions, stir to mix. Add peppers and Ginger Pickle, stir to mix. Add wine and mix thoroughly. If too dry, add 1 tablespoon of poaching liquid and mix. Make a well in the mixture, stir sauce, pour in. Stir-fry until sauce thickens and begins to bubble. Turn off heat, transfer to a heated dish, and serve.

Nutrition per serving: 198 Calories; 2g Fat; 8% calories from fat; 9g Carbohydrates; 54mg Cholesterol; 505mg Sodium.

Veal Stir-Fried with Mushrooms and Tomatoes

蕃茄蔴菇炒牛仔肉

Fan Keh Mah Gu Chau Ngau Jai Yuk

This veal stir-fry is as colorful as it is tasty, and the taste of the veal shines through. I ate a version of this in Hong Kong, but I have altered it to my taste.

8 ounces veal loin, cut into I × 2 1/2-inch slices
I cup Chicken Stock (page 37)
1/2 cup sliced fresh mushrooms (1/4-inch slices)

SAUCE

2 teaspoons soy sauce
2 teaspoons Shao-Hsing wine or sherry
1/8 teaspoon salt
I teaspoon sugar
I tablespoon oyster sauce
I tablespoon cornstarch
Pinch white pepper
1/4 cup Chicken Stock (page 37)

TO COMPLETE THE DISH

I 1/2 teaspoons peanut oil
2 teaspoons minced ginger
I teaspoon minced garlic
1/2 cup chopped scallions, white portions cut into
  1/4-inch pieces
1/2 cup fresh tomatoes, diced
I tablespoon Shao-Hsing wine or sherry

Yield:
4 servings

1. In a wok bring I cup of chicken stock to a boil over high heat. Add veal and blanch for 10 seconds. Remove veal with a strainer and drain. Bring stock back to a boil, add mushrooms. Stir to immerse and blanch for I minute, until softened. Remove to strainer with veal. Remove stock for future use. Wash and dry wok and spatula.

2. Combine sauce ingredients. Reserve.

3. Heat wok over high heat for 30 seconds, add peanut oil and coat wok. When a wisp of white smoke appears, add ginger, garlic, and scallions, stir to mix and cook for 30 seconds. Add tomatoes and mix well, cook for I minute. Add veal and mushrooms and stir together. Add wine, mix well. If mixture is dry add a tablespoon of stock. Cook and stir for another minute. Make a well in the mixture, stir sauce, pour in, stir to combine thoroughly. When sauce thickens and bubbles, turn off heat. Transfer to a heated dish and serve.

Nutrition per serving: 174 Calories; 1.5g Fat; 9% calories from fat; 4.5g Carbohydrates; 54mg Cholesterol; 429mg Sodium.

Veal with Green Tea Leaves

Loong Jin Ngau Jai Yuk

Cooking with tea leaves is common in China, particularly in such tea-growing regions as Hangzhou, because fresh, not dried or fermented, leaves are available to cooks. Dry leaves work almost as well, as you will see. Generally shrimp are favored to be cooked with green tea, but I believe the taste of veal, though decidedly different, complements the tea flavor equally as well. If you use cornstarch instead of tapioca starch, the sauce will be cloudier.

6 ounces lean veal loin filet

1 1/2 teaspoons Shallot Oil (page 40)

Pinch of salt

2 teaspoons of green tea leaves

1/2 cup boiling water

3/4 cup Chicken Stock (page 37)

2 tablespoons cloud ear mushrooms, soaked in hot water for
    30 minutes, washed 3 times, drained (1/2 cup)

6 thin asparagus, cut into 1/4-inch pieces on the diagonal
    (3/4 cup)

1 stalk celery, cut into 1/4-inch dice

SAUCE

5 tablespoons brewed green tea

2 tablespoons oyster sauce

1 1/2 teaspoons soy sauce

1 1/2 teaspoons sugar

1/2 teaspoon white vinegar

2 teaspoons Shao-Hsing wine or sherry

2 1/2 teaspoons tapioca starch (or cornstarch)

TO COMPLETE THE DISH

> 1 teaspoon minced ginger
>
> 1 teaspoon minced garlic
>
> 2 tablespoons scallions, white portions, cut into 1/4-inch pieces on the diagonal
>
> 1 tablespoon Shao-Hsing wine or sherry
>
> 2 water chestnuts, peeled, cut in half, then thinly sliced

Yield:
4 servings

1. Toss sliced veal with 1/4 teaspoon Shallot Oil and salt, and reserve, refrigerated, for 1 hour.

2. Brew the tea: Place tea leaves in a bowl. Pour boiling water into bowl. Cover bowl and allow to brew for 10 minutes. Strain the tea. Reserve tea and leaves separately.

3. Heat wok over high heat, add chicken stock and bring to a boil. Add cloud ears, asparagus, and celery, stir and cook for 1 minute, or until asparagus turns bright green. Turn off heat, remove vegetables with a strainer, and drain. Reserve stock for future use. Wash and dry wok and spatula.

4. Combine sauce ingredients. Reserve.

5. Heat wok over high heat for 30 seconds, add remaining Shallot Oil and coat wok. When a wisp of white smoke appears, add ginger, garlic, and scallions, stir to mix and cook for 30 seconds. Add reserved veal, stir to separate. Add wine, mix well. Add reserved green tea leaves, water chestnuts, and peppers, stir to mix well. Add reserved cloud ears and asparagus and mix thoroughly. If mixture is too dry add 1 tablespoon of brewed tea. Make a well in the mixture, stir sauce, pour in, stir and mix well. When sauce thickens and bubbles, turn off heat, transfer to a heated dish, and serve.

Nutrition per serving: 165 Calories; 1.5g Fat; 8% calories from fat; 9g Carbohydrates; 54mg Cholesterol; 430mg Sodium.

黑椒牛仔肉 Black Pepper Veal

Hok Jiu Ngau Jai Yuk

Here is a prime example of what the chefs of Hong Kong can do with what is essentially a Western concept. To cook veal, still novel, with a sauce based on black pepper is quite European indeed. This is my adaptation of their adaptation.

8 ounces lean loin of veal filet, cut into 4 equal portions
I1/4 teaspoons Shallot Oil (page 40)
Pinch salt

SAUCE

2 tablespoons oyster sauce

I1/4 teaspoons sugar

I teaspoon soy sauce

I teaspoon dark soy sauce

I tablespoon Shao-Hsing wine or sherry

2I/2 teaspoons cornstarch

I/2 cup Chicken Stock (page 37)

TO COMPLETE THE DISH

3/4 teaspoon crushed black peppercorns

2 large shallots, cut into I/4-inch dice

I teaspoon minced ginger

I teaspoon minced garlic

I/4 teaspoon sesame oil

I tablespoon thinly sliced scallion greens

Yield:
4 servings

I. Toss the veal with I/4 teaspoon of Shallot Oil and salt, and allow to marinate, refrigerated, for I hour.

2. Heat a Teflon-coated skillet for 45 seconds, until very hot. Place the 4 pieces of veal in it and pan-fry for 1 minute on each side. Turn off heat, transfer to a dish, reserve.

3. Combine sauce ingredients. Reserve.

4. Heat wok over high heat for 30 seconds, add remaining Shallot Oil and coat wok. When a wisp of white smoke appears, add crushed black pepper, stir and cook for 20 seconds. Add shallots, ginger, and garlic, stir and mix well. Cook for 1 minute. Stir sauce, pour into wok, stir until it comes to a boil. Add reserved veal, cover with the sauce, and allow it to return to a boil. Turn veal over and cook 1 minute. Turn off heat, add sesame oil, stir and mix well. Transfer to a heated dish, sprinkle scallions over veal and serve with cooked rice.

Nutrition per serving (without rice): 166 Calories; 2.5g Fat; 13% calories from fat; 4.5g Carbohydrates; 72mg Cholesterol; 476mg Sodium.

Chapter 7

湯 Soups, Glorious Soups

In China soups have many guises. They are foods, to be sure, liquids that are meant to nourish, but they are also the embodiments of custom and metaphor and, as in other cultures, medicinally curative. A particular soup, it is said, will provide one with interior balance; another will halt the graying of hair; another will clear congestion. In many places in China, a restaurant will brew a soup as a pharmacist might concoct a prescription.

At the table, soup is the ultimate family food. It is never ladled into bowls then delivered to the dining table, as is the custom in many other cultures. Soups come in large tureens, vast pots, from which bowls are filled at the table. And soups are the ultimate accompaniment in China. One dines on different dishes, with a soup at hand to help digestion.

Rarely, if ever, is soup served as a first course. Custom has it that to do so would indicate to one's guests that a host is miserly, that he feeds his guests soup to fill their stomachs with liquid, so that he will not have to serve too many subsequent dishes. At the Chinese table one might enjoy a bit of vegetable, a couple of bites of meat, perhaps a shrimp, then reach for his soup bowl for a couple of sips of the liquid that will clear his palate.

On the other hand, a pork soup, by itself, is said to provide lubrication for the body and may be eaten alone. A soup with chicken is regarded as a brew of richness and elegance.

When I first moved to Hong Kong from my home near Canton, I lived for a time in Kowloon with my *Ng Gu Jeh,* or "Number Five Aunt," my father's younger sister, a busy woman who operated a small sundry store that sold everything from canned fruits to cigarettes, ice cream to breads, and all manner of prepared foods. I recall that she was also known

279

in the community as *Ng Gah Jeh,* or "Number Five Sister," or by the nick-name *Ng Gu,* or "Miss Five." Miss Five's servants were always cooking, making spring rolls to sell, brewing soups, selling cakes and sweets, but always she would interrupt whatever she was doing when Sunday arrived. For that was soup day.

And what a soup she made! Chunks of pork and baby cuttlefish, mushrooms and lotus root, all cooked together in a thick stock. Such a soup was certain to make all members of her family come home on Sundays, which I am sure was her intent. My aunt would always quiz her guests about what they might have eaten during the prior week. She would nod, then put out her soup, announcing that it would cleanse them.

And we ate soup in many ways; as an accompaniment to other dishes; occasionally, but not often, as a palate-cleansing course of its own. We would pour soup, with its vegetables, or meat, or fish, over rice and eat it as a one-dish meal. There were always distinctions to be made with soup, and I have made them in this book. You will find soups in other sections, to be sure, but in those instances the soup is in a way secondary to what it is cooked with; more a vehicle. In this section, the soups are the important thing, and the ingredients adorn them.

As you travel about China you will see hundreds, thousands, of small roadside eating places, almost all of which serve soup in some fashion. There are even soup restaurants devoted to the theme of "beautiful," as they say. In Hong Kong there are several restaurants that go by the name of *Ah Yee Lang Tong,* which translates as "Beautiful Soup from Number Two." The theme of these restaurants is that if you are not receiving good soup from your number one wife, then you had better seek out number two for good soup. My husband, occasional chauvinist that he is, suggests that what is being suggested has nothing whatever to do with soup. But I pay no attention to him.

Soups lend themselves to lightness in diet, to healthful eating, to low fat consumption, as you will see from my recipes. The secret to such soups is, of course, the stocks from which they are made. Stock recipes are included in this book's introduction, and you will discover that every soup, from whatever region, is based upon these stocks.

Enjoy good soup from number one.

木瓜荳腐湯

Papaya and Bean Curd Soup

Muk Gua Dau Fu Tong

This is a soup from my childhood. Papaya was plentiful in Sun Tak when I was growing up. It is a fruit much admired by the elderly who believe that it should be eaten often by young nursing mothers. But you need not be a young mother to enjoy this colorful and nourishing soup.

> 5 cups Vegetable Stock (page 36)
> I slice ginger, 1/2 inch thick, lightly smashed
> I papaya, unripe, peeled, seeded, cut into 1/2-inch dice
>   (2 cups)
> 1/2 cup green peas, fresh or frozen
> 2 cakes fresh bean curd (8 ounces), cut into 1/2-inch dice
> Generous pinch white pepper

**Yield:
6 servings**

1. In a pot bring stock and ginger to a boil over high heat. Add papaya, allow to return to a boil. Lower heat to simmer, cook 5 to 7 minutes, until papaya is tender. Add green peas, allow to return to a boil. (If fresh peas are used, allow to cook 2 to 3 minutes.)

2. Raise heat to high. Add bean curd, stir to mix well. Add white pepper, allow to return to a boil. Boil for I minute. Turn off heat, transfer soup to a heated tureen and serve.

Nutrition per serving: 90 Calories; 2.7g Fat; 26% calories from fat; 12g Carbohydrates; 0mg Cholesterol; 320mg Sodium.

White Pearl Soup

Jun Jiu Dau Fu Tong

This simple soup is called jun jiu, *or "white pearl," because of the light color and size of the diced fresh bean curd with which it is made. An example of subtle humor—pearls are expensive, bean curd inexpensive—so one may eat "pearls" without spending a lot of money.*

4 ounces turkey cutlet, cut into 1/4-inch dice

MARINADE

> 1 1/2 tablespoons Shao-Hsing wine or sherry
> 3/4 teaspoon sesame oil
> 2 1/2 teaspoons tapioca starch (or cornstarch)
> 1 teaspoon sugar
> 1/4 teaspoon salt

TO COMPLETE THE DISH

> 4 cups Chicken Stock (page 37)
> 2 cakes fresh bean curd (8 ounces), cut into 1/4-inch dice
> Generous pinch white pepper
> 3 tablespoons minced fresh coriander (cilantro)

Yield:
4 servings

1. Marinate turkey in marinade ingredients for 15 minutes.

2. Place stock in a pot, cover, and bring to a boil over high heat. Add bean curd, stir, allow to return to a boil. Add turkey and marinade, stir and mix well. Allow to return to a boil. Add white pepper, stir in. Turn off heat, transfer to a heated tureen, sprinkle with minced coriander, and serve.

Nutrition per serving: 147 Calories; 4.5g Fat; 27% calories from fat; 4g Carbohydrates; 30mg Cholesterol; 342mg Sodium.

Bok Choy Beef Soup

Bok Choy Ngau Yuk Tong

白菜牛肉湯

This was a favorite soup when I was growing up in Hong Kong. My other aunt Lo Gu Jeh would make this soup, really an autumn and winter soup, in the summer simply because she said bok choy was at its sweetest and tenderest. The small amount of beef is just a complement to the bok choy.

2 ounces lean London broil, julienned

Marinade

1 teaspoon Shao-Hsing wine or sherry
1/2 teaspoon sesame oil
1 1/2 teaspoons oyster sauce
1/2 teaspoon soy sauce

To complete the dish

5 cups Chicken Stock (page 37)
1 slice ginger, 1/2 inch thick, lightly smashed
1/2 pound bok choy, washed, drained, and cut into 1/2-inch pieces, separating leaves from stalks

Yield:
6 servings

Allow beef to rest in combined marinade ingredients while you prepare the soup. In a pot bring chicken stock and ginger to a boil over high heat. Add bok choy stalks, stir and immerse. Allow to return to a boil, cook for 3 minutes. Add bok choy leaves, stir and immerse, cook 2 minutes more. The bok choy should be tender at this point. If not, cook for 2 more minutes. Add beef and marinade, stir, bring back to a boil. Turn off heat, transfer to a heated tureen, and serve.

Nutrition per serving: 73 Calories; 2.5g Fat; 29% calories from fat; 4.5g Carbohydrates; 9mg Cholesterol; 482mg Sodium.

Tianjin Bok Choy Soup

Tianjin Bok Choy Tong

This sweet vegetable with its white stalks and pale green leaves is also known as Tientsin bok choy, in the old Chinese spelling of the city for which it is named, or napa cabbage. The Chinese know it as wong nga bak, or "yellow white tea," a reference to its coloring.

6 cups Chicken Stock (page 37)

1 slice ginger, 1/2 inch thick, lightly smashed

2 teaspoons oyster sauce

1 teaspoon Shao-Hsing wine or sherry

1/2 teaspoon sesame oil

1 teaspoon soy sauce

Pinch white pepper

1 pound Tianjin bok choy, stalks separated, washed, drained, cut into 3/4-inch pieces on the diagonal

1 package of bean thread noodles (2 ounces), soaked in hot water for 30 minutes, cut into manageable lengths

Yield:
6 servings

In a large pot place stock, ginger, oyster sauce, wine, sesame oil, soy sauce, and white pepper. Cover and bring to a boil over high heat. Add Tianjin bok choy, stir and immerse, allow to return to a boil. Lower heat to medium, cook for 5 minutes, until stalks are tender. Add bean thread noodles, allow to return to a boil. Turn off heat, transfer to a heated tureen, and serve.

Nutrition per serving: 62 Calories; 2g Fat; 28% calories from fat; 4.5g Carbohydrates; 0mg Cholesterol; 460mg Sodium.

Tianjin Bok Choy Chicken Soup

Tianjin Bok Choy Gai Tong

In this soup, the sweetness of the bok choy, this "yellow white tea," is emphasized by pairing it with chicken. The soup becomes new, fresh, and different.

5 cups Chicken Stock (page 37)

1 slice ginger, 1/2 inch thick, lightly smashed

Pinch salt

1 pound Tianjin bok choy, cut into 1/4-inch pieces across

2 teaspoons oyster sauce

2 teaspoons soy sauce

1 tablespoon Shao-Hsing wine or sherry

Pinch white pepper

4 ounces chicken cutlet, julienned

Yield:
6 servings

In a pot bring stock, ginger, and salt to a boil over high heat. Add bok choy, immerse, stir, and allow to return to a boil. Add oyster sauce, soy sauce, wine, and white pepper and cook for 5 to 7 minutes until bok choy stalks become tender. Add chicken, stir to mix. Allow soup to return to a boil. Boil for 1 minute. Turn off heat, transfer to a heated tureen, and serve.

Nutrition per serving: 73 Calories; 2.5g Fat; 28% calories from fat; 4g Carbohydrates; 16mg Cholesterol; 470mg Sodium.

Watercress Soup with Meatballs

Sai Yeung Choi Tong

Watercress was, to my grandmother, a food that cooled the body's heat and provided interior balance, a fine Buddhist notion. She never would have eaten watercress with beef, however. So with apologies to her, I offer this pleasant, unusual soup.

MEATBALLS

4 ounces lean ground beef

Pinch salt

1/4 teaspoon sugar

1/2 teaspoon soy sauce

1/2 teaspoon oyster sauce

I teaspoon Shao-Hsing wine or sherry

I 1/2 teaspoons cornstarch

1/2 egg white, beaten

SOUP

3 1/2 cups Chicken Stock (page 37)

I cup cold water

I slice ginger, 1 inch thick, lightly smashed

2 bunches of watercress, each cut in half, loosened and
    washed thoroughly

1/2 teaspoon baking soda (optional)

**Yield:
4 servings**

I. To make the meatballs, place all ingredients in a bowl, and stir clockwise, with chopsticks or wooden spoon, until mixture is quite soft and blended. If mixture is too soft, add a bit more cornstarch. Form into 12 small balls.

2. To make the soup, in a pot bring the stock, water, and ginger to a boil over high heat. Add meatballs, allow the liquid to return to a boil. When meatballs float to the top, they are cooked. Add watercress and allow soup to return to a boil once again. Turn off

heat, transfer to a heated tureen, and serve. (To give the watercress a bright green color, add baking soda to the soup when meatballs are added.)

Nutrition per serving: 116 Calories; 3.5g Fat; 27% calories from fat; 4g Carbohydrates; 27mg Cholesterol; 567mg Sodium.

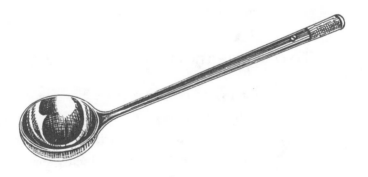

Bean Curd and Sour Mustard Pickle Soup

Dau Fu Seun Choi Tong

This is another soup from my childhood in Sun Tak. My grandmother, Ah Paw, loved this bean curd soup with its slight sourness and would tell us not only that it was good for us, but that it intensified our appetites.

2 ounces lean pork loin, julienned

MARINADE

2 teaspoons oyster sauce

I teaspoon soy sauce

I teaspoon cornstarch

Pinch white pepper

TO COMPLETE THE DISH

4 cups Chicken Stock (page 37)

I cup cold water

4 ounces sour mustard pickle, thinly sliced

I slice ginger, I inch thick, lightly smashed

Generous pinch white pepper

I tablespoon Shao-Hsing wine or sherry

I tablespoon soy sauce

2 tablespoons white vinegar

2 cakes fresh bean curd (8 ounces), julienned

2 tablespoons minced fresh coriander (cilantro)

Yield:
6 servings

I. Marinate pork in the combined marinade ingredients for 15 minutes.

2. In a pot place stock, water, mustard pickle, ginger, and white pepper. Cover, and bring to a boil over high heat. Add wine and soy sauce and allow to return to a boil. Lower heat and allow to simmer 5 minutes. Add pork and marinade, stir well, allow to return to a boil. Add vinegar, stir and blend. Return to a boil and add bean curd, mix and allow to return to a boil. Cook for 1 minute. Turn off heat, transfer to a heated tureen, sprinkle with minced coriander, and serve.

Nutrition per serving: 89 Calories; 3g Fat; 28% calories from fat; 3g Carbohydrates; 9mg Cholesterol; 333mg Sodium.

Spinach Soup with Shrimp

Har Mai Bor Choi Tong

This is truly a classic of traditional Chinese home cooking. Dried shrimp are used widely throughout China, and in those times when refrigeration was not universal, shrimp were dried and kept for months. When I was a child, our cooks would cook small fresh shrimp then allow them to dry in the sun for storage and future use. This process concentrates and intensifies their taste. If dried shrimp are unavailable, you may use fresh shrimp.

2 tablespoons dried shrimp (or 4 ounces fresh medium shrimp)

1/2 of a 2-ounce package of bean thread noodles

6 cups water

1/2 teaspoon baking soda (optional)

1 1/2 teaspoons salt

1 pound spinach, washed thoroughly, drained, leaves broken in half

5 cups Seafood Stock (page 38)

1 tablespoon white wine

1 tablespoon minced ginger

1 1/2 teaspoons Garlic Oil (page 39)

Yield:
6 servings

1. Soak dried shrimp in warm water for 20 minutes, until softened. Remove, drain, reserve. (Alternately cut fresh shrimp in half lengthwise, reserve.) Soak bean thread noodles in hot water for 30 minutes, remove, drain, cut into manageable lengths, reserve.

2. In a large pot bring water, baking soda, and salt to a boil over high heat. Add spinach, immerse and cook until it turns bright green. Turn off heat, run cold water into pot, drain. Set aside. Rinse, dry pot.

3. Place stock in large pot with wine, ginger, and shrimp. Cover and bring to a boil over high heat. Lower heat and simmer for 5 minutes. Stir until spinach is completely covered by soup. Bring back to a boil. Add bean threads and mix well. Allow to return to a boil again. Turn off heat, add Garlic Oil and stir to mix well. Transfer to a heated tureen and serve.

Nutrition per serving: 54 Calories; 2.5g Fat; 27% calories from fat; 2g Carbohydrates; 21mg Cholesterol; 476mg Sodium.

Sole and Lettuce Soup

Sahng Choi Lung Lei Tong

This is my variation of a Cantonese traditional soup. In Canton, fresh carp, filleted, would be used. Carp is widely available in Chinese and Asian markets, but the soup is as tasty when made with sole, flounder, or sea bass, which are generally easier to obtain. I use sole in this version. Whichever fish you use, always have fillets cut from the meaty portion of the fish.

8 ounces fresh sole fillet, sliced across into 2 × 1/4-inch sections

MARINADE

1/2 teaspoon White Peppercorn Oil (page 41)

1/4 teaspoon salt

1/2 teaspoon sugar

I teaspoon cornstarch

I teaspoon Ginger Juice (page 43) mixed with 2 teaspoons Shao-Hsing wine or sherry

I teaspoon soy sauce

TO COMPLETE THE DISH

4 cups Seafood Stock (page 38)

I cup water

I slice ginger, I inch thick, lightly smashed

I head iceberg lettuce, shredded (5 cups)

I tablespoon White Peppercorn Oil (page 41)

Yield:
6 servings

1. Marinate fish slices in combined marinade ingredients in a bowl for 10 minutes, reserve.

2. In a pot bring stock, water, and ginger to a boil over high heat. Add lettuce, stir, allow to return to a boil. Add fish and marinade, stir, allow to return to a boil again. Turn off heat, stir in the White Peppercorn Oil, transfer to a heated tureen, and serve.

Nutrition per serving: 60 Calories; 1.6g Fat; 25% calories from fat; 3g Carbohydrates; 7mg Cholesterol; 424mg Sodium.

Winter Melon Soup with Shredded Pork

Yuk See Dong Gua Tong

This soup illustrates perfectly the unique quality of the winter melon. This white melon, which on the outside looks like a watermelon, is basically without taste, but it absorbs beautifully the tastes of foods with which it is cooked.

5 cups Chicken Stock (page 37)

6 Chinese black mushrooms, soaked in water 30 minutes, stems removed, julienned

1/4 teaspoon salt

1 slice ginger, 1/2 inch thick, lightly smashed

1 pound winter melon, peeled, seeded, and sliced

2 ounces lean pork loin, shredded

Yield:
6 servings

In a large pot place stock, mushrooms, salt, and ginger. Cover and bring to a boil over high heat. Lower heat and allow soup to simmer for 5 minutes. Raise heat back to high. Add melon and stir well to mix, allow to return to a boil. Cover pot, lower heat, and allow to cook 3 minutes, as on next page or until melon is tender. Raise heat back to high, add pork, stir to separate. Allow the soup to return to a boil again. Turn off heat, transfer to a heated tureen, and serve.

Nutrition per serving: 57 Calories; 1.9g Fat; 28% calories from fat; 2g Carbohydrates; 9mg Cholesterol; 417mg Sodium.

Silk Squash Chicken Soup

See Gua Tong

The silk squash is an odd-looking but fine-tasting vegetable. It is shaped like a cucumber, but with ridges along its length, which must be pared down before the silk squash can be used. It was a special food when I was young, for it was available only two months each year, at the beginning of the summer. It's now more easily available.

I 1/2 **pounds silk squash**

4 cups Chicken Stock (page 37)

I **cup cold water**

I **slice ginger, I inch thick, lightly smashed**

4 ounces lean chicken cutlet, julienned

I **teaspoon Coriander Oil (page 41)**

Yield:
6 servings

1. Wash squash. With a peeler pare its ridges, but do not remove all of the green outer skin. Roll cut the squash: Starting at one end, cut diagonally into slices approximately 3/4 inch. Turn squash one-quarter turn between each cut.

2. In a large pot place the stock, water, and ginger. Cover and bring to a boil over high heat. Add squash, stir and immerse, allow soup to return to a boil. Lower heat to medium and cook for 5 minutes, or until squash is tender. Raise heat back to high, add chicken, and mix well. Allow soup to return to a boil. Turn off heat, add Coriander Oil, and stir well to combine. Transfer to a heated tureen and serve.

   Nutrition per serving: 60 Calories; 2g Fat; 27% calories from fat; 3.3g Carbohydrates; 16g Cholesterol; 450mg Sodium.

Hot and Sour Soup

Seun Lot Tong

Is there a more familiar soup than this in the Chinese kitchen? I suppose not. It would be difficult to find anyone who does know about, or has not tasted, some version of this soup with its origins in China's north and west. This version uses no oil in the preparation, and the flavor remains absolutely true to the soup's tradition.

5 cups Chicken Stock (page 37)

1 slice ginger, 1/2 inch thick, lightly smashed

40 tiger lily buds, soaked in hot water 30 minutes, washed, hard ends removed, cut in half

2 tablespoons cloud ears, soaked in hot water 30 minutes, washed three times to remove grit

1/2 cup bamboo shoots, julienned

1/4 teaspoon salt

1 1/2 teaspoons Hot Pepper Flakes (page 42)

3 tablespoons red wine vinegar

4 ounces lean pork loin, shredded

3 tablespoons cornstarch mixed with 3 tablespoons cold water

2 large eggs, beaten

1 1/2 teaspoons dark soy sauce

2 cakes fresh bean curd (8 ounces), cut into 1/3-inch strips

2 tablespoons finely sliced scallion greens

Yield:
6 servings

1. In a large pot place stock, ginger, tiger lily buds, cloud ears, bamboo shoots, and salt. Cover pot and bring to a boil over high heat. Lower heat and simmer for 10 minutes. Add Hot Pepper Flakes and vinegar and stir in. Turn heat back to high and return soup to a boil. Boil for 2 minutes. Add pork, stir and cook for 2 minutes more.

2. Stir cornstarch mixture and pour into soup, stirring to combine thoroughly. Add beaten eggs in the same manner. Add soy sauce and mix well. Add bean curd strips, stir and bring soup back to a boil. Turn off heat, transfer to a heated tureen, sprinkle with sliced

scallions, and serve. (If you wish soup to be hotter, you may add another 1/2 teaspoon of Hot Pepper Flakes before transferring to tureen.)

Nutrition per serving: 173 Calories; 5.5g Fat; 27% calories from fat; 2.5g Carbohydrates; 87mg Cholesterol; 361mg Sodium.

荳腐蕃茄豚菇湯 Bean Curd, Tomato, and Mushroom Soup

Dau Fu Fan Keh Mah Gu Tong

I created this dish to take advantage of the summer season in my state when absolutely marvelous tomatoes are plentiful. It was the same in southern China in hot summer. Tomatoes were at their best then, juicy, sweet, and meaty, perfect for this bean curd soup. I associate another memory with tomatoes; when they were in season I was on holiday from school.

I pound ripe tomatoes, cut into 1/2-inch dice

2 cakes fresh bean curd (8 ounces), cut into 1/2-inch slices

4 cups Chicken Stock (page 37)

I piece ginger, 11/2 inches thick, lightly smashed

Generous pinch white pepper

I tablespoon Shao-Hsing wine or sherry

I tablespoon soy sauce

4 ounces fresh mushrooms, cut into 1/2-inch dice

2 tablespoons minced fresh coriander (cilantro)

Yield:
6 servings

In a pot place tomatoes, stock, ginger, and white pepper. Cover and bring to a boil over high heat. Add wine and soy sauce, stir in, lower heat to medium, and allow soup to cook 10 minutes. Raise heat to high, add mushrooms, allow to return to a boil. Cook for 2 minutes. Add bean curd and bring back to a boil for I minute. Turn off heat, transfer to a heated tureen, sprinkle with minced coriander, and serve.

Nutrition per serving: 74 Calories; 2.5g Fat; 28% calories from fat; 6g Carbohydrates; 0mg Cholesterol; 538mg Sodium.

大
荳
菜
湯

Tomato and Soy Sprout Soup

Dai Dau Choi Tong

This soup is rooted in the family kitchens of Shanghai. It comes from the kitchen of my friend Rosanna Wong. Her mother believes that soybean sprouts lower the body's heat, helping its balance, while tomatoes provide needed vitamins, and bean curd provides protein. This is a dish of good health.

I teaspoon peanut oil

I1/2 teaspoons minced ginger

I teaspoon minced garlic

2 large ripe tomatoes (I pound), cut into I-inch pieces

6 ounces soybean sprouts, washed and drained

41/2 cups cold water

I1/4 teaspoons salt

2 teaspoons sugar

I cake fresh bean curd (4 ounces), cut into 1/4-inch dice

Pinch white pepper

Yield:
6 servings

Place a large pot over high heat for 30 seconds and add peanut oil. When a wisp of white smoke appears, add ginger and garlic, stir. When garlic turns light brown, add tomatoes, stir and cook for I minute. Add soybean sprouts, stir and cook for 2 minutes more. Add cold water, salt, and sugar, stir and mix well. Cover pot, leaving a small opening at the lid, lower heat to medium. Cook for 5 minutes or until soybean sprouts become tender. Raise heat back to high, add bean curd and white pepper and return to a boil. Boil for I minute. Turn off heat, transfer to a heated tureen, and serve.

Nutrition per serving: 53 Calories; 1.5g Fat; 25% calories from fat; 7g Carbohydrates; 0mg Cholesterol; 395mg Sodium.

Egg Drop Soup

Dan Far Tong

The Chinese name for this very famous soup translates as "egg flower soup," to denote how the eggs spread and flower as they come into contact with the broth. It is a simple soup, a staple in Canton and in other parts of China as well.

3 cups Chicken Stock (page 37)

I cup cold water

3 large egg whites, beaten

3 scallion greens, trimmed, finely sliced

Yield:
4 servings

In a pot bring the stock and water to a boil. Then remove the pot from the flame and add beaten egg whites steadily, beating them into the soup as you pour. Add the sliced scallions, stir in. Remove to a heated tureen and serve.

Nutrition per serving: 44 Calories; 1.5g Fat; 30% calories from fat; 0g Carbohydrates; 0mg Cholesterol; 312mg Sodium.

酒 Ginger Shrimp Soup

Jau Tong

 The Chinese words for this soup, jau tong, *translate as "wine soup," or more familiarly, "drunken soup," to indicate its wine content. Well, you surely will not become intoxicated with the wine, but I believe you will immensely enjoy the taste of ginger.*

8 ounces large shrimp (18), shelled, deveined, and washed

4 1/2 tablespoons Shao-Hsing wine or sherry

1/8 teaspoon white pepper

6 cups Seafood Stock (page 38)

1 1/2 cups cold water

1 large piece ginger, smashed well

2 scallions, cut into 1/4-inch pieces on the diagonal

Yield:
6 servings

1. Marinate the shrimp in 1 1/2 tablespoons of Shao-Hsing wine or sherry and white pepper for 30 minutes.

2. As the shrimp marinate, in a large pot place stock, water, and ginger. Cover and bring to a boil over high heat. Leave a small opening at the lid, lower heat and simmer for 30 minutes. Raise heat back to high, add remaining wine, allow to come to a boil. Add shrimp and marinade and stir. Add scallions and mix. When shrimp turn pink and begin to curl the soup is ready. Turn off heat, transfer to a heated tureen, and serve.

Nutrition per serving: 76 Calories; 2g Fat; 25% calories from fat; 1.5g Carbohydrates; 45mg Cholesterol; 303mg Sodium.

Beef and Ginger Soup

Ngau Yuk Gung

When I was making this soup, my husband asked why I had not added the word tong *to its Chinese description. I told him this was not a tong, it was a gung. "Oh," he said, "and what is a gung?" It is a thickened soup, one to which tapioca starch is added, a classic of Cantonese tradition. He loves it.*

4 ounces lean sirloin, ground

I teaspoon tapioca starch mixed with 1/3 cup Chicken Stock (page 37)

4 cups Chicken Stock (page 37)

2 tablespoons shredded ginger

I tablespoon Shao-Hsing wine or sherry

I teaspoon soy sauce

1/2 teaspoon sugar

1/8 teaspoon white pepper

3 tablespoons tapioca starch mixed with 5 tablespoons cold water

I scallion, greens finely sliced

Yield:
6 servings

I. Combine beef with the tapioca starch-chicken stock mixture and blend well. Set aside.

2. In a pot place 4 cups chicken stock with shredded ginger. Cover and bring to a boil over high heat. Boil for 2 minutes, add wine, return to a boil. Add soy sauce, sugar, and white pepper, stir, return to a boil. Place beef mixture into pot slowly, stirring as you do, until the beef blends well. Allow to return to a boil. Stir the tapioca starch-water mixture and pour into broth gradually, stirring as you do. Continue to stir until the soup comes to a boil. Turn off heat, transfer to a heated tureen, sprinkle with sliced scallions, and serve.

Nutrition per serving: 89 Calories; 2.6g Fat; 26% calories from fat; 4g Carbohydrates; 17mg Cholesterol; 360mg Sodium.

福建米粉湯

Fujian Rice Noodle Soup

Fukien Mai Fun Tong

I cooked this soup very often when I was growing up, when Fujian was still known as Fukien. This dish from that southern Chinese province is quite famous.

8 ounces packaged dry rice noodles

I ounce small dried shrimp (2 tablespoons)

I teaspoon peanut oil

I slice ginger, 1/2 inch thick, lightly smashed

I tablespoon Shao-Hsing wine or sherry

4 Thai chilies, minced

3 cups Chicken Stock (page 37)

I teaspoon soy sauce

1/2 teaspoon salt

Pinch white pepper

4 ounces lean pork loin, shredded

1/2 teaspoon sesame oil

2 scallions, finely sliced

2 tablespoons minced fresh coriander (cilantro)

Yield:
6 servings

1. Soak rice noodles in hot water for 30 minutes, until softened. Drain, reserve. Soaked dried shrimp in hot water for 20 minutes. Drain, mince, reserve.

2. Heat pot over high heat for 20 seconds, add peanut oil. When a wisp of white smoke appears, add shrimp and ginger, stir and cook for 30 seconds. Add wine, mix well. Add chilies, stir in briefly. Add stock, soy sauce, salt, and white pepper and stir in to mix well. Cover the pot and bring to a boil. Add pork, stir to separate. Add rice noodles and allow soup to return to a boil. Turn off heat, add sesame oil and scallions and stir in to mix well. Transfer to a heated tureen, sprinkle with minced coriander, and serve.

Nutrition per serving: 105 Calories; 3.3g Fat; 28% calories from fat; 6g Carbohydrates; 23mg Cholesterol; 381mg Sodium.

Cross the Bridge Rice Noodle Soup

Guor Kiu Mai Fun Tong

It is said in Hangzhou that once, when a scholar was studying for imperial court advancement, he would move away from his wife and family, either to a remote part of his house or away from home, so he would not have distractions. To be so remote was associated with being "across a bridge." So the scholar's wife would make this noodle soup and carry it to him.

3 cups Chicken Stock (page 37)

3 Thai chilies, minced

6 ounces lean pork loin, julienned

I teaspoon soy sauce

8 ounces packaged dry rice noodles, soaked in hot water 20 minutes, drained

1/4 cup Chinese chives, washed, cut into I-inch sections

Yield:
4 servings

In a pot place stock and chilies. Cover, and bring to a boil over high heat. Add pork, stir in, allow to return to a boil. Add soy sauce and stir well. Add chives and stir to mix. Add noodles and stir to mix. Allow soup to return to a boil. Turn off heat, transfer to a heated tureen, and serve.

Nutrition per serving: 201 Calories; 6g Fat; 26% calories from fat; 9.7g Carbohydrates; 42mg Cholesterol; 580mg Sodium.

Chapter 8

Tong Soi and Other Sweets

Elaborate desserts do not exist in China. In general most meals, including festive banquets, close with fresh fruit, often resting upon mounds of crushed ice. Occasionally, as is the custom in Hangzhou, fruit courses can be works of fruit sculpture and plate arrangements wherein carved fruit becomes composed still life. In general, however, a Chinese dessert is sliced fruit.

This is not to say that sweets do not exist in China. Sweet rice cakes with candied fruit, nuts cooked with sweet syrup, and all manner of candies are found in China, but these are generally served with tea, as sweet snacks rather than as desserts. In Shanghai particularly, and later in Hong Kong, a tradition of Western-style cakes, pastries, and cookies arose, but these too are treats to be enjoyed in the teahouse, not as the end of a dinner.

Some Chinese desserts are sweet soups, many made with cooked or pureed fruits, others are known as *tong soi*. These are very simple soups in which fruits, vegetables, nuts, herbs, even flower blossoms are cooked with sugar and water. In fact the words *tong soi* translate simply as "soup of sugar water." To the Chinese these soups are tonics and are advantageous to one's health, and are said to help the body to become *ching bo leung*, or "clean and clear." An adage has it that a rich man will enjoy a soup made from the swallow's nest, whereas a poor man's bird's nest soup is a tong soi.

These are very much family soups, and often they are eaten at the conclusion of a meal, particularly one that has contained a substantial amount of fat or oil, for it is felt the sugar soup will cool the body and restore any imbalance caused by intakes of fat. It is not uncommon to find tong soi made with chrysanthemums, lotus and cassia flowers; with small pearl-like balls of processed tapioca flour; with sweet potatoes and taro; with red beans; and with walnuts, almonds, and peanuts. In this section I have included three tong soi recipes, which I hope will inspire you to experiment with different fruits and vegetables that will lend themselves to sweetness.

When I was a child, I remember having all manner of tong soi, which of course my brother and I loved. But I recall that often the workers who farmed the fields around our house in Sun Tak would be given tong soi in the mornings before work, usually soups made from chunks of taro root or sweet potatoes cooked in sugar water. This was, my grandmother explained to me, a way to give them a good supply of energy.

In general our dessert soups were enjoyed in the summer months. It was felt that in the summer the body's heat tends to increase, so that fruit or sweet soup, usually clear, would tend to reduce its temperature and restore its balance. What makes these soups unusual is that they may be eaten hot or cold. Other sweet soups are made to be eaten hot, soups such as traditional ones made with sweetened red bean paste or lotus root paste; or with sweet black sesame seeds, or even sweetened peanut soups. This may come as a surprise to many, because the Chinese are not particularly recognized for their sweet soups. But more and more they are finding their way onto menus.

In cities like Hong Kong, Canton, and Shanghai, where I expect there are more sweet teeth than in other cities, the whole range of Chinese sweet soups is available. Which is not to suggest that there are not sweet soups in other parts of China, which there are. Even in New York's Chinatown, for example, a small restaurant opened recently that features an entire menu of tong sui.

I would urge you to seek out authentic sweets. Do not even open a fortune cookie (which are not even Chinese). Forget about sweet canned pineapple and chocolate ice cream. Have a tong soi. Better yet, make one.

Tea Pear Soup

Chun Pei Dun Seut Lei

This marvelous tong soi *was served to me a while ago at the Man Wah restaurant in the Mandarin Oriental Hotel in Hong Kong. Its name is fascinating; it translates as "pear boiled with old skin," the "old skin" being dried tangerine peel. I found it so exquisite that I resolved to make it myself. What results is my adaptation of this pear cooked with jasmine tea. I thank Chef Lau Sik Kwan for his inspiration.*

I piece dried tangerine peel

1 large lemon

1/2 cup plus 1 tablespoon sugar

2 teaspoons jasmine tea leaves

5 cups water

4 medium Bosc pears, ripe but hard (5 ounces each)

Yield:
4 servings

1. Soak tangerine peel in hot water for 10 minutes, until softened. Cut into fine julienne. You should have 1/2 tablespoon of peel. Place in a bowl.

2. Discard ends of lemon and cut into 8 slices. Remove peel from 4 of the slices, to prevent bitterness. Place all slices in bowl with tangerine peel, add 1 tablespoon sugar, and toss to coat evenly.

3. To brew the tea, boil 5 cups of water. Place tea in a teapot. Pour water into pot and allow to steep 3 minutes.

4. Peel the pears. Core them from the bottoms, leaving each pear with its top intact. Discard the skins, but place cores and pulp into bowl with lemon, tangerine peel, and 1/2 cup sugar. Add peeled pears to bowl and mix. This will ensure that the pears will not turn brown.

5. Place contents of bowl in a large pot. Pour in the tea. Bring to a boil, uncovered, over high heat. Lower heat to simmer. Leave slight opening at the lid of the pot and simmer for 45 minutes. The pears should soften, but still have a bit of resistance to a spoon.

6. To serve, place each pear into a soup or dessert bowl. Strain flavored jasmine tea and pour it equally into the bowls with the pears. There should be about 2 3/4 cups of the flavored tea.

Nutrition per serving: 190 Calories; 1g Fat; 4.7% of calories from fat; 20g Carbohydrates; 0mg Cholesterol; 0mg Sodium.

Steamed Papaya

Dun Mok Gua

This dessert soup, with the flesh of the papaya softened and sweetened by the tong soi inside of it, is a delight. The sugar, water, and papaya combine during the steaming and condense beautifully. My grandmother said this traditional tong soi cleansed and cooled the body. It may have done that, but it tasted good too. Often bird's nest was added to this, in which case not only were you cooled and balanced, but your skin became youthful.

4 papayas, ripe but firm (3/4 pound each)

I small brick sugarcane sugar, cut into 4 equal pieces
   (or 4 tablespoons brown sugar)

I cup water

Yield:
4 servings

1. Wash papaya thoroughly. Dry, cut each through and across, I 1/2 inches from the top, just as the shape begins to broaden. Reserve the tops. Scoop the seeds from each and discard. Place each papaya in a steam-proof Pyrex custard cup. If it moves about, pad it with foil so that it will not move about during steaming. Into the cavity of each papaya add a piece of sugarcane sugar and 1/4 cup of water. Water should be 1/4 inch from opening.

2. Place tops on papayas, then place cups in a steamer and steam for I hour and I5 minutes. After 45 minutes, shielding your hand with a mitt, lightly squeeze each papaya to see if it has softened. If soft, it can be removed and served. Otherwise steam for the time noted. This variance is due to the variances in fruit ripeness and firmness. When done remove cups from steamer and serve individually.

Nutrition per serving: I80 Calories; Ig Fat; 5% calories from fat; 33g Carbohydrates; 0mg Cholesterol; 4mg Sodium.

芋
頭
西
米
湯

Sweet Taro Root Soup

Wu Tau Sai Mai Tong

This tong soi is a traditional sweet of the Chiu Chow people of southern China. Most often taro root is prepared as a vegetable; boiled, steamed, or fried. In this preparation it becomes sweet, quite like a fruit, with a fine aroma. When buying taro root for this dessert ask the grocer for the sort that has tiny veins of purple threaded through it. These taro roots have a special sweet fragrance when cooked, called bun long wu. *Mention this; your grocer will know what you mean.*

1/3 **cup tapioca pearls**

43/4 **cups water**

I **small whole taro root, peeled, washed, cut into** 1/2-**inch dice (3 cups)**

I1/2 **bricks sugarcane sugar (or 6 tablespoons brown sugar)**

Yield:
6 servings

I. Soak the tapioca pearls in I1/4 cups of cold water for I hour.

2. In a large pot bring taro, 31/2 cups water, and sugar to a boil over high heat. Lower heat, leave a small opening at the lid of the pot, and simmer for 20 minutes, or until soft. Turn off heat, allow soup to cool 5 minutes. Pour off I cup of soup and reserve.

3. Place rest of soup and taro root in a blender and puree. Return puree back to pot. Pour reserved soup into the blender, rinse and pour into pot. Turn heat to medium, and bring back to a boil, 2 to 3 minutes. Stir to avoid sticking. When it begins to boil add tapioca pearl and water mixture. Continue to stir until it returns to a boil. Turn off heat, remove to a heated tureen, and serve in dessert bowls.

Nutrition per serving: 83 Calories; 0g Fat; 0% calories from fat; 21g Carbohydrates; 0mg Cholesterol; 5mg Sodium.

酸
桃
蜜
瓜
湯

Pickled Peach and Melon Soup

Seun Toh Mut Gua Tong

As I have noted before, Chinese desserts are customarily fresh fruit, often iced. Here is my version of a cold fruit dessert, with an addition of crisp water chestnuts.

1/2 cantaloupe (1 3/4 pounds), peeled, seeded, and cut up into large pieces, to yield 1 1/4 pounds (see note)

1 Pickled Peach (page 46), cut in half, seeded (see note)

3 tablespoons Pickled Peach liquid (page 46)

2 water chestnuts, peeled, cut into 1/4-inch dice

4 sprigs fresh mint

Yield:
4 servings

Place half the melon, half the Pickled Peach, and all of the Pickled Peach liquid in a blender and blend until coarse. Add remaining melon and peach and blend into a thick puree. Pour into 4 serving bowls, sprinkle with the diced water chestnuts, garnish each with a sprig of mint, and serve.

Nutrition per serving: 51 Calories; 0g Fat; 0% calories from fat; 17g Carbohydrates; 0mg Cholesterol; 15mg Sodium.

Note: Both the melon and the pickled peach must be very cold for this dish. I recommend placing them in a freezer for 30 minutes, after you have prepared them.

Mango and Pickled Pears Soup

Mong Gua Seun Lei Tong

This sweet and tart soup is an ideal choice for a summer meal, another of my variations on the theme of cold fruit desserts. The mango and the Pickled Pears should be very cold. If mango is at room temperature place in freezer for 30 minutes.

I large mango (I pound), peeled, pitted, and cut into pieces
I Pickled Pear (page 46), cored and cut into pieces
1/2 cup Pickled Pear liquid (page 46)
4 ice cubes
1/2 Pickled Pear, cut into 1/8-inch dice

Yield:
4 servings

Place mango pieces, whole Pickled Pear pieces, pickling liquid, and ice cubes in a blender and blend into a smooth puree. Pour into 4 dessert bowls or cups. Sprinkle diced Pickled Pears on top of each and serve.

Nutrition per serving: 65 Calories; less than Ig Fat; negligible calories from fat; 16g Carbohydrates; 0mg Cholesterol; 0mg Sodium.

紅
荳
蓮
子
湯

Red Bean and Lotus Seed Soup

Hung Dau Lin Jee Tong

This soup is a must, a tradition at New Year's feasts and wedding banquets. Lotus seeds, or lin jee, *indicate to the Chinese that in the case of newlyweds they should have a child every year; and at the New Year, the wish is for the family in general to have more children. It is believed that red beans,* hung dau, *build up one's strength, making it all the easier, I expect, to have all of those children. Even if you are not so inclined, I believe you will enjoy this festive soup.*

> 7 cups cold water
>
> I package (14 ounces) red beans, washed 3 or 4 times to remove grit, drained
>
> 1/2 package (3 ounces) lotus seeds, washed, drained
>
> I piece dried tangerine skin, soaked in hot water 10 minutes until soft
>
> 3 bricks sugarcane sugar (or 3/4 cup brown sugar)

Yield:
6 servings

I. In a large pot place water, red beans, lotus seeds, and tangerine skin. Cover and bring to a boil over high heat. Lower heat to simmer. Leave a small opening at the pot lid and simmer for I hour and I5 minutes to I hour and 30 minutes, until beans become tender.

2. When beans are tender and open, and lotus seeds soften, add sugar, stir. Raise heat to medium and cook for 5 minutes, or until sugar dissolves and blends. (If brown sugar is used, there will be no need to cook for 5 minutes. Simply stir to blend). Turn off heat, pour into a heated tureen, and serve.

Nutrition per serving: 149 Calories; less than Ig Fat; less than 1% calories from fat; 39g Carbohydrates; 0mg Cholesterol; 2mg Sodium.

It is fitting that I conclude this book on a sweet note. I would like to add that which was said at our family meals in Sun Tak. We would say, *"Ho ho sik,"* which means "good eating."

Metric Conversions

SOLID WEIGHT CONVERSIONS

Standard	Metric
$^1/_2$ ounce	15g
1 ounce	30g
2 ounces	60g
3 ounces	90g
4 ounces	120g
5 ounces	150g
6 ounces	180g
7 ounces	210g
8 ounces - $^1/_2$ pound	240g
9 ounces	270g
10 ounces	300g
12 ounces	360g
14 ounces	420g
16 ounces-1 pound	480g

LIQUID CONVERSIONS

Standard	Standard	Metric
1 tablespoon	$^1/_2$ fluid ounce	15ml
$^1/_4$ cup	2 fluid ounces	60ml
$^1/_2$ cup	4 fluid ounces	125ml
$^2/_3$ cup	5 fluid ounces	150ml
$^3/_4$ cup	6 fluid ounces	165ml
1 cup	8 fluid ounces	250ml
1$^1/_4$ cups	10 fluid ounces	300ml
1$^1/_2$ cups	12 fluid ounces	375ml
2 cups	16 fluid ounces	500ml
2$^1/_2$ cups	20 fluid ounces	600ml
1 quart	40 fluid ounces	1.25ml

Index